D1251177

JUVENESCENCE

ROBERT POGUE HARRISON

JUVENESCENCE

A Cultural History of Our Age

The University of Chicago Press   Chicago and London

The University of Chicago Press, Chicago 60637
The University of Chicago Press, Ltd., London
© 2014 by Robert Pogue Harrison
All rights reserved. Published 2014.
Paperback edition 2016
Printed in the United States of America

25 24 23 22 21 20 19 18 17 16   2 3 4 5 6

ISBN-13: 978-0-226-17199-9 (cloth)
ISBN-13: 978-0-226-38196-1 (paper)
ISBN-13: 978-0-226-17204-0 (e-book)
DOI: 10.7208/chicago/9780226172040.001.0001

Library of Congress Cataloging-in-Publication Data

Harrison, Robert Pogue, author
Juvenescence : a cultural history of our age / Robert Pogue Harrison.
pages ;   cm
Includes bibliographical references and index.
ISBN 978-0-226-17199-9 (cloth : alk. paper)
ISBN 978-0-226-17204-0 (e-book)
1. Youthfulness—Philosophy. 2. Neoteny. 3. Maturation (Psychology)
4. Age—Philosophy. 5. Aging—Anthropological aspects. I. Title.
BF724.2.H373 2014
305.2—dc23
2014029541

♾ This paper meets the requirements of ANSI/NISO Z39.48-1992 (Permanence of Paper).

to Andrea Nightingale

CONTENTS

PREFACE

This book grapples with a simple question that has no simple answer: how old are we? By "we" I mean those of us who belong to the age of juvenescence that began in America in the post-war period and gradually spread eastward, moving against the westerly drift of civilization that the ancients called *translatio imperii*.

There is no way to engage that question without probing the phenomenon of human age in all its bewildering complexity; for in addition to possessing a biological, evolutionary, and geological age, humans also possess a cultural age by virtue of the fact that they belong to a history that preceded their arrival in the world and will outlast their exit from it. Like other life forms, we humans undergo an aging process, yet the historical era into which we are born has a great deal to do with how that process unfolds, even at the biological level. We are a species that, for better or for worse, has transmuted evolution into culture, and vice versa. Thus a seemingly simple question — how old are we? — places us in an unfamiliar region where, among all the life forms on earth, we find ourselves alone and without definite coordinates.

Culture's powerful evolutionary force has gone into over-drive at present, transforming our kind in fundamental ways even as we speak. Genetically, humans have not changed for the past several thousand years, or so we're told, yet today's thirty-year-old woman on the tennis courts of San Diego seems more like the daughter than the sister of Balzac's *femme de trente ans*. In my father's college yearbook, I see the faces of fully grown adults the likes of which I never encounter among my undergraduates. In earlier ages, twelve-year-old boys looked like little adults, their faces furrowed by the depths of time. By contrast, the first-world face of today remains callow, even as it withers away with age, never attaining the strong senile traits of the elderly of other cultures or historical eras. The difference lies not merely in our enhanced diets, health benefits, and reduced exposure to the elements but in a wholesale biocultural transformation that is turning large segments of the human population into a "younger" species — younger in looks, behavior, mentality, lifestyles, and, above all, desires.

How is such juvenescence possible? Is there a biological substrate in our species-being that sponsors it? How can we be getting younger — as individuals as well as a society — even as we continue to age? And what future, if any, does our juvenilization have in store for us? These are questions that surround and traverse the core question of how old we are from the historical point of view. I have chosen to engage them through a multifaceted approach that takes into account the relevant biological and evolutionary factors, while keeping my primary focus on the broad lineaments of Western cultural history. Indeed, I have found it necessary to offer in these pages what amounts to a philosophy of history as well as a philosophy of age as such, for in the human realm age and history remain inextricably bound up with one another.

This book is at best ambivalent toward the unprecedented juvenescence that is sweeping over Western culture, and many other cultures as well. At the very least, I seek to gauge the risks it entails for our future, assuming we have one. As it convulses the historical continuum with increasing vehemence, our era has rendered the world an alien place for those who were not born into its neoteric novelties — for those who are not native to the new age, as it were. At the beginning of his "Doggerel by a Senior Citizen," W. H. Auden wrote, "Our earth in 1969 / Is not the planet I call mine." This feeling of world-expropriation has grown far more intense for many citizens of the planet since 1969. An older person has no idea what it means to be a child, an adolescent, or a young adult in 2014. Hence he or she is hardly able to provide any guidance to the young when it comes to their initiation into the ways of maturity or their induction into the public sphere, for which the young must eventually assume responsibility, or pay the consequences if they fail to do so. It has yet to be seen whether a society that loses its intergenerational continuity to such a degree can long endure.

One of the claims of this book is that our youth-obsessed society in fact wages war against the youth it presumably worships. It may appear as if the world now belongs mostly to the younger generations, with their idiosyncratic mindsets and technological gadgetry, yet in truth, the age as a whole, whether wittingly or not, deprives the young of what youth needs most if it hopes to flourish. It deprives them of idleness, shelter, and solitude, which are the generative sources of identity formation, not to mention the creative imagination. It deprives them of spontaneity, wonder, and the freedom to fail. It deprives them of the ability to form images with their eyes closed, hence to think beyond the sorcery of the movie, television, or computer screen. It deprives them of an expansive and embodied relation to nature, without which a sense of connection to the universe is impossible and life remains essentially meaningless. It deprives them of continuity with the past, whose future they will soon be called on to forge.

We do not promote the cause of youth when we infantilize rather than educate desire, and then capitalize on its bad infinity; nor when we shatter the relative stability of the world, on which cultural identity depends; nor when we oblige the young to inhabit a present without historical depth or density. The greatest blessing a society can confer on its young is to turn them into the heirs, rather than the orphans, of history. It is also the greatest blessing a society can confer on itself, for heirs rejuvenate the heritage by creatively renewing its legacies. Orphans, by contrast, relate to the past as an alien, unapproachable continent — if they relate to it at all. Our age seems intent on turning the world as a whole into an orphanage, for reasons that no one — least of all the author of this book — truly understands.

Juvenescence has no interest in promoting a doomsday vision of the future. I do not offer prophecies here, if only because our age makes it impossible to predict the outcome of the upheavals it relentlessly provokes. At present, no one can say whether the storm of juvenescence that has swept us up in the past several decades will lead to a genuine rejuvenation or a mere juvenilization of culture. All will depend on whether we find ways to bring forth new and younger forms of cultural maturity. Nothing is more important in this regard than resolving to act our age. I mean our historical age. The past does not cease to exist simply because we lose our memory of it. A multimillennial history lurks inside us, whether we are aware of it or not. We may be the "youngest" society in the history of human civilization, yet we are also the oldest — and getting older, decade by decade, century by century, millennium by millennium.

I faced two choices when I set out to write this book: to make it ponderously long or keep it mercifully short. I opted for the latter. Since I was also determined not to oversimplify the matters at hand, the result is a book that may seem at times baffling in its essayistic approach to a highly complex nexus of questions, yet I would not turn it over to the reader if I felt that it lacked an intrinsic narrative logic and inner core of coherence. It is a book that trusts its reader to stay the course, however circuitous it may be.

ACKNOWLEDGMENTS

I would like to thank Epicurus for his philosophy of gratitude, since being grateful for the has-been inoculates one against despair over the future. A love of Epicurus is one of the bonds I share with my friend and colleague Andrea Nightingale, to whom this book is dedicated and who, over the years, has read more drafts of its chapters than she or I can tally. I am grateful to my friend Antonia for her generosity (the other supreme Epicurean virtue) and for reading almost as many chapter drafts as Andrea. My thanks also go out to the following friends who read previous drafts of some of these chapters or offered special inspiration for them: Weixing Su, Samia Kassab, Florence Naugrette, Inga Pierson, Hans Gumbrecht, Laura Wittman, Heather Webb, Susan Stewart, Dan Edelstein, Pierre Saint-Amand, Rachel Falconer, Rachel Jacoff, Florian Klinger, Christy Wampole, Elizabeth Coggeshall, Niklas Damiris, Helga Wilde, Gabriele Pedullà, Dylan Montanari, and Kelly in Rome. Special thanks also to Yves Bonnefoy for inviting me to deliver a series of lectures at the Collège de France in May 2010. Those four lectures on "Le phénomène de l'age" allowed me to bring this book into much clearer focus. Finally, I am grateful to my editors Alan Thomas (University of Chicago Press), Sophie Bancquart (Le Pommier), and Michael Kruger (Hanser Verlag) for their encouragement and enthusiasm for this book.

To the Reader

One of my extracurricular activities is hosting a radio show on Stanford University's radio station, KZSU 90.1. That show is called *Entitled Opinions (about Life and Literature)*, and for the better part of a decade, it has hosted hundreds of guests, in conversation about various intellectual topics. Since the topics and authors I deal with in this book have been the subjects of some of my radio shows, I would like to cite a few of the latter here as an audio supplement to my discussion in the pages that follow. All are available on the website http://www.stanford.edu/dept /fren-ital/opinions/ and as iTunes podcasts, downloadable for free: Karen Feldman, "On Hannah Arendt" (May 15, 2007); Thomas Harrison, "On the Emancipation of Dissonance" (March 7, 2006); Martin Lewis, "On the Discipline of Geography" (November 9, 2011); Andrew Mitchell, "On Martin Heidegger" (October 18, 2005) and "On Friedrich Nietzsche" (May 26, 2009); Andrea Nightingale, "On Plato" (November 25, 2009); Marjorie Perloff, "On the Poetry and Politics of Ezra Pound" (November 15, 2005) and "On W. B. Yeats" (March 18, 2008); Rush Rehm, "On Greek Tragedy" (March 15, 2011); Richard Saller, "On the Social Institutions of Ancient Rome" (October 26, 2011); Thomas Sheehan, "On the Historical Jesus" (January 21, 2006); Kathleen Sullivan, "On the Founding Scriptures of America" (May 2, 2006); and Caroline Winterer, "On Classicism in America" (January 18, 2011). Many other shows could be added to this list, yet these are the among the most pertinent ones for this book in the *Entitled Opinions* archive.

On Citations

This book does not contain numbered footnotes or endnotes. Notes and references have been consigned to the sections entitled "Notes" and "Works Cited" in the back matter.

Both when young and old one should devote one-self to philosophy in order that while growing old he shall be young in blessings through gratitude for what has been. The life of the fool is marked by ingratitude and apprehension; the drift of his thought is exclusively toward the future. Forgetting the good that has been, he becomes an old man this very day.

EPICURUS

ONE

Anthropos

The Intriguing Phenomenon of Age

Nothing in the universe — be it the newborn infant or the universe itself — is without age. If a phenomenon does not age it is not of this world; and if it is not of this world, it is not a phenomenon.

We have on the whole a poor understanding of the essence of age, perhaps because our intellect evolved to deal more with objects in space than with the enfolded intricacies of growth, duration, and accumulation. Certainly we find it easier to spatialize time — to think of it as a linear or chronological succession of present moments — than to fathom the multidimensional, interpenetrating recesses of age. Indeed, we have a stubborn tendency to reduce age to "time," yet what is time if not a prodigious abstraction, a *flatus vocis*? Only age gives time a measure of reality.

The most sophisticated philosophers think of age as a function of time, yet a careful phenomenological analysis reveals that we should instead think of time as a function of age. After all, any concept we may have of time has a way of growing old, of succumbing to an aging process. The same holds true for eternity, which shares in the general mortality of phenomena. Eternity no longer appears to us as it did to Plato, when he and his fellow Greeks turned their gaze to the stars. Nor does it appear to us as it did to Dante, when he and his fellow Christians contemplated the celestial spheres. Indeed, eternity has been largely subtracted from our ever-expanding cosmos, which we now believe had a beginning and will eventually have an end. Hence one could say that eternity has for all intents and purposes disappeared from our phenomenological horizons, that it has aged itself out of existence.

In *Creative Evolution* (1907) the French philosopher Henri Bergson exposed in compelling fashion traditional philosophy's stubborn tendency to conceive of time geometrically rather than organically, yet for all his deep thinking about *la durée* and organic form, Bergson never put forward a philosophy of age. He offered merely another philosophy of time — one founded on biological rather than chronological paradigms. That represented a significant corrective and contribution, to be sure, yet there is more to the phenomenon of age than biology can account for, for humans are biological beings who create transbiological institutions that put cultural and historical elements into play in ways that Bergson, along with most other philosophers, leaves largely unexamined.

All living things obey an organic law of growth and decay, and in that respect human beings are no exceptions. According to the riddle of Sphinx, we walk on four legs in the morning, two legs at noon, and, if we live long enough, end up on three legs in the evening. Yet after he enters the city of Thebes, confident that he has solved the riddle, Oedipus discovers that there is far more to the story than that. The story in fact begins before birth and continues after death. In other words, unlike other living things, *anthropos* is born into humanly created worlds whose historical past and future transcend the individual's lifespan. These worlds, which the Greeks called the *polis*, are founded upon institutional and cultural memory, conferring upon their inhabitants a historical age that is altogether different in nature than biological age. Since no human being lives outside of such worlds, with their legacies and traditions, we could say that humans are by nature "heterochronic" in their age, that is, they possess many diverse kinds of ages: biological, historical, institutional, psychological. By and by we will see how these various "ages" intersect with one another—both in individuals and in civilizations—yet here let us simply note for the record that, once *anthropos* arrives on the scene, the phenomenon of age increases in complexity as least as much as it did when life first gained a foothold on our planet.

The one thinker from whom one would expect an explosive philosophy of age, especially as it relates to the human component, is Martin Heidegger. Heidegger thought more radically about time than any philosopher before or after him, yet he too, like the metaphysical tradition he labored to overcome, had little to say about age. Heidegger taught us that time is ostensive— that it is a kind of movement, or *kinesis*, that allows the phenomenon to appear and be taken up in thought and word. He also taught us that time's disclosive dynamism has its source in Dasein's finite temporality. Why he made no effort to link Dasein's temporality to its age, even in the straightforward sense of the stages of life, is hard to fathom, for when it comes to Dasein's existential determinations, age remains as fundamental as thrownness, projection, fallenness, being-unto-death, and being-with-others. Yet for some reason in *Being and Time*, as well as in Heidegger's later thought, Dasein remains essentially ageless.

I find this surprising because one could say that age is to time what place is to space. Nowhere in his corpus is Heidegger more compelling than when he reveals how place, in its situated boundedness, is more primordial than space. In exemplary phenomenological fashion he shows how the scientific concept of homogeneous space derives from, or is made possible by, Dasein's disclosure of the "there" of its own situated being. One would have expected from Heidegger a similar analysis of how age, in its existential and historical primordiality, figures as the measure, if not the source, of Dasein's finite temporality and, with it, of the chronologically governed concept of time. Such an analysis would have given him the occasion to show that the constant finishing action of time takes place in and through the unfolding of age, day in and day out, year in and year out, era after era, epoch after epoch. Unfortunately, nowhere in his corpus does Heidegger ponder age as the boundary of finitude that allows time, in its ostensive character, to disclose the world of phenomena.

Let me briefly attempt to point out how much goes unaccounted for, phenomenologically speaking, when one fails to ground time in age, or to derive the former from the latter.

I would begin by remarking that every phenomenon has its age, or better, its *ages*. Why the plural? Because entities become phenomena only where they are perceived, intended, or apprehended. Hence the phenomenon brings together at least two independent yet intersecting ages: the age of the entity and the age of the apprehender. A young boy and his grandfather in an old-growth forest of the Pacific Northwest may cast their eyes on the same giant redwood, yet they do not see the same phenomenon. Because of their age difference, it appears one way to the boy, another to his elder. The sky I see today is more or less the same blue spectacle it always was, yet it's not the same sky of old. When I was seven it was my body's covenant with the cosmos; by twenty it became the face of an abstraction; today it's the dome of a house I know I will not inhabit for too much longer; shortly it will be the answer to what today still remains a question.

It does no good to say that I "project" my age onto phenomena. The sky has always appeared to me as something ageless; yet its agelessness appears differently as I age. My only access to the sky, and to the world of phenomena in general, is from within my own noncelestial age. If identity means self-sameness through time, age is the latent element that introduces a differential into identity's equation, hence into the appearance of things. To express the same thought in slightly different terms: I do not lend the phenomenon my age; rather, the phenomenon reaches me through forms of reception and perception that pertain to my age. One could speak in a more Kantian vein and say that time is not the same form of intuition in childhood as it is in adulthood, or that the imagination schematizes time differently in youth than it does in old age.

Gerard Manley Hopkins's poem "Spring and Fall," where an older speaker addresses a young girl, gives poetic expression to what I have stated more prosaically about the age differential in the phenomenon's self-manifestation:

> Margaret, are you grieving
> Over Goldengrove unleaving?
> Leaves, like the things of man, you
> With your fresh thoughts care for, can you?
> Ah! as the heart grows older
> It will come to such sights colder
> By and by, nor spare a sigh
> Though world of wanwood leafmeal lie;
> And yet you will weep and know why.
> Now no matter, child, the name:
> Sorrow's springs are the same.
> Nor mouth had, no nor mind, expressed
> What heart heard of, ghost guessed:
> It was the blight man was born for,
> It is Margaret you mourn for.

Although Margaret's emotions here lack credibility—young girls do not typically shed tears over the falling of autumn leaves—the poem draws attention to two important phenomenological facts. The first is that the aging process effects changes in the phenomenon's perception. The second is that human perception is, at some level, always a self-perception. The difference between the child and the adult in the poem is that the adult presumably knows "why" he weeps, while Margaret presumably does not. She has yet to understand that "sorrow's springs are the same."

That last assertion may in fact be dubious, or even downright false—sorrow's springs are *not* always the same—yet the truth of Hopkins's poem lies not in its propositional claims but in its revelation that, as the heart grows older, the same phenomenon accrues a different meaning: a meaning intimately bound up with the age of the perceiver.

The Italian poet Giacomo Leopardi also held that things appear differently to perception with age. In his pessimistic worldview, youth has a tendency to see infinite promise in the phenomena of nature. Autumn leaves, moonlight, the open sea—these are intimations of future happiness. By inviting youth to experience its beauty in the mode of promise, nature is unspeakably cruel, since that promise is and always was only an *inganno*, a deception. As he puts it in his poem "A Silvia": "O natura, o natura. / Perchè non rendi poi / quel che prometti allor? Perchè di tanto / Inganni i figli tuoi?" ("O nature, o nature. Why do you not deliver on what you promised back then? Why do you deceive your children so?"). In Hopkins's case, age reveals in time the implicit truth naively perceived in the phenomenon by a young girl; in Leopardi's case, it reveals in time the deception that was implicit in the naïve perception of youth. Again, neither one nor the other vision need be empirically "true." What is important—at least for our purposes—is that, unlike the history of philosophy, the history of poetry offers an abundance of phenomenological insight into the way truth reveals itself in and through the unfolding of age.

If time is disclosive of truth, as Heidegger maintained, and if truth in turn is age-bound, as I maintain, then what is absolutely true at one stage of life is at best only relatively true at another. When I first read the opening verses of T. S. Eliot's *The Four Quartets* many years ago, I had no doubts that I had stumbled upon the timeless truth of time itself:

> Time present and time past
> are both perhaps present in time future,
> And time future contained in time past.
> If all time is eternally present
> all time is unredeemable.

> What might have been is an abstraction
> remaining a perpetual possibility
> only in a world of speculation.

For a young person, Eliot's lines about the "might have been" resound with an ominous oracular truth. It puts enormous pressure on one to take seriously Nietzsche's doctrine of the eternal return of the same (i.e., that we are fated to repeat all the moments in our life over and over again, eternally), or to take Rilke at his word when he writes, in his ninth *Duino Elegy*, "Us the most fleeting. Once / everything, only *once*. *Once* and no more. And we, too, / *once*. Never again." These theses — eternal return and the "once only" — sympathize with one another, in that both affirm that reality consummates itself in the real, and only in the real. Yet the truth of that proposition holds far more sway over a young person than an older person, if only because the former feels under a much greater imperative to realize his or her potential than does an older person, whose life, for better or worse, has already begun winding down toward a narrative conclusion, even if it has not yet reached a biological end.

While I believe that the real shines forth as the crown of the possible, I am no longer convinced, as I was when I first read Eliot's lines, that the possible finds its redemption only in actualization. I have arrived at an age where the relation between time and reality has undergone a shift that makes me more prone to believe that the punctuality of our lived moments are like sparks arising from, and returning to, that indeterminate source that the pre-Socratic philosopher Anaximander called the *apeiron*, the unbounded matrix. This *apeiron* is not nothingness. Nor is it an "abstraction remaining a perpetual possibility only in a world of speculation." Its overbearing potentiality penetrates the phenomenon and gives it depth, density, and opacity, suffusing it with a recessive latency of unrealized potential. I could put the same thought differently by saying that this vast ocean of potentiality on which actuality drifts like a single glass wave gives buoyancy and depth to our experience of the real.

There are further complexities at work in the human inflections of age. If I say I am sixty years old, what exactly does that mean? What or who is this I? Is it a body, a mind, a soul, or an aggregate of the three? Even if, for the sake of argument, we call it only a body, we are still not dealing with a simple sum. My body is at once sixty years old and several billion years old, since all of its atoms originated a few seconds after the Big Bang, hence are as old as the universe itself. Moreover, a body does not age uniformly in all its parts. The age of a weak heart is not that of a sound kidney. One may turn old in one part of the body and stay young in another over the course of years. As John Banville's protagonist remarks about his Italian neighbors in the novel *Shroud*: "They age from the top down, for these are still the legs . . . they must have had in their twenties or even earlier" (3–4). In sum, the body too is heterochronic.

My body contains a brain. Is my brain the same age as my mind? Surely not, for unlike the brain, my mind is linked by affiliation and inheritance to other minds, both past and present. In Yeats's "A Prayer for My Daughter" we read, "My mind, because the minds that I have loved, / The sort of beauty that I have approved, / Prosper but little, has dried up of late . . ." Like Yeats, I have loved minds as old as Anaximander and Plato. That makes my mind, whose thought is informed by theirs, over two thousand years old. Whether that makes it older or younger than my brain is anybody's guess.

As for my soul—or what used to be called the soul, before it curled up and disappeared from the scene of history—I am at least as old as Moses, Homer, and Dante, whose legacies form part of my psychic selfhood. And if I am ever reduced to searching the depths of my unconscious, I will most likely find that I am also as old as the archetypes of prehistoric myth.

The year is 2014. Do I—or this composite that attaches to my first-person singular—belong to my historical age? Certainly there is more nineteenth century than twenty-first century in my temperament; more celestial spheres than general relativity in my projected universe; more ancient Athens than

World Wide Web in my cultural geography. Conversely, when I consider how mired Western civilization still is in the swamps of atavisms, how snail-slow we still are in our efforts to get beyond the follies of the past and realize the promise of modernity, then I feel that historically I am not yet born, that I am sixty minus a century or two. Yet for all this untimeliness, I cannot deny that I am also a child of my age, for I cannot fully belong to a world that does not include the likes of Radiohead.

To say that age is "relative" is to understate and even misstate the issue. Certainly one's lived experience of age is relative to one's race, class, gender, culture, nation, and education. In certain societies, a fifteen-year-old boy can hardly imagine what it means to be a fifteen-year-old girl in that same society, or what it means to be a boy of his age in a very different society. Beyond these special relativities, however, there is a more general relativity, whereby being fifteen years old means something altogether different at the dawn of the third millennium than it did at the dawn of the second or first millennium, to say nothing of prehistory. Yet be it special or general, relativity in its basic concept can only take us so far when it comes to the complex manifold that constitutes a person's true age. I mean the manifold of body, mind, and soul, each of which has an enfolded dynamic of its own. The concept of relativity does as much to obscure as to clarify the bewildering nexus that keeps this manifold mysteriously united in a single person, even as it remains in a state of constant flux, unfolding its unity in what we call — vaguely enough — time.

The human nexus in question remains bound to a first-person singular, and that first-person singular remains bound to a given historical era (history funnels itself through the first-person singular, one could say). Historical eras, in turn, unfold within a larger framework of what have traditionally been called cultural ages. The ancients, for example, spoke of a golden age, a silver age, a bronze age, and so forth. Giambattista Vico spoke of the age of gods, the age of heroes, and the age of men. Later in this book, with Vico's help, we will see that the phenomenon's appearance is conditioned by a society's cultural age as much as it is conditioned by an individual's existential age; in other words, the changes that a society's cultural mentality undergoes in historical time play a formative role in how the phenomenon reveals itself to those who share in that mentality. All of which confirms my contention that what is true at one stage of life, or at one stage of history, is at best only partially true at another—in sum, that truth has its age, or better, its ages.

Anthropos

We like to think that the rational mind—its capacity for abstract thought, its ability to calculate and manipulate the forces of nature, its power to devise, design, and discover—is evolution's greatest achievement to date, yet consider the following: we have built computers able to defeat the most intelligent chess players in the world, but when it comes to building a machine that can challenge an animal's ability to move effortlessly through a room without bumping into objects in its path, we are woefully inadequate. Our ratiocinative powers are relatively easy to reproduce artificially, while our sensory motors, depth perception, reflexes, and bodily coordination present a near hopeless challenge to the science of robotics. Why?

The answer has to do once again with age. On the scale of evolutionary time, our intelligence is altogether neoteric—its reasoning capacities emerged only a few thousand years ago—while evolution has had billions of years to perfect the kinetic functioning of living organisms. From an evolutionary point of view, the rational mind is so young that, by analogy, we humans reason the way a neonate moves and behaves—awkwardly, gropingly, struggling to exert control and agency over its motions. That's one reason, among many others, that we should be wary of letting our cognitive powers reshape our world and take full charge of our future destiny.

In addition to being "young" from an evolutionary point of view, human intelligence has a congenital connection to youth.

Human beings' exceptionally prolonged childhood has allowed us to develop our intelligence no less than our intelligence has allowed us to prolong our childhood. Nothing is more extravagant, in the "youthful" sense, than human intelligence. It is the source of our timidity as well as our temerity. It has enabled us both to avoid danger and to court it. It has fostered the blessings and barbarisms of civilization, and has made us the most terrified and, at the same time, the most terrifying species ever to roam the earth.

Life throws everything that lives into risk, peril, and uncertainty. The biotic hovers insecurely on the border of opportunity and extinction. While all life is vulnerable, human beings remain far more exposed in their mode of being than any other living species, for we dwell in the openness of possibility, including the possibility of annihilation, and have found a way to turn that openness into conscious knowledge. At some fundamental level, knowledge arises as a human response to the novelty and strangeness that our exposed condition reveals in the world around us, as well as the world *inside* of us. The world in its disquieting wonder is forever new and strange to *Homo sapiens*, the way it is for the human young.

In *The Gay Science* Nietzsche asks what people really want when they seek out knowledge. His answer:

> Nothing more than this: Something strange is to be reduced to something *familiar*. And we philosophers — have we really meant *more* than this when we have spoken of knowledge? What is familiar means what we are used to so that we no longer marvel at it, our everyday, some rule in which we are stuck, anything at all in which we feel at home. Look, isn't our need for knowledge precisely this need for the familiar, the will to uncover under everything strange, unusual, and questionable something that no longer disturbs us? Is it not the *instinct of fear* that bids us to know? And is the jubilation of those who attain knowledge not the jubilation over the restoration of a sense of security? (300–301)

There is much to ponder in this psychological account of the will to know, yet we should approach with caution Nietzsche's claim that "the instinct of fear bids us to know," for if fear alone could motivate the will to know, all of living nature would seek after knowledge. It requires a distinct form of anxiety—a tear in the fabric of instinct, reflex, and routine—to jolt a species into conceptual mediation, sense-making, and language. In short, into consciousness. This tear must come from *within* the being of *Homo sapiens*, in such a way that its lacerations provoke a self-awareness that takes cognizance of the surrounding world in its enigma. The ancients suggested as much when they declared that human consciousness first sprang from wonder, which can take the form of marvel, puzzlement, or dread. In one form or the other, it arises as a response to the overwhelming strangeness of the world, above all the strangeness of our being in it.

There is no wonder without self-awareness, and where wonder prevails, the dictum "nothing new under the sun" does not apply. Human consciousness in its heightened self-awareness both engenders and reacts to novelty. The new startles. It unsettles. It awakens. It calls for attention, apprehension, and adaptation. Where there is life there is neophobia, for in the natural world the new usually entails disruption and danger. Yet here too human beings are exceptions, for alongside our natural, self-preserving neophobia, there coexists a counterstrain of neophilia. Humans dwell in the midst of the new like children who are at once attracted by and suspicious of novelty. Had our species not been endowed with this neophilic counterstrain from the start, it is unlikely that we would have wandered to the uttermost ends of the earth, invented tools, disclosed the realm of intelligibility, and let loose upon the natural world the altogether unearthly powers of human thought.

Such unearthly powers can arise only in a species that is at once exuberant and tormented. Humans have a self-consuming inclination to love what they dread, aggress what they love, and seek out what they shrink away from. The Renaissance humanist

Francesco Bondini put it well in his 1574 treatise *Lezioni sopra il Comporre delle Novelle*:

> Much more amazing [than the wonders of the natural world] is the human intellect especially in its moments of perversity: love can lead us to destroy the object of love, as Deinara destroyed Hercules; in Oedipus we can see a trust in reason lead to its own overthrow; amazingly, it is as if in the human intellect there were a living force that destroyed the rationality of that intellect and the arguments that rationality might employ so as not to fall into such error. (Kirkpatrick, *English and Italian Literature*, 237)

Whether it resides in the human intellect or elsewhere, this "living force" is thoroughly odd, such that no amount of knowledge can domesticate its perversity. Thus any "jubilation over the restoration of a sense of security" that knowledge provides will invariably give way to new forms of dread, time and again, for the terror lies so not much in the world as in ourselves.

This is the essence of the anthropological affirmation that opens the famous first stasimon of Sophocles's play *Antigone*, otherwise known as the Ode on Man: "There is much that is strange, but nothing / that surpasses man in strangeness." The Greek word *deinos* can mean strange, marvelous, or terrifying. All three connotations come into play here. The chorus goes on to declare that man — *anthropos* — sails forth on mountainous waves in the dead of winter, subdues the earth with his plow, snares the "light-gliding birds," and draws fish up from the abyss of the sea; that he has yoked the stallion and the formidable bull; that "he has found his way / to the resonance of the word / and to wind-swift all-understanding"; that he has devised shelter, found cures for illness, and created law and justice. For all his resourcefulness, however, he often comes to ill through his rashness (*tolma*) and finds himself *apolis*, without city. Try as he may, he is powerless to escape what eventually claims whatever lives, namely death: "Everywhere journeying, inexperienced and without issue, he comes to nothingness."

If man is strange, so too is this ode that sings his praises, for it ends with the chorus turning away in horror from the *anthropos* who braves the abyss, willfully challenges powers that could easily overwhelm him, and makes himself the master of all things, even though he has little mastery of himself or of other men and women (the Antigone play reveals as much in its power struggles and tragic drama). After offering a wondrous account of what makes humankind so inventive, venturesome, and innovative, the chorus declares: "May such a man never frequent my hearth; / May my mind never share the presumption / of him who does this." Why this repudiation?

Composed of Theban elders, the chorus in its recoil gives voice to a senile point of view — call it the point of view of seasoned wisdom — which stands over and against the youthful recklessness of *anthropos*. I say "youthful" because the young Antigone, in her defiance of powers that could easily annihilate her, figures in the play as a paragon of the *anthropos* under description. Her uncle Creon is her elder, yet he too is impetuously "young," ideologically speaking, for in his haste to establish law and order, he disregards a number of ancient truths, among them that unburied bodies mean unfinished business. In his zealous championing of a new civic law, or *raison d'état*, he allows his "trust in reason [to] lead to its own overthrow," as Bondini puts it in the passage quoted above. It is not by chance that, at the beginning of the play, the elders of the chorus twice refer to Creon apprehensively as the "new" king of Thebes. In Greek, the word *neos* means both young and new.

If we take *anthropos* as the human species, we could say that, in its concluding words of repudiation, the Ode on Man expresses the intrinsic wariness that accompanies humankind's incautious neophilia. I mean the neophilia that drives man to explore, discover, challenge, subdue, and overreach himself in unprecedented acts of defiance. What dismays the Theban elders is that this man, for reasons unknown, undertakes his ventures with a deliberate disregard for all that human society — with its traditions, customs, and self-preserving institutions — laboriously defends itself against, namely disaster and the nihilism of death. Perhaps *anthropos*, in his more daring aspects, is not "old" enough to fear the chasms of death lurking in the seas, mountains, and people into whose territories he ventures.

After its powerful, heroic portrait of man, the chorus's prudential ethic comes across as thoroughly antiheroic, yet we should keep in mind that the human species may well have gone extinct had it lacked this kind of trepidation, which serves to counterbalance its willful exposure to appalling perils and challenges. A neophiliac audacity may be the necessary precondition for finding one's way into language and the "wind-swift all-understanding" of human intelligence, yet in itself it is not sufficient. If what the ode declares is true — that "nothing surpasses man in strangeness" — there is every reason to suspect that the cowering anxiety and anthropological dread expressed by the chorus play an equally, if not more, important role in the emergence of human self-awareness. No external danger can induce it. Only man in his outrageous self-transcendence can terrify himself into consciousness. Only from the fissure between prudence and reckless daring can *anthropos*, in all his strangeness, break forth into the realm of meaning.

What does man's "age" have to do with his breakthrough into the openness of meaning? There is much that is strange, yet nothing is stranger than the age of man. Sophocles's ode, after all, belongs to a play about a young woman who is both the sister and daughter of Oedipus. The brother she seeks to bury, in defiance of Creon's decree, is also her uncle. It takes a strange man indeed to challenge the Sphinx and get her to plunge herself into the abyss — a man far stranger than the conventional *anthropos* who walks with four legs in the morning, two at noon, and three in the evening.

Oedipus enters the city of Thebes, apparently victorious over the Sphinx, only to discover, in due course, that the emplotment of life is more perverse than he had suspected. Only later does the riddle he presumed to have solved draw him into the vortex of its intrigue, revealing in the twists and turns of his subsequent life story that there is more to human age than a straightforward sequence of stages. Let Oedipus serve as a warning that two legs are not always what they seem, especially when you suffer from a wound in one foot, and that the line stretching from childhood to senility forms only one of the threads that entangle human existence in the sprawling web of age, at the center of which lies a knot. It is to this knot that we must now turn our attention.

Neoteny

Just how old is the human species? With this question I do not mean to ask how long ago *Homo sapiens* evolved into its present-day form. The chronology of hominization holds a special fascination, to be sure, yet what concerns us most here is the "age difference" between humans and their primate ancestors. It is with questions about the anatomy of that age difference that I propose to proceed.

We who have become the awesome creature described by Sophocles's Ode on Man—we who, with our intelligence, have practically evolved beyond the animal kingdom—did we become the most "advanced" species on earth by advancing beyond the adult stages reached by the ancestors in our remote phylogenetic past? Certainly many people thought so after the German biologist Ernst Haeckel first proposed his famous theory of recapitulation in the nineteenth century. Haeckel's catchphrase still has a familiar ring to it: "ontogeny recapitulates phylogeny," that is, individuals in their fetal development repeat or pass through the various stages of their species' evolution. Thus the human embryo's temporary gill-like slits represent vestiges of the ancient adult fish from which we evolved many millions of years ago, just as its webbed feet and its makings of a tail represent vestiges of our amphibious and early mammalian ancestry. According to Haeckel, humans evolved into their present form by means of adaptations built on the foundations of antecedent morphological stages. In other words, the human embryo, in its ontogenetic development, first recapitulates and then surpasses the adult ancestral forms of its evolutionary history.

Recapitulation offered a powerful theory of human evolution — and in modified form is making a strong comeback today — yet the morphological evidence worked against its main premise. In 1920 the Dutch anatomist Louis Bolk pointed to over twenty features that human adults share in common with juvenile primates and various mammalian embryos. For example, our round, bulbous cranium resembles the craniums of fetal and infant apes more than those of mature apes (see chapter notes for elaboration). Likewise, our facial characteristics bear an uncanny resemblance to those of young, but not adult, primates (with apes the juvenile face is relatively straight, but as they grow older it begins to project outward, with "positive allometry"). Human females share with female mammalian embryos the ventral orientation of the vaginal canal, but in other species the canal rotates back as the females develop, while in human females it doesn't. Our unopposable big toe is something most primates share in common with us in their early, though not later, stages of development. These are only some of the impressive neotenic — or youth-retaining — traits enumerated by Bolk in support of his "fetalization theory," which held that humans are basically juvenile apes whose natural development (into adult apes) has been indefinitely retarded. Thanks to this retardation, humans remain "paedomorphic," or childlike in form, throughout their entire lives. Bolk put it even more boldly: "Man, in his bodily development, is a primate fetus that has become sexually mature."

In his novel *After Many a Summer Dies the Swan*, Aldous Huxley used Bolk's fetalization theory to dramatic effect. The fifth Earl of Gonister and his lover have managed to prolong their lives for over two hundred years by ingesting carp guts. When the immortality-seeking American millionaire Jo Stoyte and his hired scientist Obispo set out on their quest to discover the secret of their longevity, they discover that the earl and his lover have turned into apes. Astonished to see the earl groveling on the floor, Stoyte asks what has happened to them. "Just time," answers Obispo. "The foetal anthropoid was able to come to maturity" (355). It is tempting to ask whether human civilization has been feeding on carp guts of late—analogically speaking—but that is a speculation we will put aside for the moment.

The technical term in biology for the fetalization phenomenon described by Bolk is "neoteny," a word that combines two Greek roots: *neos*, meaning new or young, and *teinein*, meaning to stretch, tend, or retain (related to the Latin *tenere*, to hold). In evolutionary biology, neoteny refers to the persistence of fetal, larval, or juvenile features in adult organisms, as well as to a general slowing of the rate of development that makes it possible to retain juvenile features in later stages of the life cycle.

Bolk's fetalization theory soon went the way of recapitulation, that is, it passed into the annals of flawed, obsolete science, not so much because of the morphological evidence, which remains compelling, but because the explanatory mechanism Bolk proposed to account for it was not scientifically credible. Bolk speculated that a general modification in our hormonal balance put the brake on human development, but it was simply not plausible that hormonal changes could provoke such complex morphological transformations. Moreover, Bolk had no adequate explanation for our many characteristics that are not paedomorphic in nature, including some that are clearly gerontomorphic. These he merely wrote off as "secondary," in much the same way recapitulationists had written off the paedomorphic characteristics.

Had Bolk embraced Darwinism rather than contended against it, his fetalization theory might have fared better in the history of science. Unfortunately his hostility toward the concept of adaptation caused him to seek an explanation for paedomorphosis in the wrong place, in inner hormonal modifications rather than in the external environment. It was Stephen Jay Gould who, half a century later, resurrected and rehabilitated

Bolk's "central insight," as Gould calls it, by divorcing it from its explanatory apparatus and integrating it into the current Darwinian concept of "mosaic evolution," which holds that a wide diversity of environmental factors influence morphology, hence that different parts of the human body evolved under different local pressures. In such a scheme, paedomorphosis and gerontomorphosis can coexist in human anatomy without contradiction. Here is how Gould summarizes his conclusions about the role of neoteny in the hominization process:

> I believe that human beings are "essentially" neotenous, not because I can enumerate a list of important paedomorphic features, but because *a general, temporal retardation of development has clearly characterized human evolution. This retardation established a matrix within which all trends in the evolution of human morphology must be assessed.* This matrix does not in itself guarantee a central role for paedomorphosis, but it certainly provides a mechanism for such a result, if this result be of selective value. This mechanism was utilized again and again in human evolution because retarded development carried a set of potential consequences with it: prolongation of fetal growth rates leading to larger sizes and the retention of juvenile proportions. Is not such a system the proximate cause for the evolutionary increase of the human brain? (*Ontogeny and Phylogeny*, 365; italics in original)

Gould backs up his claims that retardation is a fundamental matrix of human evolution by providing a cogent Darwinian framework within which to understand the selective advantages of neoteny. By allowing us to retain various juvenile traits in adulthood, retardation maximizes our adaptive flexibility. When the external environment, for whatever reason, undergoes rapid transformations — and most leaps in human evolution have occurred as a direct result of such upheavals — we are better able to cope with the new circumstances, since as children of neoteny we rely less on a set of conservative, specialized features and more on the enhanced plasticity, adaptability, and learning abilities of youth.

If Gould is correct, retardation is the source not only of our paedomorphic traits but also of the two interrelated characteristics that, more than any others, distinguish us from other animals: our greater intelligence and our greater capacity for socialization. The former has its source in our prolonged fetal growth rates, which allow our brains to grow to a much larger size than those of other primates; the latter has its source in our prolonged infancy and childhood, which enhance the learning process and in turn enhance intelligence. Taken together, these two characteristics account for that distinctly human strategy of survival we call culture. Only a creature with an inordinately delayed development comes to rely more on learning than on instinct, or pursues modes of survival that depend mainly on education, memory, and acquired skills. And only a creature born into the support structures of human society has the luxury of prolonging its juvenile development so extensively. In sum, our genius as a species lies in our reluctance to grow up.

Much doubt still surrounds the role that neoteny played in our evolution, yet in the overall scheme of how we became human, one cannot overstate the importance of delayed development, which reaches deep into our species-being in ways that go well beyond the paedomorphic traits. We humans spend a much larger portion of our lives growing up (roughly thirty percent) than even our closest relatives in the animal kingdom. We spend the better part of a year in the womb, and when we are born we are still essentially embryos. The reason our embryonic growth continues for so long after birth has to do with the exceptionally large size of the human brain. Were we to complete our embryonic growth inside the womb, our heads would be too big to exit the vaginal canal.

If culture is evolution by other means, delayed development is the garden — or kindergarten — where youth's capacity for learning has flourished under carefully cultivated circumstances. Only *Puer discens*, the learning child, could become *Homo sapi-*

ens. By extending the learning process dramatically, and in some cases indefinitely, delayed development has handed our destiny over to our own ingenuity, or what the Ode on Man calls our "wind-swift all-understanding."

To summarize, human neoteny is neither regression nor arrestation but a modified type of development that brings juvenile traits to new levels of maturity, where they are preserved in their youthful form. We could think of it this way: toward the end of his life Einstein claimed that his breakthroughs in physics were due to the fact that, in mind and in spirit, he had remained a child his entire life. Now Einstein's mind obviously did not cease its development when he was still a child. What he meant was that he never stopped asking more probing and technically sophisticated versions of those basic questions that parents never quite know how to answer: Why is the sky blue? How old is God? Why can't I see the wind? It takes a childish sort of inquisitiveness to wonder what an atom is made of, or under what conditions time might move backward, or what light would look like to someone traveling at its speed on a parallel beam. Einstein's mind continued to grow in capacity and complexity while holding on to its intrinsic wonder, curiosity, and love of the marvelous. In that sense his mind was not unlike Bolk's "primate fetus that has become sexually mature." Which is another way of saying that he was quite a genius.

To this I would add that neoteny resists the tyranny of legacy. To delay the rate of development entails not only a reluctance to grow up but a reluctance to reproduce a fixed and senile form that links us to ancestry by the laws of repetition and identity. In that regard neoteny gives humans a greater species freedom, both *from* the genetic dictates of the past and *for* new, as yet unrealized, possibilities. By holding on to the plasticity of youth for much longer periods, and in some cases throughout our entire lives, we have expanded our evolutionary options considerably, becoming over time a lighter, freer, more agile, and adventuresome species. In short, a more intelligent and youthful species. Or better, a more intelligent — because more youthful — species.

The Ode on Man in *Antigone* offers us a glimpse into the more terrifying side of this youthful openness to wonder, discovery, and knowledge of the world. The determination to boldly go where no one has gone before takes us to the moon and into the arcana of chromosomes; it gives us the microchip and the atom bomb. Yet for all the novelties it has brought into the world since Sophocles composed the ode, there is one part of the ongoing human story that doesn't change. Even if our youthful intelligence one day succeeds in rendering death optional rather than necessary, what the chorus says about *anthropos* will remain true: "everywhere journeying, inexperienced and without issue, he comes to nothingness." Thus, if our genius derives from our reluctance to grow up, our wisdom derives in turn from our heightened awareness of death. As we will see more in depth in the next chapter, it is when the two work together — and not against one another — that human culture flourishes.

The Albino Gorilla

Storytelling is a basic trait of the human species, a childlike way we have of making sense of the world's enigmas, above all the enigma of our being in it. There is every reason to believe that the first human stories came into being not in verbal but dramatic form, communicating plot, character, and emotion through ritualized enactments, costumes, masks, and the human body's extraordinary mimetic powers. Language would have entered the picture only later, much the way spoken dialogue came after the pantomime, title cards, and expressive gestures of silent film.

Giambattista Vico — the eighteenth-century Italian thinker whose theory about the ages of civilization I will discuss in the next chapter — was no doubt right when he claimed that the animistic myths of human prehistory arose from two interrelated characteristics that are endemic to early human childhood: the child's inability to think abstractly and its prodigious figurative imagination. Vico writes:

So that, as rational metaphysics teaches that man becomes all things by understanding them ... this imaginative metaphysics [of early humans] shows that man becomes all things by *not* understanding them ... and perhaps the latter proposition is truer than the former, for when man understands he extends his mind and takes in the things, but when he does not understand he makes the things out of himself and becomes them by transforming himself into them. (§405, 130)

The earliest human stories were almost certainly projective personifications of this sort, with actors transforming themselves into the protagonists of their narratives. This imaginative capacity to project — to believe, make believe, and suspend disbelief — is one that human beings, whatever their biological or historical age, never lose. It is one of humanity's basic neotenic traits, where neoteny now shifts from the biological to the cultural sphere.

Since our topic here is the "age difference" between *Homo sapiens* and their primate ancestors, let me invoke a story that may help us penetrate some of the thick shadows surrounding the psychic elements of this difference. Titled "The Albino Gorilla," it appears in Italo Calvino's book *Mr. Palomar*, published in 1983. Before discussing it in detail, we should remark that the gorilla in Calvino's vignette is not a fictional animal but a once famous denizen of the Barcelona zoo. Captured in 1966 while still an infant in Equatorial Guinea, the gorilla died in 2003, some eighteen years after Calvino himself passed away. Named Copito de Nieve, or Snowflake, because of his white fur and light skin pigment, he was the only known albino gorilla in existence. He sired several offspring during his long life in the zoo, none of which inherited his albinism and none of which outlived him. Copito de Nieve lived to the ripe old age of forty (the average lifespan of gorillas in the wild is roughly twenty-five), and Calvino would have seen him when the gorilla was still in his teens. Let us turn now to the story.

During his visit to the zoo in Barcelona, Mr. Palomar—"a nervous man who lives in a frenzied and congested world"— sees Copito de Nieve in his walled garden yard. Even though he is still young, the gorilla "has the look of an old man." Indeed, "the great ape suggests to Mr. Palomar's mind a remote antiquity, like mountains or like the pyramids." The impression of antiquity comes from the archaic prototype of the gorilla's body, which has endured unchanged across the ages and to which Copito de Nieve, despite his albino hide, has remained perfectly faithful. Nevertheless, this particular ape seems different from others of his kind, not simply because of his snowy coat but because he appears to suffer from the confinement of his species-being. He lives in "an enclosure surrounded by high masonry walls, which gives it the appearance of a prison yard," writes Calvino, yet one could say that the cage enclosing this gorilla is first and foremost the evolutionary limit that nature has imposed on his species.

Copito de Nieve manifests the anguish of his condition (or so Mr. Palomar imagines) by holding an old rubber tire tight to his chest. His mate also has a tire, but for her "it is an object of normal use, with which she has a practical relationship, without problems: she sits in it as if it were an easy chair, sunbathing and delousing her infant." For Copito de Nieve, by contrast, who never lets go of it, "the contact with that tire seems to be something affective, possessive, and somehow symbolic." Mr. Palomar reflects: "From it he can have a glimpse of what for man is the search for an escape from the dismay of living—investing oneself in things, recognizing oneself in signs, transforming the world into a collection of symbols—a first daybreak of culture in the long biological night." Mr. Palomar suspects that such dismay may well be the source of language itself: "Perhaps identifying himself with [the tire], the gorilla is about to reach, in the depths of silence, the springs from which language burst forth, to establish a flow of relationships between his thoughts and the unyielding, deaf evidence of the facts that determine his life."

Certain notable philosophers who have thought in depth

about the difference between human and animal being would champion Mr. Palomar's perception of Copito de Nieve as a confined creature. Martin Heidegger, for example, drawing on the work of the zoologist Jakob von Uexküll, affirmed that, compared to humans, the animal is "poor in world." Wholly absorbed by its immediate field of perception, the animal is trapped within its surrounding environment. It cannot act freely, only behave instinctively. In *The Fundamental Concepts of Metaphysics* Heidegger writes, "Captivation [*Benommenheit*] is the condition of possibility for the fact that, in accordance with its essence, the animal *behaves within an environment but never within a world*" (271)—that is, never within a world of action, comportment, and the openness of meaning.

The French philosopher Henri Bergson affirms essentially the same thing in more elegant prose:

> Radical, therefore, also, is the difference between animal consciousness, even the most intelligent, and human consciousness. For consciousness corresponds exactly to the living being's power of choice; it is coextensive with the fringe of possible action that surrounds real action; consciousness is synonymous with invention and with freedom. Now, in the animal, invention is never anything but a variation on the theme of routine. Shut up in the habits of the species, it succeeds, no doubt, in enlarging them by its individual initiative; but it escapes automatism only for an instant, for just the time to create a new automatism. The gates of its prison close as soon as they are opened; by pulling at its chain it succeeds only in stretching it. With man, consciousness breaks the chain. In man, and in man alone, it sets itself free. (*Creative Evolution*, 169)

There is a strong drive these days, among theorists and ethologists alike, to discredit such assumptions about human exceptionalism in the natural order—assumptions that seem all but self-evident to most of us—yet we need not enter that debate here, since in Calvino's story the gorilla represents more of a figurative projection than a specimen. Yet what exactly does he represent? Is he a hypothetical intermediary species between the primate and the human? Does he suffer from a distinctively male—or white male—form of existential anxiety (note the difference between Copito's "symbolic" relation to his tire and his mate's pragmatic relation to hers)? Should we see in him a refracted image of the artist in his or her alienation from society? Should we see in him a psychological self-portrait of Calvino himself? A case could be made for each of these options, yet given our main concern here, let us narrow the focus down to the following question: Is Copito de Nieve a figure of human infancy struggling to break into language?

That question admits of both a negative and a positive response. To begin with the negative, we could say that a human infant is speechless, yet not in the way this gorilla is. Infantile speechlessness amounts to an overabundant potentiality for symbolization and signification; it is the babbling prelude to an irrepressible loquacity that does not yet have words at its disposal. Unlike a human infant, Copito de Nieve will never reach the springs from which language bursts forth, no matter how long he lives, for those springs are located in the depths of infancy itself. It is not by overcoming but rather by prolonging the period of speechless infancy that language is born. Copito de Nieve is already too old, too grown, too late, for that. The more he ages the more he distances himself from the source. In sum, he is doomed to remain an ape that was never quite young enough, or was not young for quite long enough, to access the realms of symbol, myth, and intelligibility. The tire that consoles him for his exclusion from the garden of meaning has all the power of a primitive symbol, yet in his case it symbolizes the gorilla's postsymbolic rather than presymbolic condition.

Even if one were to grant that the "real" Copito de Nieve in the Barcelona zoo suffered from the sort of anguish that Mr. Palomar projects onto him, the gorilla was still bound to go to his grave without uttering a word, for Calvino's vignette locates the source of language in the wrong place, namely in "man's ... search for an escape from the dismay of living." Language does not arise from a need to escape but from a desire to enter, not from frowns of impotence but from a surplus of vitality and wonder. Vico's imaginative metaphysics arises from a juvenile human urge to *become* all things, not from a perplexed need to "establish a flow of relationships between his thoughts and the ... facts that determine his life." The latter need pertains to another stage of life — if not another stage of civilization — than the one that keeps a human infant groping for the means of expression.

Unlike Copito de Nieve's privative limitations, the infant's limitations are generative, overcharged with a sense that the surrounding world abounds in magic, enticement, purpose, and agency. For Copito de Nieve to be a figure of human infancy, he would have to be so full of somatic play and plasticity, so full of mimetic buoyancy, that the overload of his imaginative energy would be ready to spill over into onomatopoeia, personification, symbolization, and eventually speech. Instead, Mr. Palomar sees in Copito de Nieve the look of a "sad giant" who "turns upon the crowd of visitors beyond the glass, less than a meter away, a slow gaze charged with desolation and patience and boredom, a gaze that expresses all the resignation at being the way he is." Resignation is decidedly *not* the disposition that gave rise to the exuberance of primitive myth, the enchantments of animism, or the totems of magic rituals.

An affirmative answer to the question posed earlier becomes possible only if we reconceive the timing of the event. While we should not take Copito de Nieve as a figure for a human infant's struggles to break into language, we could (and indeed should) see in him a personification of the sort of infancy that persists in human beings long after they have acquired the use of language. We could call it a postjuvenile infancy, of the sort that afflicts Mr. Palomar himself in his older age. How so?

Mr. Palomar concludes his meditation by thinking to himself, "Just as the gorilla has his tire, which serves as tangible support for a raving, wordless speech ... so I have this image of a great white ape. We all turn in our hands an old, empty tire through which we try to reach some final meaning, which words cannot achieve." The remarkable thing about Calvino's vignette is that it enacts for the reader the "imaginative metaphysics" that distinguishes Mr. Palomar's human freedom from Copito de Nieve's species-confinement. Mr. Palomar may be a senior adult, he may even feel weary and ponderously old within himself, yet he retains that special childlike capacity to personify the ape by projecting himself into Copito de Nieve's imagined frustrations. For it is Mr. Palomar who, trapped in a frenzied and congested world, imagines the ape's entrapment by circumstance and the "facts of life." Likewise it is Mr. Palomar who, dumbfounded by life, imagines the ape's bewilderment before a dimly perceived dimension of meaning just beyond his cognitive reach.

More importantly, Mr. Palomar imaginatively projects onto the ape the psychic "infancy" — or speechlessness — that persists not only within himself but within all human beings throughout their lives. We do not have words for the final meaning of things, that final, elusive meaning for which we grope. No matter how long we live, no matter how much we take cognizance of the so-called facts of life, there will always be something about the larger story that exceeds human understanding, defies our expectations, and frustrates our desire to grasp its ultimate purpose. However much we imaginatively "become" all things, or scientifically "understand" them, there persists in every human being an inner child who fails to comprehend the world into which he or she has been thrown — an inner child who cannot find adequate words for the elusive mystery that surround us on all sides, wherever we turn our gaze. In that sense there is an albino gorilla inside us all.

From a Common Spring

One male member of the human species claimed that the difference between having and not having a penis entails such enormous social and psychological consequences that "anatomy is destiny," by which he meant that sex determines the fundamentals of life. There is more to anatomy than sex, however, just as there is more to sex than anatomy. When it comes to destiny, we must keep in mind that human males and females evolved in tandem; neither gender is anatomically more human than the other, nor is one significantly more paedomorphic, even if human females are in certain aesthetic respects slightly more neotenous than males. If Freud's dictum is valid, then men and women, in their species-being, by and large share a common destiny.

That does not mean that gender difference among humans is not abyssal, or that men and women do not relate to one another across a chasm. In some of the most intimate respects — how we experience our life cycles, for example, or the biological aging process — the destinies of men and women diverge considerably (although not as much as some people would like to believe). The larger philosophical question here is whether the gender difference divides men and women more than it unites them, or whether, on the contrary, it serves to consolidate our common species-identity.

Some years ago I came across, in some publication or another, a peremptory declaration by a woman zoologist: "I have more in common with female baboons than I do with males of my own species." I have pondered that assertion in depth, from several points of view, and I would now respond to it as follows: Just as men and women share in common the anatomical features that make us a single species divided into two genders, so too they share in common whatever makes it possible for one gender to feel completely at odds with the other.

I intend this to mean that the gender divide, however deep it may run, is not in itself primordial. What is primordial is our human capacity to feel alienated, bewildered, and cut off from others, as if one were an anomic aberration among one's kind. This sense of inner albinism does not afflict one gender more than another. It belongs to the distinctly human experience of estrangement, especially during youth, when one is apt to feel as freakish as Frankenstein's male monster, who vents his loneliness and incomprehension in words lent him by a woman. To put it differently: among humans the youthful sentiment of exceptionalism expressed in Edgar Allan Poe's poem "Alone" applies as much to one gender as to the other:

> From childhood's hour I have not been
> As others were—I have not seen
> As others saw—I could not bring
> My passions from a common spring.
> From the same source I have not taken
> My sorrow; I could not awaken
> My heart to joy at the same tone;
> And all I loved, I loved alone.
> *Then*—in my childhood—in the dawn
> Of a most stormy life—was drawn
> From every depth of good and ill
> The mystery which binds me still.

The mystery persists — it "binds me still" — because it arises from the depths of childhood and carries over into later phases of life as the idiosyncratic core of inner selfhood. While it binds me, it does not define me, if "define" means to impose a limiting boundary. On the contrary, the mystery exposes me to the world in the mode of openness, rendering me aware of, and susceptible to, the strangeness of things both distant and near. The uncommon "source" from which I bring my passions and take my sorrow throws me into an alien intimacy with the world — the intimacy of an initiate who does not yet understand the terms of his or her initiation. It is precisely there — in that novitiate openness — that a boy and a girl, or a man and a woman, when they respond to their deepest human calling, come together as two of a kind. The more frank and sincere their encounter, the more uncanny appears the openness in question — so much so that they may feel called on to domesticate its extravagance by forming a partnership.

It is impossible to know how other species experience the aging process, and even within our own species the experience differs significantly across genders, yet whether one is male or female, childhood represents a form of destiny among humans, not in Freud's sense of anatomical determinism but in the sense that the child's inward exposure to things continues to reverberate in all later phases of the life cycle. Whether happy or unhappy, healthy or unhealthy, blessed or besieged, childhood remains every adult's psychic center of gravity, so tenacious — or neotenacious — are its early imperatives and impulses.

The paradox is that those imperatives and impulses remain active in subsequent periods of life mostly in imaginary, retrospectively inflected forms. In truth, childhood is what every adult has lost, regardless of whether one has an accurate or distorted recollection of its condition. Precisely because it persists in the mode of loss, we have a marked tendency to mythologize its golden age or transfigure its reality through selective memory, fantasy, nostalgia, and retrospective projection. Certainly the loss of childhood is our first "intimation of mortality," if not our first taste of death itself.

Interpersonal intimacy among mature human beings, regardless of gender, involves a sharing of that loss in one form or another. When it takes place between a man and a woman, their bond becomes all the more intense by virtue of the gender difference that divides them. Such sharing is rendered possible by the fact that none of us, male or female, masters the open realm of encounter, in all its mysterious strangeness. The wondrous poem "The River Merchant's Wife: A Letter," by the eighth-century Chinese poet Li Po, traces in a first-person narrative the sharing in question. In Ezra Pound's rendition, the poem reads:

> While my hair was still cut straight across my forehead
> I played about the front gate, pulling flowers.

You came by on bamboo stilts, playing horse,
You walked about my seat, playing with blue plums.
And we went on living in the village of Chokan:
Two small people, without dislike or suspicion.

At fourteen I married My Lord you.
I never laughed, being bashful.
Lowering my head, I looked at the wall.
Called to, a thousand times, I never looked back.

At fifteen I stopped scowling.
I desired my dust to be mingled with yours
For ever and for ever and for ever.
Why should I climb the look-out?

At sixteen you departed,
You went into far Ku-to-yen, by the river of swirling eddies,
And you have been gone five months.
The monkeys make sorrowful noise overhead.

You dragged your feet when you went out.
By the gate now, the moss is grown, the different mosses,
Too deep to clear them away!
The leaves fall early this autumn, in wind.
The paired butterflies are already yellow with August
Over the grass in the West garden;
They hurt me. I grow older.
If you are coming down through the narrows of the river
    Kiang,
Please let me know beforehand,
And I will come out to meet you
        As far as Cho-fu-Sa.

The first stanza pictures two children immersed in their parallel
worlds, which intersect only at their edges. The children exist
"without dislike or suspicion," which is to say alongside, rather

than with, one another. The second stanza evokes the trauma of the girl's cohabitation with her new husband, a decision we presume was made for her by her elders. She experiences her first year of marriage as an abrupt severance from the world of her childhood. Her refusal to speak indicates that she does not have the means to express the state she finds herself in, using silence as her medium of communication. The third stanza describes how, in the wake of her lost childhood, she forms a bond with her husband that projects deep into the future, beyond even the terminal limits of biological life. The fourth stanza describes another separation, this time from her husband. Yet by now she is no longer a stranger to loss; she knows better what the sounds of the overhead monkeys intimate, namely the sorrows of mortality. The last stanza describes the wife's growing aware-ness of finitude and her realization that she and her husband have become allies in the domestication of time's wilderness. In her spouse's absence, the mosses by the gate grow too deep to clear away, time decays and becomes autumnal in the bloom of youth, and she feels the hurt of age. In the last lines of the poem she is eager to go out to meet the one who dragged his feet when he left six months earlier — to meet him beyond the confines of their home, at a more expansive confine (Cho-fu-Sa) than her garden wall. Her offer to venture forth in anticipation shows that she is ready to meet him as a full-fledged adult, in affirma-tion of their domestic partnership.

In the arc of two years the river merchant's wife goes from girl to woman, becoming fully cognizant of what it takes for two adults, having left their respective childhoods behind, to secure a human home in the midst of time's self-expropriating change of seasons. In two years she has internalized her finitude and is ready to reestablish her life on that mortal basis.

We live in a very different culture — call it a different age — than the river merchant's wife. With us it typically takes about twenty years to undergo the existential maturation process she accomplishes in two. How much is gained or lost by this increas-ing delay in the onset of existential maturity is hard to say. One advantage that the likes of the river merchant and his wife have over the "emerging adults" of our own era, who spend the better part of their twenties exploring their professional, amorous, and worldview options without yet committing to any of them—or who, in Jeffrey Arnett's words, have " left the dependency of childhood and adolescence ... [but] not yet entered the enduring responsibilities that are normative in adulthood"—is that they are biologically young enough when they become full-fledged adults that their conjugal relationship has more time—and more vitality—to dispose of. We, by contrast, are often so worn out by the time we grow up that adulthood tends to exhaust rather than exhilarate us. The age of juvenescence can do only so much to remedy this growing discrepancy between our biological and psychosocial development. Eventually nature gets the better of us. (See notes for further commentary on Li Po's poem.)

The Child Progenitor

If in biology the term "neoteny" refers to a form of delayed development, in the psychological or existential realm we could use it to refer to a form of *relayed* development, in the sense that the psychic life of childhood gets relayed forward to adulthood, where it is both preserved and modified. If there did not persist in the adult psyche an inner child to whom father gods, mother goddesses, and other kinds of divinities could make their appeal, there would be no religions in the world; and if there were no religions in the world, there would be no world at all, only environments and habitats. By the same token there would be no Oedipal complexes and precious little art, poetry, science, or philosophy, all of which owe their *élan* to a certain childlike wonder before phenomena. The expectations we humans bring to bear on life—that it respond to our appeals, that our existence matter, that someone or something care about us—are essentially childish in nature. Human adulthood does not so much supersede as inflect the desires, dreams, and disappointments we carry over into our postjuvenile stages of life — even unto that "second childhood" sans teeth, sans hair, and sans eyes.

William Wordsworth composed the modern gospel of this relay of childhood sentiment. We would do well to rescue it from the Romantic clichés to which it has given rise, above all those surrounding the much-quoted verse "The child is father of the man," which occurs in Wordsworth's short poem "My Heart Leaps Up," written in 1802:

> My heart leaps up when I behold
> A Rainbow in the sky:
> So it was when my life began;
> So it is now I am a Man;
> So be it when I shall grow old,
> Or let me die!
> The Child is Father of the Man;
> And I could wish my days to be
> Bound each to each by natural piety.

In the middle of this existential arc — the arc reflected in the rainbow's covenant between the three stages of life evoked here — the "man" retrieves his earlier delight at the sight of the rainbow, relaying it forward in the hope that in his old age he will continue to respond to that sight with something of the child's primal joy. ("To that dream-like vividness and splendour which invest objects of sight in childhood, every one, I believe, if he would look back, could bear testimony," wrote Wordsworth in a letter of 1843.) While this joy seeks to remain true to itself in time, that is, to remain identical, it cannot help but differentiate itself as the aging process takes its course.

For the child, joy arises spontaneously from the radiance of the phenomenon. For the man, it has a reiterative quality, mediated by the memory of its earlier instantiations. For the old man, it will assume a contractual character, binding him to the child by what Wordsworth calls "natural piety." One could also call it "filial" piety, for it partakes of the same kind of *pietas* that

Aeneas showed his father Anchises when he rescued him from the flames of Troy, except that in this case the "man" bears a progenitor child on his shoulders into the future.

Wordsworth elaborated on this Romantic creed in his famous poem "Ode: Intimations of Immortality from Recollections of Early Childhood," for which the last three verses of "My heart leaps up" serve as epigraph. "Ode" begins with the speaker's sense that "there hath passed away a glory from the earth"—the glory, precisely, of things as they appeared in childhood. It goes on to expound a quasi-Platonic notion of a preexistent divine state from which the human soul comes forth at the moment of birth, as if birth represented a fall from heaven to earth. "Our birth is but a sleep and a forgetting" of that prenatal state, writes Wordsworth, adding that in childhood we retain a much stronger associational memory of the glory from which we were expelled—"Heaven lies about us in our infancy!"—since the neonate remains nearer to the eternal source of joy than adults do (hence the intense "intimations" of childhood). The poem continues:

> Shades of the prison-house begin to close
> > Upon the growing Boy,
> But He beholds the light, and whence it flows,
> > He sees it in his joy;
> The Youth, who daily farther from the East
> > Must travel, still is Nature's Priest,
> > > And by the vision splendid
> > > Is on his way attended;
> At length the Man perceives it die away
> And fade into the light of common day.
> > (ll. 68–77)

There would be cause for grief over the way this prison-house begins to close in on the boy, blunting his perception of things until, in later life, his ecstatic vision fades into the light of common day. If Wordsworth refuses to grieve, it is because in eternity's "embers" the dying light of childhood joy continues to shine: "Those first affections are yet the fountain light of all our day." "Our" here refers to all humanity, just as "day" refers to all that humans perceive through the light of reason, reflection, and seasoned perception. The relayed openness of youthful wonderment conditions all of human seeing and consciousness, and not just the poet's, which is why Wordsworth, in what amounts to a statement of doctrine, emphatically repeats that our first affections remain "yet a master light of all our seeing."

Childhood sentiment lies at the core of "the faith that looks through death" and informs the wisdom that comes later in the arc of life, "in years that bring the philosophic mind" (ll. 190–91). As the aging process follows its course, it submits that sentiment to a maturation whereby the grown man gains in depth and insight what he loses in awe and intensity, such that the sentiment blossoms with age rather than withering away like a dried-up seedpod. When Wordsworth declares, "To me the meanest flower that blows can give / Thoughts that do often lie too deep for tears" (ll. 207–8), the thoughts are those of an adult who delves once again, albeit in a more mature mode, into the primordial sources of childhood marvel—sources that are too deep for tears because from them flows the love of the world that binds us to life itself.

This constant return to, and revitalization of, the source turns the aging process into an exfoliation of primal sympathy. I borrow the metaphor of exfoliation from another poem, written a century and a half later than Wordsworth's "Ode," which has various affinities with the latter's gospel of natural piety. The poem—titled "Une Voix" ("One Voice")—comes from the 1965 collection *Pierre écrite*, by the French poet Yves Bonnefoy:

> Nous vieillissions, lui le feuillage et moi la source,
> Lui le peu de soleil et moi la profondeur,
> Et lui la mort et moi la sagesse de vivre.

J'acceptais que le temps nous présentât dans l'ombre
Son visage de faune au rire non moqueur,
J'aimais que se levât le vent qui porte l'ombre

Et que mourir ne fût en obscure fontaine
Que troubler l'eau sans fond que le lierre buvait.
J'aimais, j'étais debout dans le songe éternel.

We grew older, he the foliage and me the source,
He the patch of sunlight and me the depth,
And he death and me the wisdom of living.

I could accept that time showed us in the shade
his faun's face with its unmocking laugh,
I was glad when the wind that carries the shadow

rose, and dying was just troubling some obscure fountain's
bottomless water that the ivy was drinking.
I was glad, I stood in the eternal dream.

Although the word "age" never makes an appearance, its pho-
neme is embedded in three of the poem's key words: "feuill*age*,"
(foliage), "s*age*sse" (wisdom), and "vis*age*" (face). In the course
of its exfoliation, age has divided this self-same speaker into *lui*
and *moi*, "him" and "me." *Moi* holds fast to the source, to the
springs of life, while *lui* is associated with the crown of foliage
that grows out from, or thanks to, the source from which *moi*
speaks. The more the tree grows (or the person ages), the more its
foliage crowds out the sunlight. Hence the "*peu de soleil*"—the
small patch of sunlight—that remains later in life. This patch of
sunlight will eventually give way to the darkness of death, even
as *moi* remains rooted in the "wisdom of life."

The poem reveals the extent to which we conceive of the
aging process too narrowly when we view it as a progression
from youth to maturity to death. That is *one* dimension of it, to

be sure, and in this poem *lui* seems associated with this incremental diminishment of future time (foliage patch of sunlight death). Yet the poem alludes to a countermovement, whereby *moi* delves deeper into the generative ground of life (source depth wisdom of life), as *lui* branches outward and upward. The tree's foliage thrives, growing into, and crowding out, the light, thanks to the trunk's tenacious roots, which plunge ever more deeply into the source. In this simultaneous movement and countermovement — this delving and unfolding — life and death speak with *une voix*, one dual voice.

It is because *moi* holds fast to the source that he or she, like the speaker in Wordsworth's "Ode," can "accept" what time offers up. *Moi* was glad "when the wind that carries the shadow rose," for *moi* understands death not as the termination but as the fulfillment of life's potential. That is why its event hardly troubles the "bottomless water" from which the ivy drinks, like a barely detectable ripple on its surface. This vision of existential growth sees aging not as a falling away from, but as a sinking of roots ever deeper into, the source. In that regard it partakes of that "faith that looks through death," as Wordsworth called it, allowing *lui* and *moi* to "stand in the eternal dream." The tree's crown is free to sway in the wind because its roots hold firm in the ground in which childhood first came to life and opened its eyes to the world's wonder. Where the child is father to the man, the man stands in the eternal dream, not because he overcomes death but because he lives in the fullness of age, regardless of how early or late in the life cycle he dies.

Such testaments from first-person poems corroborate one of the main theses I have been advancing in this chapter: that human maturity has its source in the youth it brings to fruition. The deeper the source, the more extravagant the growth, which is another way of saying that human youth, in its neotenic relay, makes possible a capacity for spiritual maturation that has no equivalent in the animal kingdom, insofar as it opens humankind up to a wide range of psychic, and not merely organic, modes of being. When it comes to our species-being, this is the deeper meaning of the otherwise trite phrase "The child is the father of the man."

Yet before we get too carried away with the romance of the child or kneel at the altar of juvenility, we should recall what the chorus in *Antigone* had to say about the youthful spirit of *anthropos*, namely that for all his capacity for wonder, for all his openness to the strangeness of things, for all his ingenious ability to manipulate the forces of nature and devise new gadgets and tools, there persists in "man" a strange, self-destructive recklessness that can easily get the better of him and engender disaster. The fact alone that the chorus is composed of Theban elders should serve as a reminder that it is not thanks to children that our species has survived; it is thanks to their parents, teachers, leaders, and sages. Human society in its basic structures compensates for our extravagant dependence on others during infancy and childhood. It is how the adults of the species pay—and pay dearly—for the luxury of our protracted youth as well as the folly of our misadventures. If it is true that the child is father of the man, it is because the child obliges the man to become a father, that is, to develop a degree of social, political, and moral maturity that is unheard of in the animal kingdom. In the next two chapters we will look more closely, and in specific detail, at both the "genius" and the "wisdom" that define human societies and engender—each in its own way—the cultural history of our species.

TWO

Wisdom and Genius

Sapientia

Modern humans belong to a subspecies of *Homo sapiens* that goes by the name of *Homo sapiens sapiens*. Whatever the taxonomists may have had in mind when they came up with the label, its redundancy points to two kinds of *sapientia* that are fundamentally different in character. One is linked to our genius, or the intelligence in us that experiments, invents, discovers, imagines, calculates, and in general brings about wholesale change through knowledge and manipulation of the external world. The other is linked to that senile wisdom of humankind—arising from our awareness of mortality—that gave birth to the gods, the graves of the dead, the laws and scriptures of nations, the memory of poets, and the archives of scholars. (Here and elsewhere, "senile" means fully mature, not decrepit.) Of these two kinds of *sapientia* one is "older" than the other, not because it has a prior genesis but because it takes the prior—or what comes before—into its custody and safekeeping. While genius liberates the novelties of the future, wisdom inherits the legacies of the past, renewing them in the process of handing them down.

Earlier I remarked that human age assumes inordinate complexity by virtue of the fact that we inhabit humanly built worlds that outlast any individual lifetime. Unlike animals that start the life cycle over with each new generation, humans are thrown into an ongoing story, or history, whose past opens the way to a future they will not live to see come about. However diverse the forms it may take, the institutional and societal network we depend on for our survival predates our inclusion in it. When we speak of culture, then, we mean the place where our predecessors live on, not only in the memories of their loved ones but in the laws, customs, creeds, and knowledge that inform the culture in question. By enabling them to receive and transmit a heritage, wisdom confers on human individuals a cultural age that takes its measure from the span of generations and not from our biological years alone. There is no such thing, properly speaking, as an immature society, or a society devoid of wisdom. A wholly immature society, such as the one William Golding attempted to depict in *Lord of the Flies*, either implodes or gives way to authority structures that enable it to endure.

While wisdom gives the future a foundation in the past, genius effects breaks in the cultural continuum through its creative capacity to resist the dictates of tradition and generate the new—be it new tools, new knowledge, new worldviews, or new forms of expression. Through its innovations and revolutions, it effectively modifies, confounds, and adds to the reservoir of legacies that wisdom retrieves for transmission. The domestication of fire, the casting of iron, the discovery of bronze, the invention of print, the rise of the steam engine—such events in the history of genius multiply and differentiate the ages of culture (Stone Age, Iron Age, Bronze Age, Industrial Age, etc.), putting wisdom under greater pressure to reinherit a complex, dynamic, and heterogeneous past. Wisdom could hardly meet that challenge if it were not in some sense ingenious, nor could genius build upon its past achievements if it were not in some sense wise. In sum, there is a wisdom at the heart of genius that enables genius to reap the rewards of its history without having continually to reinvent the wheel, just as there is a genius at the heart of wisdom that allows wisdom to creatively transform and rejuvenate the past, while giving a measure of continuity to the otherwise discrete history of genius.

Until recently the history of genius has been characterized

by periodic "mononeisms," single momentous innovations that took their time to reorganize our modes of being in the world. Millennia separate the discovery of fire from the discovery of agriculture. Between the invention of writing and the printing press several world empires rose, declined, and fell. Only a few centuries, however, come between the printing press and the steam engine. In broad cultural terms, that is hardly any time at all, although from our contemporary perspective it seems like a galactic age, for we have become accustomed to a condition of permanent upheaval and overturning. The period since World War II has seen a delirious proliferation of major inventions, from air travel to television to the atom bomb to the birth control pill, to mention only a few of the "polyneisms" — or multiple, more or less simultaneous novelties — that have altered practically every aspect of life in human societies across the globe.

Yet even those twentieth-century inventions now seem quaintly antiquated, for in the past two decades a staggering number of new ones — many of them equally consequential — have plunged us into a polyneistic vortex the likes of which human culture has never before experienced. Nothing in our recent or remote past compares with the rate or magnitude of this change, and no one yet knows whether there is enough youthful plasticity in the human psyche to adapt to the accelerated revolutions of our frenetic genius.

These recent surges of genius, most of them originating in the West, have made it practically impossible for wisdom to carry out its basic task of synthesizing the new with the old and providing our worlds with a measure of permanence and continuity (more about worldhood and permanence in chapter 4). Even Western wisdom, which over the centuries had become especially creative, elastic, and ingenious, has been thrown for a terrible loss, helpless to bridge the chasms opened up by our volcanic genius, to the point that we now are faced with a series of unsettling questions. Can a society dispense with wisdom altogether and entrust its fate to genius alone, without self-destructing? Can it lose its historicity and still possess a future? Can we consign our cultural memory to oblivion and continue to understand what drives our actions, decisions, and the stories we tell ourselves about who we are? Is self-knowledge compatible with a delirious expansion and fragmentation of knowledge? Is rejuvenation possible without a concomitant process of cultural maturation? In order to answer such questions we must first get a better idea of what wisdom and genius are and how they have creatively collaborated with and sponsored one another in the past. Such is the burden of the next two chapters. Only then will we be in a position, in the final chapter of this book, to attempt to answer the questions themselves.

A Note on Age and Wisdom

It bears repeating that wisdom is not "older" than genius — it did not come first, either in the evolutionary or cultural sense — even if it takes the older, or the prior, into its custody. That is why we should suspend traditional stereotypes and not think of wisdom as a hoary old man or of genius as a prodigal child. True, genius often draws on youthful energies and impulses to effect its innovations, while wisdom remains prudential in its outlook, focused as it is on the challenges of stability, preservation, and continuity. Yet, as we will see in case after case in this chapter and the next, wisdom has its own forms of ingenuity, just as genius has its own ways of being wise as it goes about its ventures.

The convention that associates wisdom with old age rarely stands up to empirical scrutiny. Young people possess an intuitive wisdom that often withers away with age. We saw that Wordsworth's doctrine of natural piety ascribes to the child an otherworldly inner wisdom that makes the child "father to the man." "Bodily decrepitude is wisdom," declared Yeats in a poem I discuss in chapter 4, but H. L. Mencken, the "Sage of Baltimore," scoffed at "the familiar doctrine that age brings wisdom." A Chinese proverb states the obvious when it says, "Wisdom does not depend on age; a man of a hundred may be full of empty talk." It was because he too believed that wisdom does not depend on age that the Greek sage Diogenes Laertius advised, "Let no one be slow to seek wisdom when he is young... no age is too early or too late for the health of the soul." One cannot be foolish one's whole life long and expect that later years will bring wisdom, as if by a natural process of compensation. If it comes at all, wisdom comes to those who cultivate its resources when they are young; the benefits they later reap—the fruits by which you shall know them—grow from seeds that are sown early on. In the last chapter of this book I will return to and enlarge upon this question of a youthful cultivation of wisdom.

Montaigne is especially persuasive—in that first-person way he has of thinking aloud—when he states that, with age, a person more often retreats into prejudice, pettiness, and petulance than blossoms with sagacity. Reflecting on his youth in his late thirties, he writes, "Since then I have grown older for a great length of time, but not an inch wiser am I, I am sure." Later in his life he would write: "my wisdom may well be of the same size in both the one time and the other [i.e., in my vigorous years and my decrepitude]; but it was far prompter to do, more supple, green, gay, natural than it is at present, stale sullen, painful." About growing old, he added:

> Our humours are hard to please; present things disgust us; and this we call wisdom. But the truth is that we do not so much leave our vices as change them; and in my opinion for the worse. ... Never a soul is to be seen, or very few, who in growing old does not take on a sour and mouldy smell. A man moves toward his full and his decline as an entity, a whole. (Booth, *Art of Growing Older*, 233)

This whole pertains not only to individuals but to civilizations, which tend to "move" as wholes. Just as a person does not necessarily grow wiser with age, civilizations do not necessarily gain greater institutional or cultural wisdom as they get older. We must be wary of pushing the analogy too far, for the organic law that governs individual maturation does not govern the historical development of a civilization. Thanks to the newborn who ceaselessly infuse them with new life, civilizations may rejuvenate themselves. At any given moment a "sour and mouldy" wisdom can become supple, green, and gay again. Individuals do not have that privilege. We may contribute to a society's decline through our folly, or to its efflorescence through our wisdom, yet our personal story comes to an end long before the history it belongs to does. The purpose of wisdom, at the institutional, societal, and historical levels, is to find new ways to keep the story going, and that requires genius.

The River and the Volcano

When one thinks of Western genius one thinks above all of the Greeks. For confirmation that Western civilization remains in many respects the child of ancient Greece, we need look no further than the opening of Plato's *Timaeus*, where a character named Critias tells Socrates an "old world story" he heard from his grandfather on the day of the "Apaturia," or registration of youth, when Critias was ten years old and his grandfather over ninety. The grandfather had heard the story in his youth from his father, who had heard it from Solon the sage, who had heard it from an elderly priest during his visit to the Egyptian city of Sais. We in turn hear Critias's account to Socrates from Plato, an abbreviated version of which I shall now retell, so that the river of cultural memory might flow on.

This is what happened: during his visit to Sais, Solon is asked by his Egyptian hosts to speak of the olden days of Greece, so he begins to tell them about the first human being, Phoroneus, about Deucalion and Pyrrha, and other Greek origin stories, yet he is promptly interrupted by a venerable old priest, who declares, "O Solon, Solon, you Greeks are never anything but children, and there is not an old man among you. ... In mind and soul you are all young: there is no old opinion handed down among you by ancient tradition, nor any science which is hoary with age." The priest goes on to explain why the Greeks are so young in "mind and soul" (*psyche*).

The goddess Athena, he declares, founded Athens a thousand years before she founded Sais—a city of great age—yet the Greeks have no memory of Athens's ancient origins due to the annihilations of their former civilizations. These annihilations were brought on by periodic "declinations" of the heavenly bodies that produced meteorological and volcanic disturbances, unleashing "a great conflagration of things upon the earth." The priest goes on to recount the story of an island that, during one of these declinations some nine thousand years earlier, sank into the sea:

Many great and wonderful deeds are recorded of your state in our histories. But one of them exceeds all the rest in greatness and valour. For these histories tell of a mighty power which unprovoked made an expedition against the whole of Europe and Asia, and to which your city put an end. This power came forth out of the Atlantic Ocean, for in those days the Atlantic was navigable; and there was an island situated in front of the straits which are by you called the Pillars of Heracles; the island was larger than Libya and Asia put together, and was the way to other islands, and from these you might pass to the whole of the opposite continent which surrounded the true ocean; for this sea [the Mediterranean] which is within the Straits of Heracles is only a harbour, having a narrow entrance, but that other is a real sea, and the surrounding land may be most truly called a boundless continent. Now in this island of Atlantis there was a great and wonderful empire which had rule over the whole island and several others, and over parts of the continent, and, furthermore, the men of Atlantis had subjected the parts of Libya within the columns of Heracles as far as Egypt, and of Europe as far as Tyrrhenia. This vast power, gathered into one, endeavoured to subdue at a blow our country and yours and the whole of the region within the straits; and then, Solon, your country shone forth, in the excellence of her virtue and strength, among all mankind. She was pre-eminent in courage and military skill, and was the leader of the Hellenes. And when the rest fell off from her, being compelled to stand alone, after having undergone the very extremity of danger, she defeated and triumphed over the invaders, and preserved from slavery those who were not yet subjugated, and generously liberated all the rest of us who dwell within the pillars. But afterwards there occurred violent earthquakes and floods; and in a single day and night of misfortune all your warlike men in a body sank into the earth, and the island of Atlantis in like manner disappeared in the depths of the sea. For which reason the sea in those parts is impassable and impenetrable, because there is a shoal of mud in the way; and this was caused by the subsidence of the island.

Atlantis sank into the sea, never to rise again, whereas Athens "sank into the earth" but eventually rose again from the ashes, retaining no memory of its prior existence.

Why does Egypt have an age-old memory of what the Greeks have long forgotten? The answer has to do with geography. Thanks to the flatness of the Nile delta, Egypt has managed to weather the cataclysmic upheavals without fatal consequences, whereas the mountainous terrain of Greece causes Athens and other Greek cities to be inundated by floods and buried under layers of ash. The priest:

Whereas in this land, neither then nor at any other time, does the water come down from above on the fields, having always a tendency to come from below; for which reasons the traditions preserved here are the most ancient. ... Whereas just when you and other nations are beginning to be provided with letters and the other requisites of civilized life, after the usual interval, the stream from heaven, like a pestilence, comes pouring down, and leaves only those of you who are destitute of letters and education; and so you have to begin all over again like children, and know nothing of what happened in ancient times, either among us or among yourselves.

Note the succinctness of the priest's distinction between Greek youth and Egyptian senility, which has to do not with chronological age but with institutional stability. The "oldest" cultures are not always those that have the earliest origins but those that have maintained greater continuity with them. Although Athena founded Athens a thousand years before Sais, the Egyptians possess an unbroken memory of, and maintain strict continuity with, their deep past, while the Greeks keep losing their memory and starting all over again "like children."

The symbol of Egyptian senility is the river, of Greek youth the volcano. The priest alludes to Greek volcanism when he states that the most serious devastations — those that wiped out Greece's former civilizations — "involved water or fire." In Egypt water tends "to come from below," causing the Nile to flood, for the most part harmlessly. In Greece, by contrast, both water and fire come from above, water as rain from the sky, fire in the form of lava and ash from the mountaintops.

In its evocation of the several lost antiquities of Athens, Plato's story points to a law of catastrophism that time and again has made its presence felt in the course of Western civilization, both before and after Plato's time. These events of "rise and decline" may not be due to "declinations" in the heavens, even if nature invariably plays a leading or supporting role in our calamities, yet there is no doubt that Western civilization as a whole periodically loses its memory, disinherits its past, and surrenders its achievements to ruin. Classical Greek culture, of which Plato's corpus is a sublime flower, emerged in the wake of a prolonged "dark age" that followed the collapse of Mycenae. Homer's epics (eighth century BC) look back to its glories from within the shadows of that darkness. Classical Greece, after its great cultural flourishing, would eventually go the way of Mycenae. Along with Rome, it would succumb to ruination.

The Renaissance in its turn would look back nostalgically to the Greek and Roman worlds, which we today still refer to as our "antiquity."

These recurring ruptures in the cultural continuum — ruptures that bring about "dark ages" of destitution, oblivion, and institutional collapse — seem frequent enough to lend at least allegorical credence to Plato's parable about heavenly declinations. Today we have the privilege of seeing this volcanic process at work up close, in Technicolor, as it were, as the entire Christian-humanist civilization that slowly consolidated itself in the wake of Rome's collapse unravels before our eyes. It was said of President James Garfield that in moments of boredom or to amuse his friends he would take a pencil in each hand and compose sentences in Greek and Latin *at the same time*. If one considers that, as a student, Thomas Jefferson used to translate the Greek Bible into Latin, and vice versa, one realizes to what extent the "heavenly declinations" have unleashed their fury upon the American political class of late. It was not so long ago that a university professor in the classroom would typically leave Greek and Latin quotes untranslated. Then he began to provide translations for the Greek but not for the Latin. Nowadays he must tell his students that there were once such things as the Greek and Latin tongues, that there was once a place called Athens, and so forth. Shortly the professor won't know even that much. Or he'll know it, in a way, but not what to make of it, and when you don't know what to make of something you eventually forget about it.

Why these periodic ruptures in the cultural continuum? In the *Timaeus* Plato attributes Greek rejuvenilization to heavenly declinations, yet we should keep in mind that civilizations are brought down not only by external enemies or natural forces but sometimes collapse from within, by virtue of their own heaviness. Our age shows that a loss of cultural memory can come about despite — or maybe even because of — an excessive remembering and cataloging of the past. The more historical knowledge we accumulate — the more we overload the vast data banks of our digital memory with information about the past — the more its essential legacies slip through the cracks of our living memory. We should also bear in mind that the more our cultural memory begins to crack, the more vulnerable we become to heavenly declinations, that is, to nature's fluctuations and eruptions. Youth has several virtues, yet providing for the future is not one of them.

Children of Science

Plato's "old world story" lends itself to other types of allegorical reading related to our theme of wisdom and genius. The Egyptian priest says about the Greeks that there is not an old man among them, no memories handed down by ancient tradition, no knowledge hoary with age, for despite their culture's deep past they keep forgetting what lies behind them. That sounds like a description of modern science. Science has an ancient history that goes back millennia, yet both its visionaries and its ordinary practitioners function best when they forget the past and look forward to the next challenge. The history of science is a matter for historians, not scientists. A twenty-year-old theorem may as well belong to the annals of prehistory. As for the wisdom traditions of the past, science rarely misses an occasion to expose their ignorance concerning matters of fact. Piety and science do not mix well, and there is no greater distillation of the spirit of daring described by the Ode on Man in *Antigone* than scientific research, especially in the present age.

Like a child who is "all eyes," science gapes at phenomena, mesmerized by their shapes, sizes, quantities, and motions. It is curious about their causes, intrigued by what it does not understand, desirous to know more than conventional explanations can provide, and given to playful "what if?" hypotheses. It is less interested in inheriting what predecessors have established than in exploring what they may have overlooked. Its dominant passion is for discovery, hence it has little use for the old unless it can be viewed anew. Modern science cultivates amnesia so that it can continue to look at the world as if seeing it for the first time. Therein lies its childlike spirit.

In the Paul Klee painting rendered famous by Walter Benjamin's commentary in *Theses on the Philosophy of History*, the so-called angel of history is borne upward through the air on outspread wings, facing backward. In Benjamin's vision, all the angel sees are the accumulated ruins of the has-been. His motion is a form of aggravated aging, a flight not through space but through time's remorseless succession of ages seen from the perspective of their passing, not their coming. This is decidedly *not* an image in which we recognize the spirit of science, for science flies on the wing of another kind of angel — the angel of neoteny — who weaves in and out of enfolded spaces, forever turning a corner or rounding a bend, entering or exiting a crease of the cosmos, such that his expectant, forward-looking gaze sees anew a world it has been seen countless times before, always as if for the first time. His happiness consists in the illusion that the line of time is an illusion. Although memory engenders the storm in paradise that draws both angels upward, the angel of neoteny sees what his counterpart doesn't see, and doesn't see what the other does. This is why he seems more at home in the universe than his endlessly aging, forever older brother of grief, who bears the burdens of primogeniture.

Like Plato's mythic Greeks, science in fact has a history and an age that belie its youthful disposition. Indeed, history remains the lens through which the world appears to its fascinated gaze. Today's theorem would not exist, let alone make sense, without yesterday's theorem, just as Copernican cosmology would not exist, let alone make sense, without Ptolemaic cosmology, and so forth. If science proceeds "naively," with the demeanor of a child, it is because it ingeniously projects its memory forward and thereby forgets it even has a memory.

Such forgetting has a lot to do with the way science incorporates its latent memory in functional objects, where the knowledge that allows those objects to function erases itself in the functioning. "Have you looked at a modern airplane?" asks

Antoine de Saint-Exupéry in his 1940 essay "The Tool." What we don't necessarily see with our eye is that "the experimentation of several generations of craftsmen [allows] he who uses this instrument ... to forget that it is a machine." "Every machine," he writes, "loses its identity in its function" (65, 67, 72). Most of the objects that populate our daily lives respond to the simple command of our fingers, yet the airplane, the dishwasher, or the personal computer discretely archive an accumulated, millennial learning in their functions. Your car may be new, yet its internal combustion engine goes back to the nineteenth century, while the fundamentals of its motility go back to the invention of the wheel. No one person masters all of the science that goes into the automobile, with its various accessory features, yet the teenager applying for a driver's license operates it as effectively as the engineer who knows something about the theorems and equations behind its basic mechanics.

All of which confirms that the average first-world citizen today enjoys the luxury of remaining as innocent as a child with respect to the instruments that he or she operates, consumes, and otherwise depends on daily. We are all the beneficiaries of a history that recedes into the depths of time, no matter how insulated or monodimensional our experience of the present may be in our age of juvenescence. Such are the ancillary, perhaps unintended, blessings of science's neotenic wisdom. Saint Exupéry intuited as much when, referring to the surge of technoscientific genius of the first decades of the twentieth century, he wrote, "We Europeans have become again young peoples. ... We shall have to age somewhat before we are able to write the folksongs of a new epoch" (70–71).

Any number of "folksongs" have since been written about the so-called new epoch, which has become quite old by now, eight or nine decades later. The volcanism of the West may keep us young in "mind and soul" by causing us to lose our memory, yet nothing can change the fact that, historically speaking, we are altogether ancient, whether we take full measure of our age or not. The deep past that lodges in the object, that fades from consciousness, or that lies buried under the debris of fallen cities, does not vanish in the successive convulsions of history. It merely goes underground, sinks into the earth, as it were, from which depths it continues to determine the future, whose outcome, when it comes about, will have had several precedents across the millennia. It is, after all, an "old world story."

The more Western civilization experiences ruptures in its historical continuum, the more new elements get introduced into its fitful story — elements so new as to alter our very conception of what it means to be old. Modern science has helped turn us into one of the "youngest" societies in world history — we are younger in ways that even our relatively recent forebears could not have imagined — yet at the same time it has also increased our age enormously. Thanks to Darwin and other theorists of evolution, the human species is much older today than it was when we believed in the Bible's chronology of creation. By the same token, in this age of juvenescence cosmologists have expanded the age of the universe immeasurably; geologists have discovered "deep time"; archaeologists have dug up one antiquity under another beneath what we once considered the *fons et origo* of human civilization; and philologists have given a hoary etymological age to the everyday words we use to tweet one another anagrammatically. Science, which keeps us so young in spirit, has done more to increase our cultural as well as natural age than any Egyptian priest from Sais could have dreamed of with his old world stories. Time and again, after losing our memory and becoming like children, we eventually discover that behind us lies a history as old as the world itself and that we are not children after all. Only this time, the age of that world is greater than ever before.

Heterochrony

If geology, archaeology, and philology can effect quantum changes in our understanding of how old things are, then we should be all the more wary of the analogy between historical development and the maturation process of human individuals. This analogy finds expression in a wide variety of myths, theories, and speculations, from Hesiod to Freud and beyond. The most grandiose — and in some ways most naïve — version comes to us from the owl philosophy of Hegel, who conceived of world history as a single, unitary movement of the Spirit's self-realization, a movement that follows the course of the sun, from east to west. Here is how Hegel puts it in his *Introduction to the Philosophy of History*:

> If we continue with the comparison of history to human growth, we can say that [Asian despotism] is the boyhood stage of history, no longer behaving with the calm trust of childhood, but rather in a rowdy and aggressive way. The *Greek World* may then be compared to the period of adolescence, for here we see individualities being formed. ... The third stage of world history is the realm of abstract universality: this is the *Roman World*, the hard work of history's manhood. ... The fourth stage of world history [is] that of the medieval *Germanic World* — history's old age (if we continue with the comparison to the cycle of aging in the individual). In nature, old age is weakness; but the old age of the Spirit is its complete ripeness, in which Spirit returns to unity with itself, but as Spirit.

This return to unity was not fully realized in Europe for several centuries, he continues, insofar as "the principle of the Germanic world became a concrete reality only through the [establishment, centuries later, of the modern] Germanic nations" (96–98).

This "comparison of history to human growth" is hopelessly static in its apparent dynamism. To begin with, the four civilizations in question arose independently of one another, with the exception of modern Europe, which preserved certain genetic links with ancient Greece and Rome. To incorporate them all into a single cycle of cultural maturation is far too cunning even for Reason. Furthermore, each one of them followed its own self-propelled course of development. Rome, for example, clearly passed through most, if not all, of the stages of this so-called world history, going from the despotism of the early family patriarchs to the aristocracy of the patricians to the popular revolutions of the plebeians, and finally to the universality of empire (whether this meant that it went from youth to senility is another matter).

When it comes to the ages of history—their emergent conditions, patterns of succession, and mutual interpenetration—the thinker we have the most to learn from is not Hegel but his eighteenth-century Neapolitan predecessor Giambattista Vico, who spent much of his obscure career pondering the laws of cultural development. The fruits of his insights are contained in his *New Science*, the definitive version of which was published in 1744. Vico held that most ancient civilizations developed autonomously, along lines that were at once specific and general. Left to their own inner dynamic, they naturally passed through what he called an age of gods, an age of heroes, and an age of men. To each age—divine, heroic, and human—there corresponds a determinate type of religion, language, technology, morality, politics, and jurisprudence. *The New Science* offers a full-fledged theoretical account of how the ages are generated, transmogrified, and dissipated according to a cyclical law that Vico calls *il corso delle nazioni*, or "the course of nations." To appreciate Vico's contribution in this regard, the following brief schematic will help.

The divine age, which gets the historical *corso* underway in primitive societies, is dominated by animistic religions. An array of deities populate its world, manifesting themselves in or as the phenomena of nature. Vico calls the first age "divine" because these gods—born of the prodigious poetic imagination of the early founders of civil society—hold sway over every aspect of human destiny. Its dominant form of social organization is the extended family clan, where the family fathers reign supreme, acting as high priests possessed of severe religious and patriarchal authority. The language of divine times is predominately ceremonial, gestural, and emblematic.

The heroic age begins with a collaborative effort on the part of the family patriarchs, or "heroes," to quell the unrest and rebellions of their serfs. By forging loose federations among themselves they give rise to a ruling aristocratic class. Indeed, the heroic age is dominated above all by class distinction, with the nobles believing that they descended from gods while their serfs ascended from beasts. The language of the heroic age is largely symbolic, heraldic, and figurative.

The human age comes about after the oppressed classes gradually realize that all human beings — noble or plebeian — have one common human nature, and begin pressing for democratic reforms. The institutions of the human age thus tend toward popular justice and egalitarianism, while its mode of thought tends toward greater and greater abstraction. The language of human times is mostly discursive, legal, and analytical — prosaic rather than poetic, precise rather than passionate, denominative rather than figurative.

The New Science shows in granular philological detail how the three ages, each in its own way, configure sense perception, mental conception, and symbolic expression. In the previous chapter I remarked that the phenomenon's perception is bound up with the perceiver's personal age (the young boy and his grandfather, I claimed, do not see the same phenomenon when they gaze at the same tree). One can make the same claim for historical age — that the phenomenon appears differently in one age than in another. Vico labors in *The New Science* to render manifest the degree to which each of his three cultural ages inflects the appearance of phenomena. This is the great achievement of his singular work. Through schematic categories and vivid examples, he shows how the phenomenon undergoes fundamental transformations — both in conception and perception — as one age gives way to another. Time and again he reminds us just how hard it is, from within our modern mindset, to enter into the phenomenological horizons of earlier ages. Referring to the reconstructive challenges he faced while writing *The New Science*, Vico declares, "We encountered exasperating difficulties which have cost us the research of a good twenty years. [We had] to descend from these human and refined natures of ours to those quite wild and savage natures, which we cannot at all imagine and can comprehend only with great effort" (§338, 100).

A human-age consciousness, especially in its modern modalities, is too belated, too enlightened, and too ironic to see deities in every aspect of "sympathetic nature." We moderns have lost the vigorous poetic imagination that once perceived the sea in the guise of a god. We see things within the rational, abstract, "disenchanted" framework that our human age places around appearances. For us Poseidon is a poetic trope, a quaint anthropomorphism, rather than the true face of the sea. This is precisely Wordsworth's regret in his poem "The World is Too Much with Us," where he laments that modern consciousness can no longer animate the phenomenon with an anthropomorphic image: "Great God! I'd rather be / a Pagan suckled in a creed outworn / so might I . . . Have sight of Proteus rising from the sea; / Or hear old Triton blow his wreathéd horn."

That creed got outworn as one age gave way another, and then another, such that the sea's phenomenon — the way it gave itself to human perception — underwent a basic metamorphosis. That does not mean that its prior modalities fall into complete oblivion. As we saw, Wordsworth believed that "natural piety" preserves a trace of the enchanted modes of childish perception, relaying them forward to later stages of life. Vico believed something similar at the historical level. Although he insisted that we cannot willfully return to or readopt modalities of conception and perception that belong to prior ages, he held that the phenomenological "truth" of those bygone ages continues to infuse the sensibility and mentality of subsequent ages to one degree or another, depending on the culture or civilization in question. In sum, the ages are not immured within their own autonomous frameworks (or what some would call their "hermeneutic horizons"); rather, they convene, intersect, and overlap with one another by virtue of the fact that "the world of civil society has certainly been made by men, and ... its principles are therefore to be found within the modifications of our own human mind" (§ 331, 96). The human mind in the broadest sense — including what later would be called the collective unconscious — contains within itself active elements of its prior mentalities and "modifications."

Scholars have generally assumed that the relation between Vico's three ages is linear, progressive, and discrete. This is not the case. While the ages in Vico's scheme do indeed succeed one another, they also interpenetrate. For example, with regard to the kinds of language particular to each age, Vico remarks the following:

> To enter now upon the extremely difficult [question of the] way in which these three kinds of languages were formed, we must establish this principle: that as *gods, heroes and men began at the same time* (for they were, after all, men who imagined the gods and believed their own heroic natures to be a mixture of the divine and human natures), so these three languages began at the same time, each having its letters, which developed along with it. (§446, 149)

I take this to mean that the three types of language are copresent in any given age, although one type preponderates in the general manifold. We who belong to the human age do not speak and write *only* in prose. Gestures, symbols, and tropes also inform our language, though to a lesser degree than in earlier ages. Likewise, the mostly mute and gestural language of divine times was not *entirely* mute and gestural, but was also — though to a lesser degree — symbolic and articulate (i.e., heroic and human). The same goes for the metaphysics, politics, and customs of the three basic configurations. Each contains, in variable degrees, "heterochronous" elements, that is, elements that pertain to different ages. This is true above all for the human age, with its heavier load of legacies, its more sprawling past. That is why the image of Proteus rising from the sea is not altogether foreign to Wordsworth, and why the myths of the divine age still resonate with us, even if "we cannot at all imagine and can comprehend only with great effort" how the world appeared to the people (or remote ancestors) who first created them.

If the interpenetration of the ages means that every human society possesses heterochronous traits to one degree or another, we can say, along with Vico, that this variable quotient of heterochrony depends on a host of circumstantial factors, such as geography, climate, wars, and local institutional histories. Above all, we can say that while different civilizations follow similar patterns of development as they move from one age to another, some have higher quotients of heterochrony than others, and that in some cases the relation between ages is benign and collaborative, in other cases belligerent and abrasive.

If Roman culture appeared to Hegel more adult than Greek culture, it cannot be for the reasons that Hegel himself advanced (namely that Spirit—analogically speaking—spent its boyhood in Asia, its adolescence in Greece, and its adulthood in Rome). Borrowing from Vico's theory, we could say it was because Rome, as it developed, retained a greater quotient of its divine age in its heroic age, and a greater quotient of both in its human age. To express it otherwise: Rome was more loyal to its founding spirit and values than were the Greeks, thanks to a variety of factors (such as, again, its geography, its social networks, its senate, its agrarian traditions, its founding myths, and so on). These factors enabled the Roman human age to preserve a greater degree of continuity with its past than was the case with Greek civilization, whose historical development (as Vico observes) was altogether more fitful, less centralized, and more discontinuous than Roman civilization.

In a passage that cannot but remind us of the *Timaeus*, Vico uses the image of a river to describe the continuity of Rome's civic and political history: "Within these human governments, even as the mighty current of a kingly river retains far out to sea the momentum of its flow and the sweetness of its waters, the age of gods coursed on, for there persisted still that religious way of thinking according to which it was the gods who did whatever men themselves were doing" (§629, 234). One could call this an instance of Vico's "rheological" account of Roman wisdom, according to which the Roman divine age flowed smoothly or "sweetly" into its subsequent ages (for Greece, the eddy, vortex, or torrent would be more appropriate analogies).

Earlier I drew a distinction between the fluvial and the volcanic. Here I would draw a correlative distinction between "pious" and "insurgent" forms of heterochrony. It is the difference — figuratively speaking — between Aeneas and Oedipus. Shouldering the burden of legacy as he assumes responsibility for his people's future, Aeneas flees the flames of Troy with his household gods in hand to secure a new homeland for the House of Troy, where it can maintain its continuity in time under new conditions. In Virgil's *Aeneid* (composed during the Roman human age), Aeneas figures as a paradigmatic "hero," yet he also labors under what Vico calls the "divine" mandate of the ancestors, a mandate that makes heavy demands upon the living, not the least of which is to care for the unborn at the expense of one's own happiness and comfort. In Virgil's archetypal portrait, Aeneas represents an idealized conjunction — a pious "and" — that links Roman generations together.

Compare that pious "and" to the rebellious "but" that one finds not only in the Oedipus story but also in Greek theogonies. Behold Uranus, god of the heavens. Jealous of his offspring, he confined them all in the body of his consort Gaia (goddess of the earth). Finding the burden intolerable, Gaia gave her youngest and bravest son Kronos a sickle and urged him to take action against his father. The next time Uranus approached Gaia to lie with her, Kronos, from within his mother's womb, castrated him. From the drops of blood that fell to the earth sprang the Furies and the Giants; from the genitals, which Kronos cast into the sea, sprang Aphrodite. The defeat of Uranus, which henceforth kept heaven and earth apart, inaugurated a new "golden age" in the history of the word — that of the Titans.

That golden age would not last long, for like his father Uranus, Kronos was suspicious and fearful of his own children—with good reason, it turns out, since Uranus had warned him that he too would be overthrown by one of his sons—so he took to swallowing them as soon as they were born. Acting on advice from Gaia, Kronos's wife Rhea gave her husband a stone wrapped in swaddling clothes to swallow in place of his son Zeus. This would prove to be his undoing, for after Kronos vomited up his other children, Zeus led his brethren in battle against their father. Thus Kronos and his fellow Titans were overthrown by a younger generation of gods, the so-called Olympians, who cast the Titans into Tartarus and bound them there in chains. It is not for nothing that we find Kronos's name embedded in the ungainly word that I have used several times already in this context: heterochrony.

The gods' generational wars tell us something about the tense and agitated nature of Greek heterochrony. Rome's turbulent history was periodically convulsed by violent civil wars and internecine strife, yet there is a difference between inter- and intragenerational conflict. Zeus versus Kronos, or Oedipus versus Laius, is not the same as Romulus versus Remus, or Brutus versus Caesar, or Anthony versus Octavian. Is fratricide the malignant outgrowth of the filial piety idealized in the figure of Aeneas? Suffice it to say that a deep anxiety about generational antagonism pervades Greek myth, and that this anxiety has something to do with the conflictual, embattled nature of Greek heterochrony when compared to the more fluvial patterns of Rome. In one case, the culture's diverse ages appear more disjunctive and dissonant; in the other, they remain more continuous, flowing into, rather than erupting out of, one another. This difference is manifested at any number of levels and in any number of domains, both in the ancient world and in our modern Western world. In the following section I take a brief look at what it means to be "at home" in the volcanic pattern I have described here, with reference to our own time.

Generation Gaps

Sociologists Gunhild O. Hagestad and Peter Uhlenberg claim that modern Western societies, especially in the United States, have institutionalized age segregation by confining the young to educational institutions, adults to the workplace, and the elderly to retirement homes. Consequently the generations spend most of their time alongside rather than with one another. The domains become increasingly partitioned and contact between them correspondingly reduced. Such apartheid deprives the elderly of their traditional mentorship roles, deprives the young of a sense of larger kinship, and deprives families of what Hagestad and Uhlenberg call "social embeddedness" and "generativity," which in more traditional societies foster dialogue and interaction between the various age groups. "Generativity" is the word Hagestad and Uhlenberg use to denote the transmission of legacies from one generation to another within the domestic sphere, leading to the mutual "embeddedness" of those who inhabit it.

It is hardly surprising that societies with high quotients of embeddedness and generativity tend to maintain greater continuity with their historical past than ones that segregate the generations. The domestic interaction that takes place — or fails to take place — between the generations depends a great deal on the common world beyond the household walls, whose social, economic, and technological forces invariably find their way into the intimacy of the family domicile. Hence it would be a mistake to say that cultural heterochrony "begins at home." It begins with the public world beyond the family walls. I use the phrase "beyond the family walls" figuratively, for we know that, in our contemporary society, there is almost nothing that physical walls can do to keep the external world from invading the domestic space.

The same holds true for the so-called generation gap, a term that became popular during the 1960s, when a flourish of genius transformed the fabric of social life in Western culture. Age segregation is as much an effect as a cause of this gap. The polyneistic eruptions of the postwar period brought about such rapid and wholesale changes in the common world that the Baby Boomers came of age in what amounts to a different world than the one their parents had grown up in. When parents and children are natives of different worlds, the domestic sphere becomes heterocosmic and heterochronic in the volcanic rather than the fluvial sense.

For reasons that remain obscure, the kind of world we are born into and grow up in during our most formative years provides us with a mental framework or generational outlook that remains remarkably persistent throughout our lives, even after that world has effectively disappeared. (I am using the word "world" loosely here to refer to particular configurations of social reality, for example, the "world" of the Great Depression versus the "world" of the postwar boom. In chapter 4 I will discuss in more analytic detail what exactly the term "world" means in a broader discursive sense). To the extent that the world one is born into informs one's cultural mentality, every generation has its native mentality.

We do not fully appreciate just how much people of the same age or generation tend to have in common across classes, races, genders, and even nationalities. There is an elusive *Stimmung*, or generational disposition, that attunes people of the same age in strange, subterranean ways. Once it is formed, it tends to persist throughout all later stages of life. When I meet people of my generation almost anywhere in the world, I feel I am among my own kind, as it were. This lifelong persistence of a generational mentality acquired early in life marks another fundamental aspect of cultural neoteny.

During the 1960s it was still possible to speak of *the* generation gap in the singular, since the gap in question divided an entire generation of parents from their children. (When I say "an entire generation" I mean that segment of the population — a minority, to be sure — for whom the gap was a reality.) Nowadays it would make no sense to speak about a single generation gap, for in the past couple of decades the singular has given way to a delirious plurality. Today the gaps that exist between micro age groups are so numerous that one can no longer call them generational. If the Baby Boomers constitute a generational whole, their offspring have splintered into a multiplicity of sub-generations, making it difficult, if not impossible, to speak of generations in any meaningful way, so quickly does one world, along with its genetic mentality, get overturned by a new one. The fissures become not only more frequent but more abyssal. Today a chasm—psychological, social, verbal, and cultural—divides those who grew up with personal computers and those who did not. The same applies to the cell phone, or to video streaming, or to social media. Five or ten years of age difference now puts a young person on one side of this or that abyss, while the abysses continue to multiply. In the meantime, many of the traditional differences between one generation and another are collapsing. Adults shop at the same outlets as their children and grandchildren, literally and figuratively speaking. This strange phenomenon of generational confusion, so reminiscent of the Oedipus story, is a topic I will take up later on. For now, let us return briefly to the Greeks and continue to grapple with the knot of generational conflict.

Tragic Wisdom

One might infer from my earlier remarks about the piety of Aeneas and the Oedipal dramas of Greek theogonies that, unlike the Romans, the Greeks were long on genius but short on wisdom. Nothing could be further from the truth. Greek genius thrived to the degree that its correlative wisdom knew how to put the embattled ages into creative tension with one another, without necessarily resolving their strife. In the *Oresteia* the Erinyes' "divine" law of blood vengeance clashes with an abstract concept of justice that arose much later in the Greeks' historical *corso*, to speak with Vico. In the tense reconciliation that brings it to a conclusion, the trilogy confronts, without subter-fuge, the potentially self-destructive antagonisms that Athena's intervening wisdom succeeds in containing.

A similar clash occurs in *Antigone*, where a young woman de-fies her uncle in a dispute that involves not only two individuals but two imperatives—one much older in origin than the other. The irony of their confrontation is that the young Antigone up-holds an archaic law of kinship (burial of family members), while the older Creon appeals to the neoteric civic law of the state. As I stated in the previous chapter, there is a political naiveté about Creon that makes him appear politically immature. Through his rash actions and poor judgment he fulfills the apprehension that the chorus implicitly voices at the beginning of the play when it remarks on his status as a "new" king: "Creon, the new man for the new day ... what new plan will he launch?" (Fagles trans-lation, 174–76). Later in the play, his son Haemon will reveal himself to be politically wiser than his father when he points out the folly of insisting on his death sentence for Antigone when the citizens of Thebes so thoroughly disapprove of it.

In his book on *Antigone*, George Steiner rightly stresses that the burial motif in Sophocles—so central to *Ajax*, *Antigone*, and *Oedipus at Colonus*—"reaches back ... to far vestiges of the totemic" and that "the millennial magnetism of [*Antigone*] and of the myth it enacts draws on much older sources of psychic energy" (117). Those older sources of psychic energy adopted various masks through which they pressed their enduring claims on the Greek stage, under an intense sun that shined down on, and into, the abyssal depths of the ages, playing to the audience's anxiety about the power of ancient forces to rise up from the underworld and throw the younger Olympian order into crisis.

Beyond their thematics, Greek tragedies show a wondrous heterochronic complexity in their formal aspects as well. In many instances the choral odes—their prosodies, melodies, and theologies—well up from much older sources than the prosaic speech of the characters. The hypnotic chants and dances of the chorus give its odes a cavernous resonance, opening a subterranean depth beneath the spectacle of human suffering. In its movement and countermovement during the strophe and antistrophe, it offers choreographic images of an enduring truth that, like a dark fringe of wisdom, encircles the episodic tumult of the play's action. That most of the plots of Greek tragedies reach back into the deep history, or in some cases prehistory (some would say the unconscious), of Greek society only served to heighten the wonder and terror of this heterochronic tension.

Dramaturgy would have to wait until Shakespeare's *King Lear*—almost two millennia later—before staging anything remotely resembling such strife between the ages. It is not merely Lear's biological age ("four score and upward") that makes him so old. It's the fact that he belongs squarely to a heroic age at a time when it has already given way to a human age, with its self-reflexive consciousness, analytic abstraction, and convulsive will-to-power. Vico writes of the human age that its mentality and outlook are determined by irony, which is "fashioned of falsehood by dint of a reflection that wears the mask of truth" (*New Science*, §408, 131). This psychological capacity for reflection, which not only knows how to distinguish between truth and falsehood but also knows how to manipulate that distinction by masking falsehood behind the veneer of truth, and vice versa—this capacity for reflection, it should be noted, is not at all native to Lear's mentality. Lear cannot grasp the deadly play of irony. He must be educated into its treacheries through a series of shocks during the course of the play. Even after his baptism by fire, he still fails to fathom its perversities. It is this being-out-of-age—this belonging to an earlier, now largely obsolete age—that makes Lear so archetypically old.

Although she displays a Virgilian piety when she rallies to her father's cause, Cordelia is as much a creature of the new age as her duplicitous siblings. Her sincerity is the virtuous counterpart of the malignant insincerity unleashed by irony. Certainly such sincerity appears wholly out of place in the symbolic divestment ceremony arranged by her father at the start of the play. Cordelia's refusal to play her programmatic and emblematic role—her qualms of conscience, her judicious and delimited declarations, her prosaic weighing of the literal meaning of words—reveals just how decisively she belongs to the new, "reflective" age of irony. Lear expects of her a formal participation in a heraldic ritual; what he gets instead is a gesture of sincerity. The problem is that Lear knows nothing of sincerity and insincerity. He knows only loyalty and unloyalty. In her prosaic response to a poetic solemnity, Cordelia throws him for a loss, causing him to shrink back in bewilderment. It is the chasm that comes between one cultural age and another that causes Lear to believe that Cordelia has become a stranger to him.

In Vico's theory of the historical *corso*, human consciousness becomes ironic thanks to the faculty of reason, which subjects the superstitions and ignorance of prior ages to critical analysis, exposing the arbitrary foundations of the truths that those ages upheld as sacrosanct or normative. When it comes to establishing its authority on the basis of its own self-posted foundations, reason's task is to reveal the falsehoods that for centuries and even millennia have worn the mask of truth (that the class distinction is based in nature, for example, and not in custom; or that human society needs the authority of tradition lest freethinking lead to perdition). In his *Discourse on Method* Descartes declared that his goal was to secure, by the exercise of reason, a reliable method to distinguish between what is true and what is false, yet the will to truth has a potentially self-destructive impulse at the heart of its drive to subject all things to its disabused analysis. Reason submits to a withering critique not only the noxious falsehoods of the past but also the social and ethical principles that, while rationally unfounded, have allowed commonwealths to endure over the centuries. Thus while it has the power to liberate human beings from their ancient bondage, it also has the power to undermine the institutional foundations of society through the corrosive effects of cynicism.

King Lear endows both its villains and Cordelia with a high quotient of reason (nothing is more reasonable than Cordelia's speech to her father in the opening scene). Reason is the currency of the new age. The younger generation obsessively rationalize their actions. From a pragmatic point of view Regan and Goneril are perfectly "reasonable" when they demand that Lear reduce his retinue of knights by half, or half of the half, or even dispense with them altogether, since he has no need of attendant knights now. To this human-age reasoning, which turns need into the new religion, Lear responds with a heroic reasoning of his own: "O, reason not the need! Our basest beggars / Are in poorest things superfluous / Allow not nature more than nature needs, / Man's life's as cheap as beast's" (2.4.264–67).

In a play that abounds with rationalizations and poignant speeches, there is nothing to compare with the disabused, analytic edge of Edmund's reflections in those moments when he reasons honestly and openly to himself. His irreverence contains a compressed, insurrectional energy that makes him a metaphysical champion of the modern ideology we call our own:

> This is the excellent foppery of the world, that,
> when we are sick in fortune,—often the surfeit
> of our own behavior,—we make guilty of our
> disasters the sun, the moon, and the stars: as
> if we were villains by necessity; fools by
> heavenly compulsion; knaves, thieves, and
> treachers, by spherical predominance; drunkards,
> liars, and adulterers, by an enforced obedience of
> planetary influence; and all that we are evil in,
> by a divine thrusting on: an admirable evasion
> of whoremaster man, to lay his goatish
> disposition to the charge of a star! My
> father compounded with my mother under the
> dragon's tail; and my nativity was under Ursa
> major; so that it follows, I am rough and
> lecherous. Tut, I should have been that I am,
> had the maidenliest star in the firmament
> twinkled on my bastardizing. (1.2.119–33)

No twentieth-century exponent of existentialism, including Jean-Paul Sartre himself, ever came close to condensing the essence of the doctrine the way Edmund does in these brilliant lines, which denounce all who would disavow authorship of their own destinies. Were it not for the ever-resourceful ruses of bad faith, which is endemic to every human age, anyone who has a modicum of modern blood in his or her veins would cheer Edmund's call to self-determination and self-responsibility.

In the most enigmatic lines of *King Lear* — the couplet that brings the drama to an end — Edgar reminds the audience of the play's dominant theme, that is, age. "The oldest hath borne the most; we that are young / Shall never see so much, nor live so long." Surely he cannot mean that he and Albany will never live as long as Lear, nor that the young will never experience as much as their forebears, yet exactly what he means eludes us, inviting us to wonder whether the new age that has supplanted Lear's heroic age is simply too agitated, too decentered, and too chaotic in its metaphysics and geopolitics to last as long as its predecessor.

We need not examine here how age-conflict in *King Lear*, as well as its resolution, differs in many respects from the strife staged by the Greek plays discussed earlier. Suffice it to say that Shakespeare's tragedies typically present a clear divide between the forces of good and evil, which is usually not the case in Greek drama, and that in Shakespeare the former almost always end up prevailing over the latter, even if the victory comes at considerable cost. However, the age-conflict in *King Lear* is decidedly *not* one between good and evil, nor does it translate into a conflict between generations. A number of younger protagonists, after all, ally themselves with Lear and Gloucester against the likes of Edmund, Cornwall, and the depraved daughters. Their triumph over the play's villains does not restore the bygone age, but merely buries it solemnly and ceremoniously, with the respect that it deserves. The final undoing of the button of Lear's heraldic vestment tells us, in symbolic language, that Lear's age has been divested of its authority ("Pray, undo this button," Lear says in his last speech). If the forces of good prevail over those of evil in the play, they do so in the sense that their ambassadors secure a degree of benign continuity, rather than violent overthrow, in the transition from one age to another. In that respect, a certain measure of wisdom does indeed win the day.

Yet this is a defensive or conservative kind of wisdom. What we do not find in *King Lear* is the kind of ingenious, revolutionary wisdom that, in collaboration with the forces of genius, brings about a veritable rejuvenation—rather than a mere stabilization—in the political, social, or cultural sphere. Indeed, so far we have dealt with the phenomenon of heterochrony almost as if it were a collection of movable parts, or discrete interacting ages, rather than a historical process of interfusion and transformation. What remains to be done is to examine in detail, with reference to specific examples, the way wisdom and genius have worked together in the past to bring veritable "neotenic revolutions." In the next chapter I discuss a select sample of such revolutions.

THREE

Neotenic Revolutions

Preamble

This chapter aims to show how the dynamic synergy between wisdom and genius has brought about various "neotenic revolutions" in the cultural sphere. The revolutions I will deal with have little to do with biology, which is where the word "neoteny" comes from, yet I am not merely engaging in loose analogies between biology and culture. As I argued in chapter 1, neoteny figures as one of the most important sponsors of our species's enhanced intelligence and socialization. Since culture is the enlarged arena in which humankind plays out its evolutionary destiny, what I attempt to throw into relief in this chapter makes full sense only in light of my discussion of biological neoteny in the first chapter, as well as my discussion of wisdom and genius in the second.

To be more specific, I understand cultural neoteny as a highly variegated process of rejuvenation whereby older legacies assume newer or younger forms, thanks to a synergy between the synthetic forces of wisdom and the insurgent forces of genius. The best way to understand how this synergy works — or how genius consolidates its revolutions by calling on the resources of wisdom — is to take up a number of case studies that bring together premise and example, the way Vico attempted to bring together "truth" and "certainty" in his *New Science*. My case studies in this chapter include the rise of Socratic philosophy, the triumph of Christianity in the ancient world, the European Enlightenment, and the founding of the American republic. I could have chosen any number of other events in Western cultural history—the Renaissance, Romanticism, the French Revolution—yet my intention in this book is to offer a *theory*, not a history, of cultural neoteny. By dealing with my examples in a decidedly schematic manner—not as researcher but as a "new scientist," so to speak—I intend above all to illustrate a thesis rather than narrate a history.

I have chosen to focus on these particular case studies primarily because of their heterogeneity. Each of these revolutions in Western cultural history has its own distinctive, noniterative character; each takes place at a different time in history; and each belongs to its own cultural sphere (philosophy, religion, ideology, or politics). Yet taken together these revolutions manifest recurrent patterns whose structures or tendencies I seek to discover here. Whether the effect is to bring a youthful cultural characteristic to a higher level of maturity or to give a senile legacy a new or younger form, in each case we will find that the novelty of the new comes to rest on the foundations of the old—indeed, that it has no other foundations on which to repose.

The word "old" is necessarily ambiguous in this context. As the antonym of both "new" and "young," it can refer to very different phenomena and thus give rise to referential ambiguity. One must learn to live with this ambiguity, the way the Greeks did with their word *neos*, which means both young and new. "New" and "young" are not interchangeable, and the new is not in itself neotenic by any means. Nonetheless, novelty and youth are related to one another in ways that frequently make one the natural correlate of the other. Cultural neoteny typically engenders the new, even as it liberates, cultivates, or makes room for what is young. Just as neoteny in these pages must be understood in terms of rejuvenation as well as renewal, so too neotenic revolutions should be understood as advancing the cause of both novelty and youth, as we will see straightaway in our first case study—the rise of Socratic philosophy in ancient Athens.

Socratic Genius

It is unlikely that someone who does not fall in love with philosophy during his or her youth will have much use for it in later years. Even most of those who *do* will not have much use for it in later years. It may be true of a life full of future that "the unexamined life is not worth living," but when it comes to a life that has lived out the bulk of its years, the Socratic credo hardly applies. At a certain age life is worth living simply because it is life. Maybe the credo should state: an unexamined youth is not a genuine youth but a premature old age. To which we might add that a self-interrogating philosophy based on critical reason is appropriate to a self-searching, critical stage in the maturation process. The Romans called this stage of life for which the study of philosophy is appropriate *adulescentia* (roughly between sixteen and thirty years of age). Certainly many Greek and Roman patricians spared no expense when it came to hiring the best dialecticians to tutor their sons, yet they expected the latter eventually to move on to more serious matters than philosophy, like getting on with their lives and assuming the responsibilities of adulthood.

Plato's *Republic* dramatizes the disinclination of the elderly to engage in philosophy during the opening exchange between Socrates and the old man Cephalus, in whose house the dialogue takes place. To Socrates's query about what he, Cephalus, considers the greatest blessing of his inherited wealth, Cephalus replies: "The great blessings of [inherited] riches, I do not say to every man, but to a good man, is, that he has had no occasion to deceive or to defraud others, either intentionally or unintentionally; and when he departs to the world below he is not in any apprehension about offerings due to the gods or debts which he owes to men." Conventional wisdom has it that Cephalus is a naive simpleton who believes that virtue is contingent upon luck and circumstance. The conventional wisdom, however, is prejudiced by Plato's sardonic portrait of the oldster. Looked at from the perspective of life and not of theoretical reason, it is a mark of wisdom and maturity on Cephalus's part to suggest that the greatest blessing of inherited wealth is the moral, not material, comfort it affords. Behind every great fortune lies a crime, said Balzac, and certainly if you have inherited a fortune you are less likely to engage in criminal activity than if you have to earn one. Socrates:

> Well said, Cephalus, I replied; but as concerning justice, what is it? — to speak the truth and to pay your debts — no more than this? And even to this are there not exceptions? Suppose that a friend when in his right mind has deposited arms with me and he asks for them when he is not in his right mind, ought I to give them back to him? No one would say that I ought or that I should be right in doing so, any more than they would say that I ought always to speak the truth to one who is in his condition.
>
> You are quite right, he replied.
>
> But then, I said, speaking the truth and paying your debts is not a correct definition of justice.
>
> Quite correct, Socrates, if Simonides is to be believed, said Polemarchus interposing.
>
> I fear, said Cephalus, that I must go now, for I have to look after the sacrifices, and I hand the argument to Polemarchus and the company.
>
> Is not Polemarchus your heir? I said.
>
> To be sure, he answered, and went away laughing to the sacrifices.

At the beginning of the *Symposium* it is the flute girl who is chased away from the banquet of philosophy. Here it is the old man who departs just as the dialogue is about to get "serious," that is to say, just as Socrates is about to treat abstract nouns as if they were real substances. Cephalus knows that, at his age, it is better to go off and make a sacrifice than to interrogate the nature of the gods with finite means, or to wonder what an ideal republic would look like, or to inquire whether justice has an essence. You may as well make your sacrifice and have the gods on your side, just in case there are any. Cephalus simply does not have time for Socratic philosophizing. Death is breathing down on him. He was hoping that the two of them might engage in pleasurable conversation ("The more the pleasures of the body fade away, the greater to me is the pleasure and charm of conversation..."), but Socrates, for all his dialogical skills, is not a charming conversationalist. He is a stingray. Nor is philosophy, as he practices it, pleasurable conversation. It is an agonistic contest.

The difference between Socrates and Cephalus lies not so much in their age — they may be the same age as far as we know — but in Socrates's lifelong retention of that youthful urge to which philosophy makes its most intense appeal. I mean the urge to seek out the meaning of reality. In his refusal to retire his quest or give up his questioning until the day he died, Socrates appears to us across the ages as a neotenic figure par excellence. Here was a man who never surrendered the inner core of his passion to the aging process, a man who heroically maintained his faith in philosophy's promise of a new life even in the face of death. That is no doubt why he was so drawn to Athenian youths, and why they in turn were drawn to him. Whether the charges brought against him were justified or not — impiety toward the gods and corruption of the youth — and whether Plato's and Xenophon's portraits of him as an older man who preferred to spend his time with boys and young men rather than with people his own age are accurate or not, there is little doubt that Socratic philosophy, in its skeptical relation to received ideas, its groping for the grounds of its own truth, and its intoxication with transcendence, appealed primarily and directly to what was most youthful in the Athenian youth: their libido, their restlessness, their desire for heroism, their capacity for wonder, their infinite expectations, their inclination to doubt, their tendency to question, their readiness to believe, and their simultaneous need for guidance and independence.

The irony here is that philosophy's love of wisdom, so seductive to youth, dreams of a maturity that would surpass that of all other elders and sages. Socrates aspired to a fully realized maturity, which no man had ever yet attained. Refusing the posture of the wise man and professing ignorance in matters of true knowledge, he played the role of the perpetual student who never graduated to the wisdom toward which he directed his desire. By blurring the distinction between teaching and learning, master and disciple, hierophant and sycophant, he turned philosophy into an interminable pedagogy in which teacher and pupil share the same love and pursue the same outstanding ends. Socrates's genius consisted in making education the means as well as the end of philosophy. It is as if Socrates proclaimed to his fellow citizens, "You are all children when it comes to wisdom. I too fall short of the ever-receding goal, but unlike you, my education is not over, I have not finished, and I will never finish, maturing." To stay the course of philosophy, or of the unending maturation process, requires a wholesale rejuvenation (or de-Cephalization) of the psyche. Surely it was only because the Greeks were so "young in mind and spirit" (*psyche*) in the first place that someone like Socrates could appear in their midst to call them to a more vigorous, more protracted, more retentive youth—a youth capable of aspiring toward a wholly unprecedented maturity of soul.

Thus it is not only because he held on to his youthful passion until the day he died, or even because he died on behalf of that passion, that Socrates remains a wondrous neotenic genius. It is because he brought that passion to a new level of reflection without compromising its inner youthful drive. His power of seduction over his younger disciples derived from this same source. To inspire as well as educate the pupils' love, a teacher must be at once older and yet of the same "spiritual" age as them. Socrates's most distinctive feature as a pedagogue is that he appeared to his disciples not in the guise of a wise old man but as a more mature incarnation of their own youthful aspirations toward an ever-receding erotic goal. The fact that they tended to love *him* more than what he himself loved indicates to what degree he incarnated, in his person, the neoteny of philosophy itself. His personhood was proof of philosophy's inextinguishable spirit of youthfulness. Socrates's legendary strength, courage, endurance, and resistance to the effects of alcohol all pointed to an inward spirit that remains young to the degree that it continues to heed the call of philosophy.

Between Socrates and Cephalus, it is impossible to say which is more "mature," for Socrates revolutionized the very measure on which such a comparative evaluation could be based. From Cephalus's point of view, someone who remains intoxicated by philosophy's promise of transcendence into his old age has simply failed to come to terms with life's sobering realities, above all the reality of finitude. From Socrates's point of view, Cephalus's perfunctory pieties, his fear of dying, his corrosive doubts and guilt before the fact of death, are morbid symptoms of the unexamined life, conclusive evidence of a failed education. ("When someone thinks his end is near," says Cephalus before going off to make a sacrifice, "he becomes frightened and concerned about things he didn't fear before. It's then that the stories we're told about Hades, about how people who have been unjust here must pay the penalty there—stories he used to make fun of—twist his soul this way and that for fear they're true"). Death for Socrates was merely a stage in an unending maturation process. Just how old, or just how young, must one be to believe that?

Platonic Wisdom

Today we tend to think of classical philosophy as a venerable old man possessed of a wisdom hoary with age, yet when Plato set out to complete the transition from *mythos* to *logos* initiated by his teacher, one of the biggest problems he faced was philosophy's lack of tradition, hence its lack of authority. The Greeks may have been children compared to the Egyptians, yet even they were not "young" enough in spirit to bow to the authority of something as neoteric as critical reason. In this respect the Greeks were not unlike the Egyptians, the Romans, and the ancients in general: authority lay with age, history, and tradition. Lacking these, critical reason lacked persuasion and credibility.

It was not enough, in other words, simply to secure the theoretical foundations of philosophy; it was also necessary to lay them on preexistent cultural foundations. Only in that way could philosophy bring about a veritable neotenic revolution, falling short of which it would hardly have flourished or established such a distinguished, long-lasting tradition. How did Plato accomplish this? How did he succeed in conferring upon reason an authority that he knew it could not claim on the basis of its reasoning alone, regardless of how rigorous such reasoning might be? Quite simply, he enlisted the ancient powers of *mythos* on behalf of the *logos*, so that the novelty of the latter might repose on, while overturning, the foundations of the former. More precisely, he called on the generative resources of myth to provide reason with what it lacked, namely a lofty antiquity. Only myth has the power to create antiquities, just as only Athena has the power to found the city of Athens. While reason projects its promise into the future and invests its aspirations in things to come, myth takes the past, the archaic, and the original into its safekeeping. Plato knew that *mythos* did not belong to a past that could be superseded; he knew, on the contrary, that the past, insofar as it recedes toward the awesome womb of origins, belongs to the realm of *mythos*. It was such a past, with all its mythic authority, that he found a way to procure for philosophy.

In sum, Plato became a mythmaker. Only in so doing was he able to secure philosophy's future. Anyone who has even a cursory familiarity with Plato's corpus knows that it features a prodigious archive of myths, some traditional, some esoteric, others of his own invention. Yet it is not simply Plato's use of myths, nor even his invention of new myths, that bring genius and wisdom together in his work. It is the way in which he invariably links his philosophical doctrines to antediluvian origins, and in so doing gives birth to the myth of philosophy itself. The pre-incarnate soul, the preexisting forms, the precosmic demiurge, the preflood city of Athens — these are only some of the founding stories by which Plato affiliated philosophy with a realm of absolute antecedence. Such affiliation is purely mythical, which is to say, it is purely sublime. From the matrix of such antecedence come all the fables, allegories, and analogies that even today still define the Platonic corpus — the winged soul, the virtuous charioteer, the ascent from the cave, the great ladder of love, all that is most unforgettable, inspired, and reinheritable in that corpus — the sum total of which adds up to one supermyth of reason's genetic appurtenance to the aboriginal transcendence in and through which the world and its universal soul first came into being.

Philosophy, and philosophy alone, accedes to the realm of primal origins, since its *logos* belongs to, or derives from, the sparks of creation itself. This *logos* is in touch with first things, with prior things (hence its "a priori" nature, as it would later come to be called) — things so prior and primordial that the traditional myths of Hellas have no effective recollection of them. Plato implies as much in the *Timaeus* when he has the Egyptian priest mock the origin stories narrated by Solon. There is a memory older than your stories remember, says the priest. Only the *logos* of philosophy can access this older memory. True knowledge is *anamnesis*, or remembrance. Knowledge is not acquired but repossessed. Philosophy does not teach us anything; it critically dismantles our narrow mental framework so that reason may recall what the preexistent soul forgot during its fall into matter. In Plato's corpus, wisdom and genius came together to make philosophy the sole legitimate heir of this lost antiquity of the soul.

It is in this vein that we must understand the myth of Socrates himself in that corpus. Socrates is merely a vessel, a midwife, a mediator who enables the student to reclaim a prenatal memory to which the traditional myths are oblivious. In his youthful spirit lurks a wisdom that predates the wisdom of all other sages. Socrates does not possess such wisdom but has intimations of its recessive anteriority. Plato's genius made a myth of Socrates, yet his wisdom made a myth of the aspirations that defined the life of Socrates. In his horizon of infinite expectation Socrates aspired to an absolute maturity—the maturity of the origin, as it were. He was forever on its trail. His lifelong commitment to a lifelong education consisted in learning how to move backward. That is the arduous labor of philosophy: to move against the flow of time to the source from which time itself first sprang into being.

Through the figure of Socrates, Plato transformed and at the same time preserved the Greek idea of *paideia*, according to which education consists in learning the lessons of the past and reinheriting its legacies. Philosophy too teaches the lessons of the past—not of the partial past but rather the absolute past of the origin, which lies out ahead of us like a prospect of maturity waiting to be realized. All of which is another way of saying that Plato did not simply effect a transition from *mythos* to *logos*; in his ingenious wisdom he made a *mythos* of the *logos* and thereby gave philosophy what it most needed if it was to found a tradition full of future: an age as old as the world itself.

The Child and the Kingdom

There are many ways in which one could speak of early Christianity as a neotenic revolution. Certainly there is something like a theology of the child in the New Testament, for example in the Gospel of Luke, where Jesus says, "I thank thee, O Father ... that thou has hid these things from the wise and prudent, and hast revealed them unto babes" (10:21). In a famous passage in the Gospel of Matthew, Jesus declares, "Verily I say unto you, Except ye be converted, and become as little children, you shall not enter the kingdom of heaven" (18:3). Yet what exactly does Jesus mean by that? What aspects of the child is he referring to when he says that in conversion we "become as little children"? The child's openheartedness, sincerity, dependence, powerlessness? In the first Epistle of Peter we read, "Wherefore laying aside all malice, and all guile, and hypocrisies, and envies, and all evil speakings, / As newborn babes, desire the sincere milk of the word, that ye may grow thereby" (2:1–2). Assuming these are the sorts of childlike qualities that the passage in Matthew is referring to — which is by no means a given — how are adults to return to, or perhaps achieve for the first time, such a childhood of the spirit? And finally, what does it mean that God's kingdom of heaven is barred to those who fail to become childlike?

These are vexed questions indeed, all the more so because they raise other questions related to the infancy narratives in the Gospels of Luke and Matthew. For example, what does the infant Jesus have to do with the child in Matthew 18? What does the infant Jesus have to do with Christian doctrine in general, assuming he has anything to do with it at all? Does the obsessive iconography of baby Jesus in the history of Christian art arise from the core of Christian doctrine, or does it represent a sentimentalizing, second-millennium phenomenon that has little to do with the Christian revolution in antiquity? Is the child — be it the child Jesus or the child of conversion — of any essential significance when it comes to Christian theology?

Martin Luther certainly believed there was a connection. In the child Jesus he saw Christianity's humanization of the otherwise inhuman transcendence of God. "True Christian divinity setteth not God forth unto us in majesty, as Moses and other doctrines do," he wrote in his *Commentary on Galatians*. "Wherefore, when thy conscience standeth in the conflict, wrestling against the law, sin and death in the presence of God, there is nothing more dangerous than to wander with curious speculations in heaven, and there to search out God in his incomprehensible power" (43). Over and against the terror of contemplating God in his cosmic sublimity, Luther urges a turn to Jesus in the manger:

Wherefore, whensoever thou art occupied in the matter of thy salvation, setting aside all curious speculations of God's unsearchable majesty, all cogitations of works, of traditions, of philosophy, yea and of God's law too, run straight to the manger, and embrace this infant, and the Virgin's little babe in thine arms, and behold him as he was born, sucking, growing up, conversant among men, teaching, dying, rising again, ascending up above all the heavens, and having power above all things. By this mean shalt thou be able to shake off all terrors and errors, like as the sun driveth away the clouds. (44)

Luther sees in the child Jesus God's self-abasement, his decision to become incarnate, not in the mode of Greek gods, who every now and then assume a human disguise, but in the mode of true embodiment—an embodiment whose reality is proven by the infant's capacity for organic growth and his natural kinship with the manger animals.

The Gospel of Matthew certainly lends support to Luther's association of human childhood with humility: "Whosoever therefore shall humble himself as this little child, the same is greatest in the kingdom of heaven" (18:4). To become as little children means to embrace the humbleness of Jesus himself, who was born in a manger and died on a cross. In such humility lies Christ's eventual exaltation, his "ascending up above all the heavens, and having power above all things," as Luther puts it. As Nietzsche never tires of reminding us, Christianity effects a transvaluation of values, turning the lowest into the highest, the highest into the lowest, such that wise men now come to pay homage to the child. The Christian term for this transvaluation is "conversion," literally a turning around, or upside down.

Saint Paul, whose epistles were composed before the Gospels, founded Christianity on a theology of conversion. Paul knew that from the perspective of worldly wisdom nothing could be more absurd than believing that a young vagrant from Nazareth named Jesus was the son of God, that he had died on the cross for our sins, and that he was raised from the dead by his Father. Paul never sought to deny the foolishness of Christian faith; on the contrary, he pitted it against the wisdom of those who scoffed at it:

> For Christ sent me not to baptize, but to preach the gospel: not with wisdom of words, lest the cross of Christ should be made of none effect.
>
> For the preaching of the cross is to them that perish foolishness; but unto us which are saved it is the power of God.
>
> For it is written, I will destroy the wisdom of the wise, and will bring to nothing the understanding of the prudent.
>
> Where is the wise? where is the scribe? where is the disputer of this world? hath not God made foolish the wisdom of this world?
>
> For after that in the wisdom of God the world by wisdom knew not God, it pleased God by the foolishness of preaching to save them that believe.
>
> For the Jews require a sign, and the Greeks seek after wisdom:
>
> But we preach Christ crucified, unto the Jews a stumbling block, and unto the Greeks foolishness;
>
> But unto them which are called, both Jews and Greeks, Christ the power of God, and the wisdom of God.
>
> Because the foolishness of God is wiser than men; and the weakness of God is stronger than men. (1 Corinthians 1:17–25)

This apology for holy foolishness is no foolish piece of rhetoric. Note how its sermon is patterned upon the figure of the cross, with its chiastic inversions. On the crux of its revelation everything is turned around, such that the loftiness of worldly wisdom is now revealed as the fool's self-deception, while the foolishness of faith is revealed as otherwordly wisdom. Such is the truth of the crucifixion: on its cross the lowest becomes the highest, the weakest becomes the strongest, the most humble becomes the most glorious. Its theology turns the world upside down, such that only a conversion, a literal turning-oneself-around, can set things straight again — no, not again, but for the first time in the history of the world.

In Paul we do not find any sentimentalizing of children or Jesus in the manger. His Christ is a Lord, not an infant. His epistles contain no baby talk but a robust, maturist challenge to Judaism and pagan wisdom. What Paul saw in Christ was the (only) way of redemption, which descends through the realm of sin, flesh, and death in order to rise in a new spiritual body. "New" here means *of another order than the old.* The new emerges in and through — it is predicated upon, literally born of — the death of the old. It was not the incunabula of Christ's birth but the nascent quality of his death that obsessed Paul. He saw in the crucifixion the birth of that "new man" who can work himself free from the old legacy of sin. If there is a theology of the child in Paul, we must look for it in his theology of renewal, rebirth, and resurrection.

That theology contains an altogether new idea of renewal, and with it a new understanding of baptism. For Paul, baptism figures not as a cleansing or purification but as a sacramental dying and rising in Christ: "Know ye not that so many of us as were baptized into Jesus Christ were baptized into his death?" (Romans 6:3). Insofar as the crucifixion frees us from our en-slavement to sin, it puts to death the "old man" who has hitherto dominated history in his service to sin: "For if we have been planted together in the likeness of his death, we shall be also in the likeness of his resurrection. Knowing this, that our old man is crucified with him, that the body of sin might be destroyed, that henceforth we should not serve sin" (6:5-6). Until now we have served this master — the old man in us — but through Christ's death "we are delivered from the law, that being dead wherein we were held; that we should serve in newness of spirit, and not in the oldness of the letter" (7:6). Paul understands baptism as a sacramental participation in Christ's death, in and through which all that is old — whatever is of this world in its secular antiquity and wisdom, whatever is subject to sin or death, and indeed, whatever is subject to *becoming old* as such — dies on the cross. Through such death we enter a new service: "Therefore we are buried with him by baptism into death: that like as Christ was raised up from the dead by the glory of the Father, even so we should also walk in the newness of life" (6:4).

Paul believed that it was the crucifixion itself that made possible this new understanding of baptism, that this event revealed the sacrament's true meaning, hitherto veiled to us. Indeed, the crucifixion *is* the true meaning of baptism. It is the baptism of all baptisms, as it were, whereby in the new order inaugurated by the incarnation the faithful are reborn as God's children. The following passage makes clear how Paul understands the term "children," theologically speaking:

> But ye are not in the flesh, but in the Spirit, if so be that the Spirit of God dwell in you. Now if any man have not the Spirit of Christ, he is none of his.
>
> And if Christ be in you, the body is dead because of sin; but the Spirit is life because of righteousness.
>
> But if the Spirit of him that raised up Jesus from the dead dwell in you, he that raised up Christ from the dead shall also quicken your mortal bodies by his Spirit that dwelleth in you. ...
>
> For as many as are led by the Spirit of God, they are the sons of God.
>
> For ye have not received the spirit of bondage again to fear: but ye have received the Spirit of adoption, whereby we cry, Abba, Father.
>
> The Spirit itself beareth witness with our Spirit, that we are the children of God:
>
> And if children, then heirs; heirs of God, and joint-heirs with Christ; if so be that we suffer with him, that we may be also glorified together. (Romans 8:9–11, 14–17).

In Matthew 18 "children" refers to youth, or to the child's youthful status or disposition (its openheartedness, its meekness, or whatever qualities one chooses to associate with the term "*little* children"), whereas here in Paul's epistles it has more to do with the child's legal status as heir or beneficiary. If conversion turns us into children, it does so for Paul in the sense that faith in Christ allows us to receive the "Spirit of adoption" and thereby to become the beneficiaries of God's forgiveness. As "joint-heirs" along with Christ, the faithful now are free to inherit God's freely given grace. Whereas in Matthew, Jesus seems to call for the infantilization of the faithful—however one wishes to interpret that call—Paul calls instead for a resolute turning away from sin through a turn toward Christ. The resoluteness of such conversion has little, if anything, to do with infantilization. Or does it?

For both Paul and Matthew faith is the precondition of God's grace. Such faith cannot be reasoned. It begins and ends with trust. When Paul speaks of faith he means not so much belief as unconditional trust—the sort of trust, precisely, that a child puts in its parents. For Paul, Christ's incarnation, and above all his crucifixion, calls on the believer to place his or her trust in the father in the mode of children. Yet we should not understand this trust childishly. It is not the innocent, instinctive, blind trust of naive, unreflecting children. On the contrary, it is an existential commitment taken with full awareness of what is at stake in the decision to put one's trust resolutely in God through Christ. In that respect the decision to become childlike—or to become the child of God—has an altogether adult character. By retrieving in his or her mature self the child's innate capacity for trust, the faithful Christian "converts" the child's trusting disposition into an adult mode. Such conversion alters, but at the same time retains, the native childlike trait, giving it a new form: that of Christian faith. In such retention lies the essence of Christian neoteny.

Paul insists time and again that through such converted trust the unbelievable (i.e., Christian revelation) becomes not only believable but certain. The otherworldly truth of Christian doctrine, closed off to the discernment of the wise, requires, for its revelation, a turn or re-turn to the child that preexists one's identity as a "Jew" or "Greek" or bearer of any other such secular label. It is to this unaging, preexistent, universal child, forever waiting to be reborn in the adult mode, that the Christian proclamation makes its ultimate appeal.

Christian Wisdom

According to Acts 26:25, Porcius Festus, a Roman governor of Judea from about 50 to 62 AD, declared to Saint Paul, "Paul, thou art mad; much learning makes thee mad." He had a point. The passage from 1 Corinthians cited in the previous section confirms that Paul's madness had a learned quality about it and that his foolishness was unusually well reasoned. In his denunciation of worldly wisdom and defense of holy foolishness, Paul not only appropriated the authority of the Hebrew prophetic tradition ("For it written, I will destroy the wisdom of the wise ..."), he also appropriated the rhetorical devices of those pagan "disputers" against whom he so eloquently stated his case. This phenomenon of subversion-through-appropriation, which recurs in various guises during the first few centuries of church history, accounts in large part for the astonishing success of the Christian revolution throughout the ancient world. To understand one of the most important aspects of that success, we must turn from the Christian proclamation to its defense, or from its genius to its wisdom, for it was thanks to the early church's response to the attacks and accusations that besieged it during its infancy that Christianity succeeded in consolidating one of the most momentous and improbable revolutions in cultural history to date.

Paul's counteroffensive in 1 Corinthians is aimed more at learned pagans than at scandalized Jews, for it was principally the former who saw in Christian beliefs mere childish nonsense (the Jews, says Paul, saw in them a *scandalon*, or "stumbling block"). Here Paul was "untimely" in a different sense than when he speaks of his belatedness vis-à-vis the Christ event in 1 Corinthians 15 (Paul never met Jesus and converted after his death). By that I mean that he was ahead of his time, for the most intense pagan attacks against the Nazarenes came well after Paul's death, in the second and third centuries AD, when Christianity had begun to spread throughout the Roman empire.

In the polemics of pagans like Lucian, Celsus, and Suetonious, we find that one of the main objections against Christianity had more to do with its lack of antiquity than its lack of credibility. Or better, its lack of credibility derived from its lack of antiquity. Celsus, for instance, claimed that his arguments against Christianity relied on "an ancient doctrine which has existed since the beginning, which has always been maintained by the wisest nations and cities and wise men," while the Christians based their doctrine on a man who was "only of yesterday," who "had not been known by name" to the world prior to now (Pelikan, *Christian Tradition*, 1:34). It is hard to overestimate the importance of the early church's response to this prevailing charge of neotericism. The problem was similar to the one faced by Plato when it came to establishing philosophy's authority in a society where authority derived from age and tradition. Arnobius, a Christian apologist, summed up the pagan objection to Christianity in these words: "Your religious observances [or so you pagans believe] precede the ones we espouse by many years, and for that reason [you assume they] are truer because fortified by the authority of age" (1:34). Christianity may well have been doomed to oblivion had the early church fathers not countered this attack to the church's own advantage.

Their response was simple: Moses is older than Homer. In brief, they pitted the antiquity of Judaism against that of paganism and claimed the former for their own Christian doctrines. Christ's word was both the correction and fulfillment of what had been prophesized in Hebrew scripture. Even as it initiated a new order of truth, the incarnation brought to its fulfillment an old order that began with Moses. Rarely did one of the apologists pass up the occasion to remark that, in the words of Tatian, "our doctrines are older, not only than those of the Greeks, but than the invention of letters." Against Celsus's claim that the Jewish prophets had "misunderstood Plato," Origen exclaimed, "Moses and the prophets [and hence the truth of Christian revelation] ... are not only earlier than Plato but also than Homer and the discovery of writing among the Greeks." Likewise Tertullian affirmed, "Moses and God existed before all your Lycurguses and Solons" (1:35).

This appropriation of Judaism's antiquity formed part of what came to be known as Christian "typology," which engaged in a "figural" interpretation of the Hebrew Bible that understood several of its characters and events as "types" that foreshadow the truth of Christian revelation. A common strategy of the *adversus Judaeos* writings of the early church fathers — "testimonies," as they were often called — was the compilation of Old Testament passages that, in the Christian interpretation, foretell the coming of Christ. Thus Psalm 110 prophetically prefigures (or "typifies") Christ's resurrection and exaltation at the Lord's side. The suffering servant in Isaiah 53 prefigures Christ in his Passion. The rebellion of the nations against Yahweh in Psalm 2 prefigures Christ's suffering at the hands of both Pilate and the Jews. And so forth. By interpreting events and characters of the Hebrew Bible as proleptic anticipations of Christian truth, the church fathers created a series of typological relations between the old and the new, between Adam and Christ, hence between the Jewish and Christian testaments. The church grounded both its proclamation and its apologies during the early centuries of its expansion on this fundamental claim, namely that Christian revelation both consummates and transcends its Judaic prehistory. Figural reinterpretation of the Hebrew Scriptures saw in the old a march toward the new, and saw in the new a "correction and fulfillment" of the old. Just as the coming of Christ revealed the "spiritual" meaning of the Hebrew law, so God's old covenant with Israel gave way to a new covenant with the "true Israel," namely the Christian church.

Historically speaking, this appropriation of the authority of Judaism did little to convert Jews to Christianity — to this day

Judaism has held its ground against the Christian claim to have inherited and liquidated its legacy — yet it was crucial to the church's evangelical mission, for it allowed the early fathers to ground their revolution on an ancient, antecedent tradition and thereby to claim, against their pagan detractors, that the coming of Christ had revealed "things hidden since the foundation of the world."

To a large extent the Christian apologists did to Greek wisdom what they did to Judaism, that is, they appropriated its authority. Following the cue of various Jewish scholars, Justin Martyr, for example, claimed that much of what was true and praiseworthy in Greek moral philosophy had in fact been derived from the Jewish scriptures. He went so far as to claim that Plato had read Moses and that Christ had been "known in part even by Socrates" (Pelikan, 1:31). To account for the anachronism of the latter affirmation, he put forward the notion of the *logos spermatikos*, or "seminal reason," which God had strewn throughout the world before the incarnation. It was this preexistent, widely disseminated *logos spermatikos* that explained the presence of those truths in pagan philosophy that accorded with Christian doctrine and allowed Socrates, Plato, and other non-Christian sages to intimate the truth that Christ would reveal fully and completely, in and through his preaching and his person. The pagans "spoke well in proportion to the share [they] had of the seminal Logos" (1:32). Thus did Justin claim for Christianity the august antiquities of the two traditions against which, but also in conjunction with which, the church consolidated its revolution: Judaism and pagan wisdom.

Justin, Tatian, Clement of Alexandria, Origen, and others apparently were not bothered by the fact that they often borrowed from Greek philosophy what they claimed the Greeks had borrowed from Hebrew scripture. Clement of Alexandria, for example, argued that Plato's cosmogony in the *Timaeus* was indebted to the Hebrews, while in fact Clement's doctrine of creation, so important for later orthodoxy, was heavily indebted to the *Timaeus*. Likewise Christian typology was clearly inspired in its methods by the pagan allegorical tradition, which had already de-anthropomorphized the Greek myths and spiritualized the meaning of the Homeric epics. Yet these same apologists who applied their allegorism to the Old Testament denounced the practice as "sophistic" when pagan philosophers applied it to pagan myth. That is one reason why the early Greek fathers held Socrates in such high esteem: he refused to allegorize Homer and simply banished him altogether.

By such means the apologists engaged their antagonists on the latter's own terms, adopting and adapting their ideas, methods, and vocabularies while holding on to the revolutionary core of the Christian proclamation. As a result they preserved an empowering measure of continuity with the traditions they were in fact overturning. This principle of continuity-in-rupture, or subversion-through-appropriation, is essential to almost all successful neotenic revolutions. At bottom there was only one way for Christianity—the child of Judaism—to remain a child. It had to become an old man. It did this by reinheriting and transforming the wisdom of its predecessors and incorporating that wisdom into its genius, in such a way as to secure a rock-solid institutional foundation for the childish trust and foolishness that to this day remain the primary means of access to the inner core of the Christian kerygma.

The Child of Enlightenment

Before turning to the next major case study—the founding of the American republic—a word about the phenomenon that helped render it possible, namely the Enlightenment. America has been called "the child of Enlightenment," yet in some respects the Enlightenment itself, at least for one of its major theorists, possesses the characteristics of a child—a child struggling to come of age and to free itself from parental authority, much the way the American colonies once struggled to become independent from the "mother country." One could say that the Enlightenment strived for a fully realized human maturity in which freedom, independence, and the law of reason would converge and become one. How so? In what way are these concepts internally related?

Hegel saw in the Reformation a crucial stage in the realization of modern freedom, yet even if we concede that Luther transferred the "external" authority of the church to the "internal" freedom of subjective conscience, this does not make Luther the progenitor of Enlightenment, as Hegel believed. Luther rejected the authority of Rome only to fall back on the authority of scripture. To enslave oneself to the authority of the written word instead of to an institution's historical mediation of its meaning amounts to constipating the prospect of freedom and postponing its advent indefinitely. Hegel failed to recognize that Galileo in fact did far more than Luther when it came to preparing the way for freedom from external authority, for Galileo proved the authorities wrong, and with them the scriptures, regarding matters of fact. Galileo incubated the modern idea of freedom by rejecting authority of *any sort* as a criterion of truth in science and by calling for the independence of reason in scientific inquiry.

Descartes wrote the declaration of that independence in his *Discourse on Method*. The first order of business in the *Discourse* was to orphan the *res cogitans*, to break the hold that authority and tradition had on it, and to exorcise it of all the past ghosts or voices that might preinhabit its cogitations, so that its autonomous "I" could come forward as a subject without paternity, ancestry, or historicity, in short, as an unengendered, fully mature subject that answers only to its self-posited rules for "rightly conducting one's reason and for seeking truth in the sciences," to quote the subtitle of the *Discourse*.

Descartes of course knew that the *res cogitans* could not in fact be born fully mature. It had to pass through a childhood of sorts, which is why at one point he wonders wistfully what it would be like "had we the full use of our reason from the moment of our birth and had we never been led by anything but our reason" (*Discourse*, 7). He intends the remark historically as well as existentially. Wouldn't it be a blessing, in other words, if human civilization could have been spared its laborious evolution from barbarism to enlightenment. No such luck. Not only does our early childhood development take place without the guidance of reason, but the age of reason itself will never fully overcome the heritage of those early, formative ages of history. Coming too late in the course of the ages, reason is doomed to contend with the tenacious customs, mentalities, and institutions of the prerational past of human society—a past whose legacies live on despite reason's attempts to dispose of them once and for all.

No one better understood how the age of reason must struggle to come of age—or how the past's stubborn persistence in the present has an infantilizing effect on reason, even after reason has come fully into its own as a critical faculty—than Immanuel Kant. Kant opens his brief essay of 1780, "What Is Enlightenment?," with the declaration "Enlightenment is man's emergence from his self-imposed immaturity." This much-cited phrase points to all the paradoxes and enigmas of the so-called age of enlightenment. By "immaturity" Kant means our reliance on others to do our thinking for us ("Immaturity is the inability to use one's understanding without guidance from another"). It is "self-imposed" when one has already reached the age of reason but continues, out of aversion to thinking for oneself, to defer to the guardians of authority ("Laziness and cowardice are the reasons why so great a proportion of men, long after nature has released them from alien guidance [*naturaliter maiorennes*], nonetheless gladly remain in lifelong immaturity"). To "emerge" from our self-imposed immaturity means to resist this unnecessary dependence and to "dare to know!" ("*aude sapere!*") (41).

Emergence consists in a long and difficult process of public education, one that requires "the freedom to use reason *publically* in all matters." Such freedom is exceptional among nations, founded as they are on the authority of their political and religious institutions, which everywhere and at all times tell us, "Do not argue! Obey!" But where the public is free to argue, as in the Prussian state of Frederick the Great (who says, "*Argue* as much as you want and about what you want, but *obey*!"), reason gradually and *naturally* becomes the tribunal to which all public arguments are referred: "Once nature has removed the hard shell of this kernel for which she has most fondly cared, namely the inclination to and vocation for free *thinking*, the kernel gradually reacts on a people's mentality (whereby they become increasingly able to *act* freely), and it finally even influences the principles of *government*, which finds that it can profit by treating men, *who are now more than machines*, in accord with their dignity" (46). "In accord with their dignity" means in accord with their adultlike ability to think and act for themselves.

To the question "Do we presently live in an *enlightened* age?" Kant answers, "No, but we do live in an age of *enlightenment*." That is like saying, we are mature enough to be on our way to maturity, though we have not yet become mature. While "man" is ready and even over-ready to emerge, his ability to think for himself is still in an underdeveloped state. His reason has been infantilized for so long by the tutors, and he, in his fear of independence, so willingly conspires with their tutelage, that his maturation is unnaturally delayed. Nature, for her part, has done her job. She has given man the ability to reason and made him ready for independence (*naturaliter maiorennes*). It is *history*, or the inertia of the past, that makes him hesitant to grow up. An age of enlightenment, as opposed to an enlightened age, is one that finds itself in the midst of this unnatural delay in the historical maturation process.

But who exactly is the "man" Kant speaks of? Is he the Prussian citizen of the 1780s? Is he the historical manifestation of world spirit in a particular stage of its development? Whoever he is, the prospects for his maturity are ever-receding. One of the most telling features of Kant's brief essay is the consistent adoption of the perspective of the child, never of the adult, in its pages, where the word "man" invariably refers to the wards, not the wardens, to the guarded, not the guardians, to the tutored, not the tutors. These latter, "who have so benevolently taken over the supervision of men [and] have carefully seen to it that the far greatest part of them (including the entire fair sex) regard taking the step to maturity as very dangerous, not to mention difficult" (41), are presumably of another cultural age than the ones whom they supervise and in whom they discourage independence. They are the custodians of the cultural senility from which the age of enlightenment, in its efforts to come of age, seeks liberation. As for "man," he is a potential adult who for the moment remains a child of enlightenment.

From the perspective of Vico's *New Science*, which predates Kant's essay by several decades, the process of "emergence" described by Kant is nothing other than the fitful transition from an age of heroes to an age of men, or from an age founded on the "certainty" of authority to one based on the "truth" of reason. *The New Science* reminds us that such transitions have occurred before, and that the age of men, while it may be more rational, just, and humane than prior ages, contains its own potential dangers and naivete. One of them is reason's tendency to hallucinate its self-sufficiency and to assume that coming of age means reason's independence from, rather than its reinheritance of, the past's legacies. In its Cartesian drive to ground itself on its own self-posited, autonomous foundations — rather than on the foundations of history — reason (for Vico) runs the risk of annulling rather than fulfilling the accumulated wisdom of the ages it supersedes.

Indeed, half a century before the French Revolution, Vico saw in the human age a distinct danger that the claim of reason — founded not upon particular traditions of certainty but upon the universality of truth — could become militantly ideological, and that ideology in turn could degenerate into new forms of tyranny, if not terror. (We who belong to the end of the human age, as it were, have seen this story unfold in several versions over the past few centuries.) To conceive of freedom and independence absolutely rather than relatively is, for Vico, a sign of reason's congenital immaturity—its naive belief in the abstract universality of its own law and its determination to subject the past to the endless accusations of its self-righteous tribunal.

Vico saw in the age of reason another, related danger, namely that it would become altogether "monolingual," in the sense that its abstract, prosaic language would no longer be fluent in the divine and heroic languages from which it was born. His excavation of the "poetic wisdom" of the ancients aimed to reeducate an age that had been swept up in a Cartesian enthusiasm for a universal language of reason (mathematics), that is, to reeducate them in those other languages, so as to help assure that the age of reason would remain properly heterochronous, heterocosmic, and heterolinguistic—in short, that it would remain pregnant with historicity, rather than abolish its historical and cultural memory altogether. That is why Vico's life work was dedicated to repossessing the languages of the dead, reanimating their scripts, and retracing the "ideal eternal history" that gave birth to the modern nations from out of the womb of poetic wisdom.

Mainstream Enlightenment thinking, by contrast, called for genius to free itself from the authority of wisdom. Vico did not champion the opposite cause; he was by no means a cultural conservative. He called instead for the marriage of genius and wisdom, so that the human age might become the heir rather than the orphan of history. Such was the "newness" of his new science—it sought to retrieve what was oldest so that the new age could become genuinely new, rather than merely novel. Genuine newness entails the rejuvenation, rather than the repudiation, of that from which it seeks freedom and independence. Nowhere does this dynamic become more evident in its mechanisms than in the founding of the American republic, to which we will now turn our attention.

Declaring Independence

The founding of the American republic represents one of the great neotenic revolutions in political history. Wherein lay its success? How did the American "child of Enlightenment" come to maturity without losing its youth, as it were? The Declaration of Independence, the Constitution, and the Gettysburg Address are the scriptures to which we might look for an answer. Indeed, the fact that the nation is founded upon such scriptures is already part of the answer.

The republic's allegiance to reason is written into the Declaration of Independence, and with good reason. One cannot base a claim to independence on faith, while one most certainly can base it on reason. Reason and independence have this much in common: both appeal to their own intrinsic maturity; both presume to rest not on the ground of external authority but upon their own self-supporting, self-legitimating foundation. We may appreciate, therefore, just how critical is the concept of the "self-evidence" in the opening lines of the Declaration:

> We hold these truths to be self evident: that all men are created equal; that they are endowed by their Creator with certain inalienable rights; that among these are life, liberty, and the pursuit of happiness; that to secure these rights, governments are instituted among men, deriving their just powers from the consent of the governed.

The self-evident is independently and manifestly true. It shows its truth in and of itself, without need of external appeals. The concept of self-evidence already contains within itself the concept of independence.

How crucial, then, was that slight revision that Jefferson and his colleagues made to the Declaration before presenting their draft to the Congress. The unrevised version read, "We hold these truths to be *sacred and undeniable*..." In that minor revision lies the entire modernity of the American nation. A sacred truth has a transcendent source that lies beyond the bounds of self-confirmation. At stake is the difference between a matter of faith (on which universal agreement, in the wake of Protestantism's fractures, is impossible) and the self-justifying claims of reason (on which *all* men, being *equally* capable of reason, can and must agree). Whatever else it may declare, the Declaration declares the independence of reason from faith, and on this rock — the rock of reason — the American nation built its state.

Yet what could be *less* self-evident — when one looked objectively at history, nature, or human society in the eighteenth century — than the equality of men, or government by consent of the governed? Everywhere one turned one saw only inequality and oppression, nowhere inalienable rights and consent. To what or to whom, then, are the Declaration's "truths" self-evident? Answer: to the eye of reason, which sees beyond the evidence of the particular to the self-evidence of the universal, beyond the evidence of the *is* to the self-evidence of the *ought*.

Let us not misunderstand the nature of reason's independence from faith in the Declaration. While it entails reason's separation from faith, it also entails reason's rejuvenation of the language and heritage of faith, such that the two (reason and faith) remain related by bonds of kinship, the way America remained related to England even after the former gained political independence from the latter. This becomes all the more clear when one recalls the famous Pauline definition of faith in the Letter to the Hebrews, which in the King James translation reads, "Now faith is the substance of things hoped for, and the evidence of things unseen" (Hebrews 11:1). The evidence of things unseen is "self-evident" if one has faith in reason's truth, as most Enlightenment thinkers did. Certainly the equality of men, inalienable rights, government by consent, and other such truths derived from the "laws of nature and of nature's God" are things unseen, things hoped for, things never yet known to have existed on earth except in thought and hope. Insofar as such truths lie beyond the evidence of facts and history, they are tenets of faith—the faith of reason, as it were. Or better, they are solemn prophecies that foretell a completely new (hoped for) foundation of legitimacy for the world's nations: government by consent of the governed. In that sense the Declaration's appeal to the self-evident does not reject but creatively renews the "sacred and undeniable" origins of its declared tenet of faith.

At Gettysburg, Lincoln proclaimed that the founding fathers had brought forth on the American continent a "new nation." He intended the word "new" the way the Puritans intended it when they spoke of a new England, or the way Paul intended it when he spoke of the new Adam given birth by the coming of Christ. We must, that is, understand the word "new" in the Christian, conversional sense of *another order than the old*. The fathers brought forth a new nation not simply by basing its institutions on the dictates of reason and thereby preparing the way for a secular, modern republic, but by successfully subsuming faith's battered heritage into the natural law on which they based their claims to independence, nationhood, and democracy. (The "laws of nature," from which nations derive their legitimacy, are still the laws of "nature's God.") Those fathers successfully separated reason from faith through an incorporation, transformation, and strategic retrieval of faith's futural legacies.

We find here the same phenomenon that we uncovered in the neotenic revolutions discussed earlier, namely rupture that takes the form of continuity, albeit a new kind of continuity. In this case, continuity-in-rupture informs the founding law of the American republic: separation of church and state. The separation of church and state is not just one law among others in the Constitution, it is the law that grounds the Constitution's ultimate authority. The state is the basis of our union—it legislates the sphere of our interaction—while the church marks our (right to) separateness from one another. Every native of the nation, regardless of race, ethnicity, or religious faith, is born into this separation. It is what constitutes the American citizen. Yet here too we find the futural persistence or afterlife of faith, for while separation of church and state is a law of the American state, it has a distinctly Christian origin, traceable to the phrase uttered by Jesus in the synoptic gospels: "Render unto Caesar the things which are Caesar's, and unto God the things that are God's" (Matthew 22:21). This Christian understanding of separation of church and state is newly retrieved and politically realized in the republic's founding.

One should say, to be even more specific, that separation of church and state retrieves or realizes radical Protestantism's protests against the Church of Rome, which in its worldly ambitions had failed to maintain the separation. Certainly the most ardent apologist for the separation of church and state in American history was the seventeenth-century fanatical Puritan Roger Williams, founder of the colony of Rhode Island. Williams wanted to protect the sanctity of the church from profanation by the state, while the framers wanted to protect the state from interference by the church, yet in this difference lies a fundamental continuity that tells us just how much of the Christian heritage was incorporated into the founding principles of the "new nation."

If neoteny in the biological realm means the retention of juvenile characteristics in postjuvenile stages of development, what we have in the founding of the American republic is the cultural obverse of that process: a new nation successfully carrying over into its youth a number of older elements from the heritage of nations. This obverse pattern, by which a senile trait assumes a novel or rejuvenated form, or takes on a new life in a separate and independent context, is equally fundamental to the mechanisms of cultural neoteny I have been exploring in this chapter. We will see it at work once again in the following section.

The American Constitution

The conventional image of America as a young nation that fetishizes youth, and whose popular culture promotes what Norman Podhoretz once called "a poisonous glorification of the adolescent," obscures the fact that America is also one of the oldest of modern nations, in more ways than one. Its Constitution, for example, has endured longer than any national constitution extant today. That alone would suggest that "the wisdom of ages is interwoven into [it]," as Aaron Hall from New Hampshire put it in an oration of 1789 (Wood, *Creation of the American Republic*, 594). Only a constitution that was conceived in "wisdom and maturity," as its framers claimed at the time, could age as well as the American Constitution has aged.

As I remarked at the beginning of this chapter, wisdom is not naturally correlative to old age, and the same can be said for "maturity," if by that term we mean something other than biological development. When the framers spoke of the "wisdom and maturity" of the Constitution, they were referring to its long-term projection into an uncertain future, and the future's tendency to fall back into the senile ways of the past. Wisdom and maturity provide for the future in a way that youthful enthusiasm rarely does. Youth is forward-looking, to be sure, yet it tends to relate to the future in the mode of hopeful expectation rather than to view it as a stage for likely misadventures and calamities. To provide for the future (*pro-videre*, to look ahead) means above all to look at its prospect with suspicion and apprehension, making provisions for what might go terribly wrong. The geopolitical failures of communism had several proximate causes, yet in the final analysis communism's downfall had a great deal to do with its blind ideological faith in the future, its conviction that history would inevitably rally to its cause, and its belief that the future would redeem rather than reenact the sins of the past.

The American Constitution shows no such trust in the future. It certainly does not trust human nature, any more than the framers' Puritan ancestors did. Roger Williams, whom I invoked earlier, spoke of a "rotten nature, from whence (from *within* the Lord Jesus tells us) proceed all the rotten and hellish Speeches and Actions" of history. The Constitution keeps alive this Puritan pessimism regarding human nature and seeks to defend the new nation from its potential malignancy. James Madison spoke of a "degree of depravity in mankind" that governments cannot redress but at most can contain or redirect toward the common good. "If men were angels," wrote Madison, "no government would be necessary (*The Federalist* no. 51; February 6, 1788). Yet even if "the better angels of our nature" exist, the American Constitution does not trust them to prevail when it counts the most. It trusts only its own soberly conceived network of constraints, precautions, and safeguards, all of which have but a single political aim: to create a form of government that would amend — not rewrite — the text of original sin.

Although they inherited a distinctly Puritan pessimism about human nature, the framers rejected the traditional claims of Christian princes that their monarchies are based on a providential mandate from God to shepherd and tutor people who, in their fallen state, could hardly be expected to administer their own welfare. The reason they rejected the hallowed assumption that government remains above the corruption of human nature is because they had learned the lessons of more radical theorists like Machiavelli, Hobbes, and Locke, who — against the presumption of the traditional ruling classes — taught that governments are rooted in the same "rotten nature" from which proceed all the hellish speeches and actions of individuals. The extreme distrust of human government that underlies the Constitution's sublime architecture of checks and balances and separation of powers derives from this premise, as well as from the framers' historical memory of power's deeply entrenched patterns of abuse.

Save us from those who would give us a just government. The Constitution does not seek to create a just government but to place limit after limit upon government's power to encroach upon the freedom and rights of individuals. Kant defined Enlightenment as an emergence from our self-imposed immaturity, by which he meant that Enlightenment is *not* a set of laws but our capacity and willingness to exercise critical reason in the public sphere. If reason is the faculty that sets and observes limits, as Kant believed, the American Constitution exercises that faculty by limiting the government's ability to consolidate power in any one of its branches and assuring that the separation of powers will remain intrinsic to the framework itself. The result is a dynamic political system that pits the states against the central government, the House against the Senate, the president against the Congress, the courts against Congress, the Senate against the president, the people against their representatives, the state legislatures against the senates, the electoral college against the people, and so on. By dividing power against itself in as many ways as possible, the Constitution constitutes, in the fullest and most concrete sense of the term, a "critique" of state power. The critical reason that informs its document founds a critical system of government that refuses to trust the very institution of government it embodies.

The genius of the Constitution lies in the way it overturns the traditional foundations of sovereignty and invests it in "we the people." Yet here too the wisdom and maturity of its conception come into play, for the Constitution does not trust "the people" any more than it trusts their traditional wardens. The framers in fact had an almost paranoid fear of democracy, or what they called "tyranny of the majority," believing that unbridled democracy was the greatest threat to their republic. "People, if unrestrained, seldom judge or determine right," wrote Madison, echoing the sentiments of his fellow Federalists. In his *Defence of the Constitution*, John Adams remarked that history teaches one basic, cautionary lesson: that the people, when unrestrained, "have been as unjust, tyrannical, brutal, barbarous, and cruel, as any king or senate possessed of uncontrollable power" (Wood, 578). Maybe a viable democracy must be based on this kind of underlying distrust of democracy. The Constitution's apprehension about unrestrained democracy is evident in its provisions for the indirect election of the president through the electoral college system, and the election of senators through the state legislatures. Such apprehension underlies the Constitution's implicit assumption that it is we the people whom "we the people" should fear the most. Several dark antiquities haunt the shadows of this clairvoyant and in many ways prophetic fear.

The lack of confidence in the ability of people, when unrestrained, to "judge or determine right" lies at the heart of one of the most conflicted issues debated at the Philadelphia Convention: the role of the Senate. While almost all the delegates agreed that the national legislature should be bicameral, it was far from clear what role an upper house would play. Would it be equivalent to the English House of Lords, that is, a separate body representing the interests of the rich and well-born? Would property conditions be placed on senators? Would they be elected by the representatives, or by popular vote, or by some other process? Would they hold office for life? While several questions remained unresolved, there was a general consensus that the House of Representatives — precisely because its members were elected directly by the people — needed to be offset or supervised by a separate body composed of sober, mature statesmen who would act, as George Mason put it, "with more coolness, with more system, and with more wisdom, than the popular branch" (Wood, 553). The words most frequently used to describe what a Senate would bring to the government were "weight and wisdom," "permanency," "steadiness and wisdom," "stability and energy," "knowledge," "more extensive information than can be acquired in a short time," "knowledge and firmness" that would serve "check the inconsiderate and hasty proceedings of the first branch" (556).

Initially it was imagined that the senators themselves, by dint of their excellence of character, would provide the wisdom and maturity necessary to maintain the government's stability, yet it quickly became apparent that there was no way to institute a system that would assure the election of the nation's wisest citizens. In the final analysis the Senate's function was reconceived and redefined by the framers as simply a further distribution and separation of the government's power, "a division of power in the legislature itself" (559). It would fulfill its role merely by virtue of its place in the system. This transfer of wisdom, maturity, and experience away from individuals and directly into the Senate's formal function within the system is typical of the Constitution's refusal to entrust the government to the moral character either of the representatives, the senators, the president, or the electorate itself. The Constitution trusts only its own critical system, devised to foresee and thwart the profane impulses of human nature.

By the time the Constitution got ratified the political theories of Montesquieu — once a major source of inspiration for the American revolutionaries — had become largely irrelevant to the founder's thinking about republicanism. Montesquieu had argued that enlightened republics are founded on public virtue, but "Montesquieu had never study'd a free democracy," declared William Vans Murray. The failure of ancient republics, he added, was due to their attempt "to force the human character into distorted shapes," while the American republic gives "fair play" to that character (Wood, 611). James Wilson's remark that there had been introduced "such particular checks and controls . . . into the very form of government as to make it advantageous even for bad men to act for the public good" meant precisely that: that the role of public virtue had been taken over by the critical interplay of the governing system itself.

To the degree that it does not trust people to behave virtuously or wisely, the Constitution provided in its own founding legislation the virtue and maturity on which the nation's stability would depend. In so doing it transformed, rejuvenated, and renewed various august heritages: Greek and Roman traditions of republicanism, Christian doctrines, and Enlightenment thought, to mention just a few of the major ones. By incorporating "the wisdom of ages" in its scripture, the framers to a great extent freed America's citizens from the need to think, remember, and judge aright. The Constitution does that for us, for the most part. As long as its Constitution lasts, the American republic preserves the maturity of its birth, allowing its citizens the luxury of becoming like children, without having to "begin all over again," like Plato's postcataclysmic Greeks.

Alas, if only it were so simple.

Gettysburg

One of the reasons the American Constitution has endured so long and aged so well is because subsequent generations have always assumed that the framers — or the political system they put in place — know better than they do when it comes to how the republic should govern itself. The founding fathers are our national gods. We dare not tinker with their work, for we know not what we do. Our foolishness could only vitiate what they conceived in wisdom. Somewhere in our national consciousness we understand that, compared to them, we are like children, that our fragile union depends on following the letter of their laws, heeding their intentions, and doing their will, otherwise we are lost. Thus do the fathers continue to infantilize us.

Yet the one responsibility the Constitution cannot absolve us from is that of preserving its integrity. This is principally the charge of the Supreme Court — America's council of elders, as it were, whom age and experience have qualified to take on the task of assuring that our newly enacted laws remain faithful to and consistent with the Constitution's intent. The hermeneutic challenge for these succeeding generations of elders is to provide words for the Constitution where it contains none — words consistent with those it does contain.

Yet as I remarked at the beginning of my second chapter, age does not always bring wisdom. Nor does the existence of a separate branch of government devoted to preserving both the letter and spirit of the Constitution guarantee that its members, however senior they may be, will show wisdom in their judgments. There are times when the Constitution cannot do our thinking for us, and when the members of the Supreme Court behave like fools, knaves, and villains. Ralph Waldo Emerson in his 1854 lecture on the Fugitive Slave Law:

You relied on the constitution. It has not the word *slave* in it; and very good argument has shown that it would not warrant the crimes that are done under it. ... You relied on the Supreme Court. The law was right, excellent law for the lambs. But what if unhappily the judges were chosen from the wolves, and give to the laws a wolfish interpretation? ... These things show that no forms, neither constitutions, nor laws, nor covenants, nor churches, nor bibles, are of any use in themselves. The Devil nestles comfortably into them all. There is no help but in the head and heart and hamstrings of a man. Covenants are of no use without honest men to keep them; laws of none but with loyal citizens to obey them. To interpret Christ it needs Christ in the heart. The teachings of the Spirit can be apprehended only by the same spirit that gave them forth. (*The Spiritual Emerson*, 200–201)

Such antinomianism is irrefutable. When the republic's very founding falls into crisis, as it did over the issue of slavery, the Constitution cannot save us; rather, the citizens of the American republic are the ones who must the save the Constitution by resolving upon its intent: not the intent of its letter, but of its spirit. In such moments of national crisis, the Supreme Court reveals its impotence, or worse, its blind partisanship. That is when the nation as a whole must go to war to decide what its Constitution means — what it *will* mean henceforth, and hence what it will have meant from its inception.

It was Abraham Lincoln who, at a critical moment in the republic's history, mobilized the effort to rescue the Constitution by deciding the fate of its future authority. He did this by plunging the nation into a civil war that would "test" whether that nation, or any nation conceived in liberty, can long endure:

Four score and seven years ago our fathers brought forth on this continent, a new nation, conceived in Liberty and dedicated to the proposition that all men are created equal.

Now we are engaged in a great civil war, testing whether

that nation, or any nation so conceived and so dedicated, can long endure. We are met on a great battle-field of that war. We have come to dedicate a portion of that field, as a final resting place for those who here gave their lives that that nation might live. It is altogether fitting and proper that we should do this.

But, in a larger sense, we can not dedicate — we can not consecrate — we can not hallow — this ground. The brave men, living and dead, who struggled here have consecrated it, far above our poor power to add or detract. The world will little note, nor long remember what we say here, but it can never forget what they did here. It is for us the living, rather, to be dedicated here to the unfinished work which they who fought here have thus far nobly advanced. It is rather for us to be here dedicated to the great task remaining before us — that from these honored dead we take increased devotion to that cause for which they gave their last full measure of devotion — that we here highly resolve that these dead shall not have died in vain — that this nation, under God, shall have a new birth of freedom — and that government of the people, by the people, for the people, shall not perish from the earth.

I have commented at length on the Gettysburg Address in my book *The Dominion of the Dead* and elsewhere, hence I will not reiterate here what I asserted in those pages. Let me address instead a question I did not touch in my previous commentaries.

Some have claimed that Lincoln's Gettysburg Address usurps the intent and meaning of the Constitution, which nowhere speaks about men being created equal, or about the American nation being founded upon a dedication to that proposition. While this may be literally true, the crisis came about as a result of the failure of the literal words of the Constitution to keep the union from breaking apart. At times the letter of the law is simply dead. In such moments only the living citizens can decide its meaning and intent, by choosing sides, even at the cost of giving up their lives on behalf of their choice. Lincoln claimed in his address that the nation is founded not on a proposition but on a "dedication" to that proposition. It is the dedication that writes the proposition and gives it its grounding power. It is we the living, on the graves of those who died in dedication, who must take responsibility for the Constitution's meaning, and decide its meaning, thereby rendering its proposition historical.

The founding fathers did not found upon "this continent" the Constitution they framed for the nation. It was Lincoln who presided over that solemn event by giving the "new nation" a new founding. He did so by calling on, mobilizing, or activating the archaic unifying powers of sacrifice, victimage, and fratricide. The origin myths of Rome tell us that the blood of Remus, slain by his brother Romulus, marked the place of Rome's foundation. Cain, slayer of his brother Abel, founded a dynasty. Cadmus slayed a dragon and sowed its teeth in the earth, from which there came a harvest of armed men whom Cadmus turned against each other until they fought one another to death, except for five survivors who went on to engender the Theban nobility. America was brought forth by its Constitution as a well-conceived, fully modern nation, yet through its civil war — and Lincoln's memorializing act at Gettysburg — it placed or re-placed its nationhood on the most atavistic basis of all: the blood of the brother. Could a new nation long endure without such grounding?

The role Lincoln played in American history cannot be exaggerated. He consolidated the nation's "new birth of freedom" by securing for it an ancient sacrificial basis. He did this not only in his political life as president of the United States but above all in his political death. In his martyrdom he embodied or stood for all the victims of a civil war waged on behalf of, and against, the union. In the symbolic magnitude of its tragedy, his death became, and to this day remains, a source of unity in the union's body politic — a unity that the Constitution, for all its provisions for the future of the nation, could not provide.

Rome founded its empire on the civil wars that followed in the wake of Caesar's assassination. In Shakespeare's version of that crisis, Caesar's wife has a foreboding dream in which she sees his statue spouting blood from a hundred holes. The conspirator Decius, seeking to allay Caesar's apprehensions and lure him to the Capitol, declares, "This dream ... signifies that from you great Rome shall suck / Reviving blood..." (2.2. 87–8). And so it was to be. So too America and its Constitution have sucked reviving blood from Lincoln's death. Caesar's death preceded, and Lincoln's followed, the civil wars in question, yet the effect was the same. Why a modern nation dedicated to freedom, reason, and consent of the governed should need to draw blood from such an archaic source remains a mystery, yet it is evidence enough that, in its newness, America is as old as the oldest nations of the earth.

FOUR

Amor Mundi

Clarifications

Hannah Arendt coined the term "natality" for the ever-present potentiality for new beginnings that humans bring into the world when they are born. When it takes on historical forms, natality revitalizes the reservoir of cultural legacies by allowing past, present, and future to inflect one another in what Baudelaire called the realm of correspondences, with its "long echoes" and its "obscure and deep unity." We saw such inflections at work in the preceding chapter's case studies, where I showed in granular detail how neotenic revolutions, when successful, both break with and renew — or renew in the act of breaking with — antecedent traditions, canons, institutions, or articles of faith.

If we return for a moment to Gettysburg, we note that, in his address, Lincoln describes the natality of the American nation as a birth that has yet to be accomplished. Turning fathers into mothers (or into midwives), he says, "our fathers brought forth on this continent a new nation." The child they delivered was "conceived in liberty," yet four score and seven years later its conception had not yet been fully realized. History called on Lincoln to help complete that event by rallying to the cause of the nation's conception and helping it achieve a "new birth in freedom," as he calls in later in his speech. Such was the natality of that decisive moment when the historical destiny of the American republic, in its past and future versions, hung in the balance.

Just as natality gives birth to history, history in turn provides natality with openings and occasions for its initiatives. I speak of history here not as the bygone but as an incubator of renewal that endows the present with nascent possibilities that reach it from the future, in its subterranean correlations with the past. I will have more to say later in this chapter about how the future is born of the past and the past reborn from out of the future, thanks to a mysterious process of transmission. Meanwhile, let us note here what the previous chapter put into relief, namely that when the new does not renew — when it does not rejuvenate latent legacies — it gets old in a hurry.

A nation can build for the future, invest in the future, and undertake industrial, social, or technological projects for the future, yet if it does not find ways to metabolize its past, it remains without genuine prospects. That means that its youth remains largely stagnant, culturally speaking. The greatness of Western civilization, for all its disfiguring vices, consists in the fact that it has repeatedly found ways to regenerate itself by returning to, or fetching from, its nascent sources. The creative synergy between Western wisdom and Western genius has always taken the form of projective retrieval — of birthing the new from the womb of antecedence. Thus retrieval, in this radical sense, has little to do with revival and everything to do with revitalization.

Western natality is wildly expansive. We may be antiquarian, monumental, or critical in our attitude toward the past — we may be pious, insurgent, or blasphemous toward our predecessors — yet time and again the West has made history by renatalizing its heritage. As Paul Valéry put it in his Notebooks, "*novat reiterando*": to renew through repetition, where repetition means precisely to re-petition the source. "Make it new!" (Ezra Pound's famous injunction to modernists) does not mean to invent ex nihilo but to descend into Hades and give dead languages a new vernacular, to bring into being a younger version of an earlier form or tradition. By retrieving and transfiguring a wide variety of strains in the literary heritage, the modernists showed in their innovations that the genuinely new does not chase after novelty.

It finds ways to make the old new again, and in so doing to give it a more youthful and vibrant style.

Novat reiterando. Under this rubric Dante did to Virgil what Virgil did to Homer—he *repeated* him, not slavishly but regeneratively. Transmuting the Roman's *heroic poem* into a first-person Christian epic, Dante coerced Virgil, and with him all his other pagan sources, into a Christian framework, preserving and overturning their legacies in the process. Ovid, Lucan, Horace, Aristotle, and a host of other predecessors would, if they could, attest to the fact that Dante used and abused them, often outrageously, but they would also have to concede, however begrudgingly, that in so doing he gave them new life in a world and era to which they were not native.

A few decades after Dante gave us a full-blown medieval-Christian antiquity, Petrarch gave us a Renaissance-humanist antiquity. Petrarch became the first truly modern European not by plunging into the future futuristically but by studiously consulting the ancients and reworking their testaments into a scintillating Italian vernacular. Through his long dialogues with the dead, Petrarch inaugurated a new cultural humanism, and with it a wholly different relation to the classical past than Dante had established half a century earlier.

Prior to the twentieth century no one did more to liberate, vindicate, or express youthful sentiment than the Romantics; yet as we saw in our discussion of Wordsworth, their inner child was anything but childish. The Romantics did not sing their songs of innocence innocently. They did not babble their way into a new idiom but used a remarkably sophisticated poetics to naturalize the diction of their predecessors. It took an ingenious wisdom to give the word "bird" a more poetic resonance than "feather'd songster," or to find in the ruins of antiquity a landscape for the modern soul, or to reach back behind the age of reason to a medieval patrimony, as the Romantics did.

Nietzsche lay claim to the twentieth century by cultivating the one faculty he held more important than any other—what he called the "historical sense." In his case the historical sense took him back again and again to the Greeks, not the Greeks of the Weimar classicists nor of the Winckelmann school, but a more radical — because more radically reclaimed — tribe of ancestors. Nietzsche's transvaluation of all values represented nothing less than an exuberant transfiguration of the Greeks' tragic wisdom, as he understood. Here is how Nietzsche put it at the end of *Nietzsche contra Wagner*, the last book he worked on before his mind succumbed to darkness:

> Oh, those Greeks! They knew how to live. What is required for that is to stop courageously at the surface, the fold, the skin, to adore appearance, to believe in forms, tones, words, in the whole Olympus of appearance. Those Greeks were superficial — *out of profundity*. And is not this precisely what we are coming back to, we daredevils of the spirit who have climbed the highest and most dangerous peak of present thought. ... Are we not, precisely in this respect, Greeks? Adorers of forms, of tones, of words? And therefore — *artists*? (*Portable Nietzsche*, 683)

It was his free reprise of the Greek past — his obsessive return to that generous source — that enabled Nietzsche to become what he called a "philosopher of the future."

The West's Greek and Roman antiquity courses through its cultural history, renewing itself in a great plurality of forms. There is a medieval antiquity, a Renaissance antiquity, a Baroque antiquity, an Enlightenment antiquity, a Romantic antiquity, and a modernist antiquity. Yet where does one stop? There are Emersonian, Wagnerian, Baudelairean, Yeatsian, Joycean, Heideggerian, and Arendtian antiquities, to invoke only a few modern heroes who fetched from the same source. This wild multiplicity of antiquities is enough to make one suspect that Western culture flourishes only to the degree that it retrieves its way into the future.

These considerations, along with others I will be drawing attention to in this chapter, make one wonder about the juvenescence contemporary society is undergoing. Does it represent a veritable neotenic revolution—a rejuvenation of legacy the likes of which Western culture has never experienced before, either in degree or extent—or does it represent instead a mere juvenilization? The difference is more than terminological. Rejuvenation gives the past a future to grow into and gives the new a foundational staying power. Juvenilization, by contrast, militates against historicity and deprives the present of temporal and phenomenological depth. If cultural neoteny brings youthfulness to new levels of maturity, and gives that maturity younger forms of expression, juvenilization does the opposite. It gives youth a premature old age, and old age a callow youthfulness. We are not in a position, historically speaking, to answer the question I have just posed regarding our juvenescence. It may turn out that we who think ourselves so young are in fact suffering from a senile form of juvenility, or it may turn out that our genius is in the process of engendering historically unprecedented forms of cultural natality. It is too early to say.

Changing the World

It was high praise for the *New York Times* to call Steve Jobs "a visionary who transformed the digital age" in its obituary of October 6, 2011. Today's visionary is a transformer who contrives and concocts rather than preserves and perpetuates. There is no glory in conserving the world, only in changing it. Thus in 1983, the article noted, Jobs had succeeded in convincing the onetime chief executive of Pepsi-Cola, John Sculley, to become the chief executive of Apple with an irresistible pitch: "Do you want to spend the rest of your life selling sugared water, or do you want a chance to change the world?"

It is practically impossible for us today to appreciate how, in past eras, those who would change the world were viewed with dread and suspicion. If you cared for the world, if you made it your home, if you were cognizant of how much effort, sacrifice, and foresight it had cost your forebears to build, fortify, and incrementally improve its institutions, if you saw it as the place of your secular afterlife, then you had every reason to impute sinister tendencies to those who would meddle with the world's finely tuned configuration, thereby endangering its calibrated stability. It requires a great deal of love — what Hannah Arendt, borrowing a phrase from Saint Augustine, called *amor mundi* — to take the well-being of the world to heart and commit oneself to assuring its continuity through the generations. It is that love, and that love alone, that takes custody of the world's future. Nothing serves to bind human beings together as a polity more intensely than a heightened awareness of world-belonging. Only a shared world offers people what their shared humanity needs the most, namely a sense of cohesion between the living, the dead, and those to come.

When changing the world becomes a prime directive, a psychologist of the Nietzschean school may well suspect an *odium mundi* at work. If "odium" seems too strong a word, one could call it a certain disregard for the untold labors, efforts, and suffering that went into the world's creation. Across the millennia human beings worked themselves to exhaustion and death to build worlds that would endure, for they had a deeply rooted need to belong to an institutional order that would outlive them. Only the "late born" — and we are all late born at this stage in our history — have the luxury of taking the world for granted.

In chapter 1 I discussed the strong neophiliac strain in the human species, yet I also drew attention to the innate neophobia we share with most other living species. In the final analysis nothing runs deeper in worldly beings like ourselves — who are the only worldly species in the universe, as far as we know — than our need for a context of permanence. This is what a world is, finally — a historically based context of permanence for our transitory, mortal lives.

There are several ways that context can be shattered. One is through deliberate destruction; another is through negligence; yet another is through an overactive deployment of the creative forces that build up worlds in the first place. In the latter case especially, the world turns into a place of endless upheaval rather than quiet constancy, of shock rather than shelter, of subclinical paranoia rather than everyday sanity. The stress that comes with this kind of agitation easily engenders world-loathing, where before there was world-love. This is the self-consuming paradox of an overactive deployment of the creative forces. The more the world changes, the less those who inhabit it feel at home in it; the less they feel at home in it, the more urgent becomes the desire to change it. At a certain point the world becomes un-worldly. As the prevailing order of things fills us with dread, the will to overturn it gains momentum.

Destructiveness then can take on a glamorous and redemptive aspect. In his reflections on what he called "the destructive character," Walter Benjamin personified a certain type of heroic world-undoing: "The destructive character knows only one watchword: make room; only one activity: clearing away" (*Reflections*, 301). Benjamin's character is not motivated by odium; he does not suffer from Nietzschean *ressentiment*, since "his need for fresh air and open space is stronger than any hatred." Indeed, he is "young and cheerful," for "destroying rejuvenates in clearing away the traces of our own age." In his carelessness, this youthful character, whom "no vision inspires," does not ask himself what will replace what has been destroyed. His purpose is simply to "find a way through" the encrusted accumulations of the world's history, which he sees as so many obstacles thwarting his impulse to "make room."

There is no creative drive in the destructiveness personified by Benjamin's character ("the only work he avoids is being creative"), yet as it de-clutters the world and opens up empty space where before there was scarcely room to move, it may serve the cause of creative renewal simply by getting rid of the petrified monuments of tradition and disclosing new horizons of possibility. Where the traditionalists "pass things down to posterity, by making them untouchable and thus conserving them," the destructive character makes it his business to "liquidate" them, thus opening up the way for a new aesthetic, a new morality, or a new political order, as the case may be. There is a reckless visionary quality to this destructive character: "Where others encounter walls or mountains, there, too, he sees a way." This is why Benjamin, along with other champions of a modernity-to-come, hails the destructive character as a hero of rejuvenation whose irreverence for what exists informs a certain type of disaggregating aesthetic as well as a certain type of political militancy vis-à-vis the status quo.

From our contemporary perspective, almost a century after his portrait was drawn, Benjamin's character appears not only dated but even quaint in his late nineteenth- and early twentieth-century gestures of insurrectional impiety. His youthful assault on the world's support systems seems to have outlived its appeal, since there is little more one can do these days to shock the bourgeoisie or to tear down the pillars that held up the old world order. Hannah Arendt put it well in her essay "On Humanity in Dark Times" when she declared:

> In the two hundred years that separate us from Lessing's lifetime, much has changed ... but little has changed for the better. The "pillars of the best-known truths" (to stay with his metaphor), which at the time were shaken, today lie shattered; we need neither criticism nor wise men to shake them anymore. We only need to look around us to see that we are standing in the midst of a veritable rubble heap of such pillars. (10)

Benjamin wrote of the destructive character, "What exists he reduces to rubble, not for the sake of the rubble, but for that of the way leading through it." It turned out that the way leading through it only led back to the rubble itself, which today lies all around us as far as the eye can see, despite all the "new things" that have since been introduced into this landscape of ruins. In sum, the newness that constant change brings into the world does not replace the ruins; it does not even exist alongside the ruins; rather, it merely adds to the rubble.

Arendt does not deny that bringing down the world's pillars "could be an advantage, promoting a new kind of thinking that needs no pillars and props, no standards and traditions to move freely without crutches over unfamiliar terrain." Yet she reminds us of a crucial truth that rarely receives consideration among those who lionize the destructive character, namely that the world is one thing, while the people who live in it are another. The passage continues:

> For long ago it became apparent that the pillars of the truths [that have been shaken and shattered in the modern era] have also been the pillars of the political order, and that the world (in contrast to the people who inhabit it and move freely in it) needs such pillars in order to guarantee continuity and permanence, without which it cannot offer mortal men the relatively secure, relatively imperishable home that they need. To be sure, the very humanity of man loses its vitality to the extent that he abstains from thinking and puts his confidence in the old verities or even new truths, throwing them down as if they were coins with which to balance all experiences. And yet if it is true for man, it is not true for the world. (10–11)

From this perspective the modern era appears as a prolonged confusion on the part of critics, liquidators, and revolutionaries between what is true for human beings, on the one hand, and what is true for the world, on the other. For better or worse, our humanity is housed by the world — by its places, legacies, customs, and institutions — rather than in our psychological selves. Deprived of a world, human beings quickly lose their historicity and, instead of belonging to a continuum that generates the future from out of the past, inhabit a punctual and intransitive present.

By subjecting the world to repeated political, moral, and social convulsions, to say nothing of environmental ones, the history of the twentieth century worked against the claims of both our historicity and our humanity. Here again, Arendt puts it best:

> The world becomes inhuman, inhospitable to human needs — which are the needs of mortals — when it is violently wrenched into a movement in which there is no longer any sort of permanence. (11)

Humanity cannot do without hospitality — the offering as well as receiving of it — and that means it cannot do without a hospitable world, which alone renders us capable of showing hospitality. Hence there is a certain perversity in the fact that human beings, in their capacity as historical agents, are the ones who have brought about the violent unworlding of the world.

This perversity may not be particularly modern — we saw manifestations of it in Sophocles's *anthropos*, whose misadventures can render him *apolis*, or worldless — yet the modern era seems to have lost its chorus of elders, as it were. By that I mean that it has disinhibited the apolitical forces (in the Arendtian sense) to such an extent as to turn worldlessness into a general historical condition, precisely by pursuing a course of constant change. Arendt remarks that this sort of wrenching movement, which provokes a homeless malaise in human beings, practically guarantees any number of reactionary but feckless attempts at restoration:

> That is why ever since the great failure of the French Revolution people have repeatedly re-erected the old pillars which were then overthrown, only again and again to see them first quivering, then collapsing anew. The most frightful errors have replaced the "best-known truths," and the error of these doctrines constitutes no proof, no new pillar for the old truths. In the political realm restoration is never a substitute for a new foundation, but will at best be an emergency measure that becomes inevitable when the act of foundation,

which is called revolution, has failed. But it is likewise inevitable that in such a constellation, especially when it extends over such long spans of time, people's mistrust of the world and all aspects of the public realm should grow steadily. For the fragility of these repeatedly restored props of the public order is bound to become more apparent after every collapse, so that ultimately the public order is based on people's holding as self-evident precisely those "best-known truths" which secretly scarcely anyone still believes in. (11)

Such is the misery of certain forms of conservatism as well as radicalism, from Arendt's perspective: the latter are unable to give us a new world, while the former are unable to rescue the old one. Here too one must insist on the distinction between the world and the human agents who act within it, for it takes more than an act of political or collective will to build a world of relative permanence, or to restore an order that has been shattered. Worlds do not come into being, nor do they endure, through acts of will but through the generative and regenerative forces of what I have called the source. These forces are not "natural resources." They cannot be mastered, willed, seized, or put at our disposal. They must be summoned from the depths of world-time, which holds the historical recesses of past, future, and present together and keeps them in dynamic relation to one another. Only through such world-time can worlds come into being and cohere. Indeed, what Arendt calls "dark times" must be understood as a general deficiency in the historical power of world-formation as such.

In her preface to *Men in Dark Times*, Arendt states that the dark times her title refers to fell on the world "during the first half of the twentieth century, with its political catastrophes, its moral disasters, and its astonishing development of the arts and sciences" (vii). The "astonishing development of the arts and sciences" in this period is a matter I must skip over here. I will simply note that much has changed since 1959 — the year Arendt first delivered the address from which I have been quoting at length—yet precisely to the degree that much has changed, little has changed, or as Arendt herself put it, "little has changed for the better." The "violent wrenching" of the world into constant movement has remained constant. Indeed, the only constancy of the past several decades has been change itself, that is, constant inconstancy. The paradox of this syndrome causes those who suffer from it to hope that change—or the right kind of change—will eventually put an end to the dread it induces through its endless turnover of the new. This is a strange hope to hold to, yet it may be the only one available at a time when the unworlding of the world seems a fait accompli.

Amor Mundi and a Poem about Going

I have discussed in abstract terms how relentless change can destroy the essence of the human world, namely its permanence and hospitality, yet there is nothing abstract about our everyday experience of this destruction, which touches in intimate ways rich and poor, white and black, old and young alike. The poor are more vulnerable to the brutal disfigurations of the lived environment, while the rich can afford the luxury of insulation and artificial paradises. Artificial paradises, however, engender a desire for the genuine article that cannot be satisfied by artificial means, while insulation offers no substitute for the social, communal, and public world we share in common. At best, insulation grants one the privilege of a quieter despair than that suffered by those who bear the full brunt of the world's undoing.

As for the young and the old, the shattering of the world affects them in different yet equally unsettling ways. Later in this chapter I will discuss world-disavowal among the young. Here I will offer some analysis of the sentiments of those who are old enough to feel that *their* world is disappearing before their eyes.

The Englishman Philip Larkin—one of the least sentimental poets in the modern canon—wrote a poem four decades ago that speaks from a first-person perspective about the existential anguish that aggravated change engenders in a man who has reached a certain age. Titled "Going, Going," it reads as follows:

I thought it would last my time—
The sense that, beyond the town,
There would always be fields and farms,
Where the village louts could climb
Such trees as were not cut down;
I knew there'd be false alarms

In the papers about old streets
And split level shopping, but some
Have always been left so far;
And when the old part retreats
As the bleak high-risers come
We can always escape in the car.

Things are tougher than we are, just
As earth will always respond
However we mess it about;
Chuck filth in the sea, if you must:
The tides will be clean beyond.
—But what do I feel now? Doubt?

Or age, simply? The crowd
Is young in the M1 cafe;
Their kids are screaming for more—
More houses, more parking allowed,
More caravan sites, more pay.
On the Business Page, a score

Of spectacled grins approve
Some takeover bid that entails
Five per cent profit (and ten

Per cent more in the estuaries): move
Your works to the unspoilt dales
(Grey area grants)! And when

You try to get near the sea
In summer ...
It seems, just now,
To be happening so very fast;
Despite all the land left free
For the first time I feel somehow
That it isn't going to last,

That before I snuff it, the whole
Boiling will be bricked in
Except for the tourist parts—
First slum of Europe: a role
It won't be hard to win,
With a cast of crooks and tarts.

And that will be England gone,
The shadows, the meadows, the lanes,
The guildhalls, the carved choirs.
There'll be books; it will linger on
In galleries; but all that remains
For us will be concrete and tyres.

Most things are never meant.
This won't be, most likely; but greeds
And garbage are too thick-strewn
To be swept up now, or invent
Excuses that make them all needs.
I just think it will happen, soon.

The poem records in everyday language the discreet yet desolate reflections of a person whose state of mind has been unnerved by an apocalyptic dread. Everything he observes around him points to the inevitability of an imminent outcome, namely "England gone." The poem's center of gravity lies with the word "last," from the first line, "I thought it would last my time." The speaker's had assumed that at least England's age-old country-side would last, yet even traditionally imperishable things are perishing under the pressure of the more — "more houses, more parking allowed, / more caravan sites, more pay." There is less and less world in this age of the more, for the "more" of this particular historical moment has world-devouring quality about it.

Larkin died in 1985, and we know that England's country-side, or at least a good part of it, has indeed lasted beyond his death. Yet Larkin's poem does not advance empirical claims. The "it" of that first line refers not to "fields and farms" as such but to the speaker's inward "sense" that there would "always be fields and farms." It is this inner, psychological assurance that is nearing its end. "For the first time I feel somehow / That it isn't going to last." This "I feel" figures as the proper subject of the poem, whether or not it corresponds to a certifiable external reality. Indeed, the "I feel" — especially when it becomes a collective sentiment — will often engender the reality it either desires or dreads.

Is it because the speaker is closer to death than the "young crowd" at the M1 Café that he has such foreboding? The elderly, after all, are prone to confuse their own approaching end with the world's demise. Or have the changes, losses, and degradations taking place in England rendered manifest, beyond any reasonable doubt, the sinister death-drive of contemporary history? This is not a question that can be answered empirically. If it exists, the death-drive would be neither conscious nor intentional ("Most things are never meant"), even if it enlists "a cast of crooks and tarts" to do its work of unworlding the world. All we know is that the speaker experiences his historical present as a fast-moving rush toward annihilation, and that it is above all the speed of the process that fills him with a sense that the end is near: "It seems, just now, to be happening so very fast." The "it" here refers to the final denouement, as it does in the poem's last line: "I just think it will happen, soon."

Again, it matters little whether this subjective sense of world-demise, brought on by the magnitude and pace of change in the speaker's lifetime, corresponds to an objective state of affairs or not. In the human realm the subjective has a way of becoming objective, for history has shown time and again that the fate of the external world is bound up with what its inhabitants "feel" internally, which in turn depends on what they see taking place in their midst. For the world to last *as a world*, and not merely as a habitat, those who live in it must continue to consider it their own. Once it becomes alien to them, or once they sense that it is no longer *their* world, they withdraw their love from it. This shedding of *amor mundi* is the biggest danger the world faces today, for the *mundus* disappears along with the *amor* that took custody of its future. That is why subjective sentiment cannot be separated from objective reality when it comes to world-hood.

Giambattista Vico understood the binding power of love for world-formation. In his *Institutiones oratoriae*, or *Art of Rhetoric*, he goes through the different stages of development in an individual's life and remarks that each is marked by a specific kind of love, beginning with the self-directed love of the infant, or what Freud would later call primary narcissism. In *The New Science* he takes up again this notion that "every age has its love" (*omnis aetas amat*) and incorporates it into his theory of societal development, from barbarism to full enlightenment. Each stage of development corresponds to what we could call a world, and each entails a kind of love:

> Man in the bestial state loves [*ama*] only his own welfare; having taken wife and begotten children, he loves his own welfare along with that of his family; having entered upon civil life, he loves his own welfare along with that of his city; when its rule is extended over several peoples, he loves his own welfare along with that of the nation; when the nations

are united by wars, treaties of peace, alliances, and commerce, he loves his own welfare along with that of the entire human race. In all these circumstances man loves principally his own utility. (§341, 101)

Persisting in all the later stages of this process of development, self-love invests its desire, will, and care into the world-configurations that make up the sequence that Vico adumbrates here — family, city, nation, empire. The more expansive the configuration, the more general and inclusive is the love that holds it together. But at any moment in the sequence, love can collapse in on its intrinsically egotistic core. In Vico's theory, this usually happens at the end of a given cycle of historical development, if and when enlightened commonwealths start succumbing to what he calls the "barbarism of reflection," with its aggravated forms of irony, skepticism, and cynicism.

It would be idle to speculate about whether our present age corresponds in some programmatic way to any of the stages posited by Vico, especially since those stages, as we have seen, bleed into one another heterochronically. I bring Vico back into the discussion here only as a further reminder that *amor mundi* both suffuses and sustains the world, and that its withdrawal leaves the world ever more vulnerable to the forces that provoke its withdrawal in the first place. The question we face in our present age — an age that is both older and younger than it was when Larkin wrote "Going, Going" — is not whether we are that much closer to the end foreboded by his poem but whether a regeneration of world love is possible under present conditions. It is to that question that we must now turn.

The New Ones

Whatever comes into being historically — be it a tradition, an institution, or a worldview — begins to decay once it goes static, hence world-stability should not be confused with inert immutability. It should be conceived instead as continuous, self-renewing transformation. Unfortunately there are no firm rules for discriminating between transformational and deformational change, and the modern era, especially in the aesthetic domain, has shown time and again that regeneration, in its initial manifestations, appears to many skeptics as symptomatic of degeneration. Since objective standards do not apply, one must be cautious about passing judgments on the new, especially since, in many cases, destruction is a necessary component of genuine renewal. Yet caution must go both ways. We should also remember that change does not always mean transformation, and that it is far easier to ruin the world than to fortify it.

The world's self-rejuvenating natality depends mostly on the "new ones" (*oi néoi*, as the ancient Greeks called young people), since they infuse the world with new life, once they are ready to take custody of it. I insist on this last clause because, when it comes to the kind of transformation that preserves the world through renewal, everything depends on the culturally variegated processes by which the new ones learn what it means to become adults and assume responsibility for the world they were born into, which amounts to saying that everything depends on their education.

The young have an ambivalent relation to the world insofar as they are thrown into it without having chosen it or built it, hence they do not have a sense of ownership in its regard. Yet since they are destined to inherit it, they have no choice but to concern themselves with what it holds in store for them. This ambivalence has its roots in the condition of childhood itself, which is simultaneously oriented away from, and toward, the world. Children traditionally spend much of their time within the sheltering privacy of the home, at a safe remove from the public world their elders share in common, yet they also spend a fair amount of time at school, whose primary purpose is to introduce the newcomers to the world beyond the domestic space and prepare them to be inducted into it. As it positions them somewhere between the private and the public sphere, school teaches children what it means to assume ownership of the world they were born into. That is why societies that seek to exclude women from the public sphere and confine them to the home have no business sending girls to school, since education is an intermediary institution that teaches the lessons of citizenship and responsibility. That is also why formal schooling for girls, as well as women's access to higher education, represents one of the greatest advances of modern civilization. It gives half of humanity a foothold in the world.

To take their place in the world, the *néoi* must acquire a basic knowledge of how it came to be. When history's struggles, failures, and advances — its conflicted and stratified past — begin to inform the student's cognizance of the present, that student's relation to time — to his or her *being in time* — undergoes a maturation process. The more the present reveals itself as the outcome of the past, the more it also appears as a prelude to the future. Education does not fulfill its worldly mandate by putting an electronic device in every student's hands, or by promoting a purblind vision of the present, but rather by plunging students into the depths of history and pushing them toward those subterranean regions where the dead speak in their own untimely voices. Education becomes futural when it takes the form of a *katabasis*, a descent into the shadow realm where the reservoir of legacies has its source.

Education cannot lead one by the hand to the source, for the latter lies hidden deep within the selfhood of each young person; what it can do is show the way to the golden bough that grants the individual access to the underworld, where students may discover the source for themselves, in the first-person singular. In sum, it can show them the way to the Stygian forest of history out of which, or in which, the world as we know it came into being. In its most vital vocation, education teaches the young how to see in the dark — the dark of the living past where the future's possibilities call out across time for retrieval. There is nothing more difficult for a young person than to access within his or her selfhood the rejuvenating powers that lurk in the depths of a civilization's psyche. Those depths never cease calling on the young — summoning them, as it were — even if the call goes mostly unheeded, or fades to an inaudible whisper as youth gives way to adulthood. One must assume that the call arises from history's unconditional will to keep the story going by enlisting the young on behalf of its cause.

At the beginning of the *Divine Comedy*, Dante's pilgrim attempts to climb the mountain of transcendence, with its promise of future happiness, by following a rectilinear path up its slope, but his way is blocked by three beasts, whose allegorical meaning remains obscure. The thirteen-hundred-year-old ghost of Virgil arrives on the scene to rescue the pilgrim, telling him that the way up the mountain actually leads downward before it leads upward. "You must hold to another path," Virgil tells him. The same holds true for the future. If the young are to inherit the future they must hold to another path than the one that leads straight toward its blinding light — a path that circles back and descends into the past, away from the entanglements of the present, before it breaks into the future's *vita nuova*.

That is why education succeeds only where it resists the siren calls of contemporaneity and keeps open the dimension of the untimely. Since we make the future only out of what has been bestowed, education's first order of business is to assure that bestowal takes place, a task that requires of it to create a living cultural memory. In *Matter and Memory* Henri Bergson defined living memory as "the synthesis of past and present with a view to the future." In its ideal, education assists in the birth of this kind of synthesis.

Living memory only comes to life in the animate selfhood of the person performing the synthesis. Just as one can take the horse to the water but not make it drink, so too education can lead students into history but cannot by itself historicalize them. The transmission process that generates heirs remains mysterious. Somewhere in the recesses of self, something gets passed on and kept alive. It takes place for the most part invisibly and silently, registering its effects in the developing selfhood of the initiate much the way Dante's journey in the *Divine*

Comedy effects a spiritual transformation within the pilgrim's first-person singular. The formative place that we call the young person's soul, for lack of a better term, is where history's potential for new life take roots and germinates.

Young Love

It may or may not be empirically true that "we only learn from those we love," as Goethe affirmed, or that "the deepest insights spring from love alone," as Nietzsche affirmed, yet there is little doubt that education's unofficial currency is love. To be more precise, its mission is to educe a love of the world — the kind of love without which there could be no world at all.

What is the source of world love? Or better, *where* is the point of entry to the way that leads to it? Answer: in the interval between childhood and adulthood. It is in that interval that the seeds of *amor mundi* must be sown. This makes the mission of education all the more arduous, for from the outside there is no direct access to this inward source of love in the young person's soul. We recall Edgar Allan Poe's appeal to that source in the opening lines of his poem "Alone," discussed in chapter 1:

> From childhood's hour I have not been
> As others were—I have not seen
> As others saw—I could not bring
> My passions from a common spring.
> From the same source I have not taken
> My sorrow; I could not awaken
> My heart to joy at the same tone;
> And all I loved, I loved alone.

Before adult love can direct itself outward toward the world that citizens share in common, it must first immerse itself in the "uncommon spring" deep within of the person undergoing adultification. Without the uncommon differences that separate one person from another, the "world that comes between men," as Arendt calls it, would not have "plurality" as one of its basic constituents. The world is the locus of plurality because each of its citizens is a first-person singular. Love has the power to bind only to the degree that it also has the power to isolate, in youth, the individual it subsequently relates to others, be it personally, socially, or politically. If I may adopt for my own purposes Stein's dictum in Joseph Conrad's novel *Lord Jim*: "In the destructive element immerse!" In this case, the world-shy self-affection of the young soul is the destructive element from which *amor mundi* ultimately springs. To become an adult, in the full sense of the term, means to realize what I least suspect to be the case during my formative years, namely that all I hold most dear depends on, and comes to me through, the world into which I was born.

The reason I insist on the idiosyncratic quality of young love is because the adult self that is born of that love remains, even in its older age, a nascent entity, one whose birth continues to take place in that silent, withdrawn place of ecstatic interiority that hides in every one of us, whether we're aware of it or not. D. H. Lawrence evokes the self's native homeland in a passage that speaks directly to our concern here:

> In the very darkest continent of the body there is God. And from Him issue the first dark rays of our feeling, wordless, and utterly previous to words: the innermost rays, the first messengers, the primeval, honourable beasts of our being, whose voice echoes wordless and forever wordless down the darkest avenues of the soul, but full of potent speech. Our own inner meaning. (*Phoenix*, 759)

The god who resides in this darkest continent of the body, by which Lawrence means the animate core of life, and which I earlier called living memory, is not one of the traditional gods. It is not Yahweh, Zeus, or Jesus. "Give us gods before these," Lawrence declares in one of his poems. These earlier gods — "utterly previous to words" — are "the first messengers" who bring tidings of natality. They come alive when the self is alone enough to bring its full attention to bear on that almost inaudible voice which, like a child, is "wordless . . . but full of potent speech." In his poem "Thought," Lawrence evokes the kind of thinking that allows "the innermost rays" of the self to shine:

> Thought is the welling up of unknown life into
> consciousness,
> Thought is the testing of statements on the touchstone of
> the conscience,
> Thought is gazing on to the face of life, and reading what
> can be read,
> Thought is pondering over experience, and coming to a
> conclusion.
> Thought is not a trick, or an exercise, or a set of dodges,
> Thought is a man in his wholeness wholly attending.

No matter how removed or withdrawn from the world it may seem, it is this kind of thinking that keeps the world in being, for only "a man in his wholeness wholly attending" brings the world into full focus, allowing its "unknown life" to well up into consciousness.

This unknown life, as I have emphasized, emanates from love, and love in turn emanates from the depths of that "dark continent" of the individual's "own inner meaning." Nothing is more important in the transition into adulthood — or in the transmission of legacy — than gaining access to this place within the self where love in its self-transcending impulse binds past, present, and future together in "living memory." It is from that source that the individual acquires historicity. Such access requires a daily measure of withdrawal, silence, and solitude, for most of the essential things that come to fruition later in life are nourished in the hours a young person spends alone — reading, learning, wondering, observing, dreaming, imagining, and pondering. This being-alone-with-oneself is the "destructive element" in which the self incubates its future psychological and cultural maturity.

We live in an age that, wittingly or not, has declared all-out war on the dark continent of inwardness, silence, and attention, of the self in its wholeness wholly attending. The devices that so enthrall us, that miniaturize the world on a screen, appeal to our childlike capacity for mesmerization, to be sure, yet they also inhibit the maturation process that takes place in the continental depths. This is the most crucial maturation process of all, for it turns self-love into world-love, and turns children into adults, not only at the psychological level but at the cultural and historical level as well. Yet for some reason the age demands that we remain at all times connected to the Borg collective, that we join its hive and hear inside our heads not the call of world renewal but the incessant drone that fills the network of globalized interconnection.

Thought begins in what Plato called the silent dialogue I have with myself inside my own head. Only later does it enter into interpersonal dialogues with the citizens in the polis. Without the former, the polis is thoughtless, and the conversation we hold with one another there is mere chatter that lacks the power to promote plurality and *amor mundi*. At the end of his essay "Experience," Ralph Waldo Emerson writes the following about the two kinds of dialogue:

> I know that the world I converse with in the city and in the farms, is not the world I *think*. I observe that difference, and shall observe it. One day I shall know the value and law of this discrepance. But I have not found that much was gained by manipular attempts to realize the world of thought. (*Essential Writings*, 326)

As long as thought take places in the self's solitary dialogue with itself, an essential difference will always come between the world of thought and the world of the city. For some, this "discrepance" is considered objectionable. It must be eliminated. Yet for Emerson it constituted a law whose value may not be immediately apparent but without which there is no thought at all, hence no world to converse with in the city.

The twentieth century did not heed Emerson's call to keep the two worlds related but separate. Much of its political history consisted precisely of "manipular attempts to realize the world of thought" through totalitarian means. The irony of such attempts was that they sought to demolish the world of thought in their drive to realize it through revolution, genocide, social engineering, ideological reeducation, or other means. Here too it took Hannah Arendt to show how the primary goal of totalitarian regimes was to do our thinking for us, and to make it impossible for us to think for ourselves, precisely by filling the silence inside our heads with the constant noise of propaganda. By its very nature propaganda wars against both worlds—the world that I think, and the one I converse with in the city. This in itself is evidence enough that solitude is fundamentally "political," and that it remains crucial for the maturation process that eventually allows an individual to interact and exchange opinions with a plurality of individuals who, like him, think for themselves.

The classic variety of twentieth-century totalitarianism may be in retreat, yet the same cannot be said for the threat against the self's solitary dialogue with itself. Quietude of thought has other enemies these days than invasive propaganda. A globalized network of voices would make drones of us all, and anyone who would seek to disconnect from it hears the same refrain from every corner: "Resistance is futile." That may well be true, yet it does not change the fact that, if the world that I think disappears, the world of the city loses its converse and becomes essentially thoughtless. Nor does it change the fact that a thoughtless world is not a world at all but a hive. One can desire a hive, no doubt, yet such desire has little in common with the *amor mundi* that keeps the human world in being.

Where *amor mundi* fails to take hold, the fault does not

always lie not with parents or teachers, nor with the young's dazed indifference; sometimes the fault lies with the world itself, which fails to elicit in the young the kind of devotion that would turn them into its keepers. One reason why the world today might be failing in this regard is because it imposes its passions on the young too insistently, too chaotically, and too boisterously. When the young cannot withdraw into thought, *amor mundi* cannot gain a proper foothold among them. If "thought is the welling up of unknown life into consciousness," as Lawrence puts it, the world must take special care not to interfere with that process of transmission, given that its future depends upon it.

After Long Silence

In his 1921 poem "The Leaders of the Crowd," W. B. Yeats indicts a certain type of activist who seeks to rile up the crowd and lives in daily quest of excitement, novelty, and new love affairs. Here is what Yeats says about the "leaders" near the end of the poem:

> How can they know
> Truth flourishes where the student's lamp has shone,
> And there alone, that have no solitude?
> So the crowd come, they care not what may come.
> They have loud music, hope every day renewed
> And heartier loves: that lamp is from the tomb.

The student's lamp disperses the passions and clamor of the day, shining on what is most thoughtful, distilled, and self-gathered in books whose words transcend the oblivion of the tomb. Such books do not give expression to "timeless truths." Timeless truths do not exist. At most there exist books that surge with new life when readers uncover in them the unfinished transcendence of truth—books so pregnant with meaning that they never finish saying what they have to say.

Yeats's poem says, "Truth flourishes where the student's lamp has shone, and there alone"—in other words, it flourishes not in the books themselves but in the light that shines on them, that is to say, in the reader's concentration on them. The lamp's light comes from within the student; it comes from "man in his wholeness wholly attending," to recall Lawrence's formulation. Or to phrase it yet another way, truth comes to life in the seminal interaction between words and attention. The student need not be young nor even be in school; he or she need only read studiously or eagerly (*studium*, eagerness, from *studere*, to press forward diligently). The flourishing of truth comes as the fruit of solitude: "How can they know / truth flourishes where the student's lamp has shone, / and there alone, that have no solitude?" Just as solitude makes possible a thinking that takes the form of the self's dialogue with itself, so too being-alone-with-oneself in the presence of a book is the precondition for entering into dialogue with the words of the dead illumined by the lamp.

The active conversation with the past that takes place in the act of study is described by Niccolò Machiavelli in a famous letter he wrote to his friend and patron Francesco Vettori. After giving an account of how he spends his days on his small farm, to which he withdrew after his exile from Florentine politics in 1512, he writes of how he spends his evening:

> When evening comes, I return home and enter my study; on the threshold I take off my workday clothes, covered with mud and dirt, and put on the garments of court and palace. Fitted out appropriately, I step inside the venerable courts of the ancients, where, solicitously received by them, I nourish myself on that food that alone is mine and for which I was born; where I am unashamed to converse with them and to question them about the motives for their actions, and they, out of their human kindness, answer me. And for four hours at a time I feel no boredom, I forget all my troubles, I do not dread poverty, and I am not terrified by death. I absorb myself into them completely. And because Dante says that

no one understands anything unless he retains what he has understood, I have jotted down what I have profited from in their conversation and composed a short study, *De principatibus*, in which I delve as deeply as I can into the ideas concerning this topic, discussing the definition of a princedom, the categories of princedoms, how they are acquired, how they are retained, and why they are lost. (Atkinson and Sices, *Machiavelli and His Friends*, 264–65)

The passage corroborates what I affirmed earlier, namely that the most audacious documents or movements of the modern era often arise through studious conversations with the dead, above all the ancients. In Machiavelli's case, his queries to the dead yielded *The Prince*, a treatise that divorced politics from its traditional alliance with ethics in a manner so unprecedented that it founded the modern discipline of political science.

Machiavelli's anecdote about his ceremonious change of attire before sitting down at his desk with his student's lamp (in his case, candlelight) reminds us that studious reading takes place in the *real*, even if not physical, presence of interlocutors from the past, confirming once again that solitude is relational and dialogical rather than monological or solipsistic. Another lesson we draw from Machiavelli's anecdote is that "truth flourishes" where the student brings a regardful and reverent posture to the act of reading. One need not dress up for the occasion, the way Machiavelli did. The mere act of holding a book in a certain manner is sufficient — not the manner of narcotic mesmerization, typical of the screen reader, but the manner of self-gathered concentration that is typical of deep reading, where the lamp emanates from within the mind of the student and not from the garish glare of a computer screen.

In addition to the inner dialogue with oneself and with one's interlocutors from the past, solitude makes possible a meaningful converse with one's fellow human beings, be they friends, lovers, or fellow citizens. Indeed, meaningful dialogue with others presupposes dialogue with oneself and with the dead.

Here is where studious reading becomes existentially relevant, especially with respect to the aging process.

Consider the following poem by W. B. Yeats, called "After Long Silence":

> Speech after long silence: it is right,
> All other lovers being estranged or dead,
> Unfriendly lamplight hid under its shade,
> The curtains drawn upon unfriendly night,
> That we descant and yet again descant
> Upon the supreme theme of Art and Song:
> Bodily decrepitude is wisdom; young
> We loved each other and were ignorant.

Enfolded into one long sentence, these imbricated phrases evoke, both semantically and syntactically, the temporal depth and winding personal history the lovers bring to their renewed encounter late in their lives. The two of them are old enough that the lamplight is "unfriendly," since, were it not "hid under its shade," it would show their "bodily decrepitude." Their relationship goes back a long way, and seems to have been marked by interruptions or separations, for their present speech comes "after long silence," at a time when "other lovers" are now "estranged or dead." Like lamplight, the night is "unfriendly," either because it is a harbinger of approaching death or because the outside world has little use for the two of them now.

The poem's concluding two lines set up an interactive and perhaps even interdependent relation between the "ignorance" of youthful love and the "wisdom" that now allows the reconnected lovers to discourse upon the supreme theme of Art and Song. Only those who were exposed to the supreme theme when they were young — only those who read books in their youth, even if their reading was steeped in experiential ignorance — will be able to dialogue about it later in life. This is the meaning of the phrase "That we descant and yet again descant." When they were young they loved each other and discoursed in ignorance about Art and Song, that is, without full cognizance of the degree to which Art and Song have to do with loss — the loss of love, youth, and loved ones. Had the two lovers not been introduced to the supreme theme in their youth, had they not learned the basic grammar of Art and Song in their past — in short, had they not received a cultural education of sorts when they were young — they could not descant upon the theme "yet again" in older age. In other words, there would be little, if anything, for the aging couple to talk about after long silence.

The poem contains a crucial lesson. If one has not learned to speak as a child, one will not break into speech in old age. If one has learned nothing about song, art, ideas, history, or cultural history during one's youth, one will not be able to access their "wisdom" later in life. If one does not learn the ways of learning when one is young, one will not know how to graduate to another mode of being in older age. Such is the seminal neoteny of education. It is the student's lamp that, later in life, gives us something to say to one another once the lamplight becomes unfriendly. If wisdom has its source in youthful ignorance, it is because the maturation process yields a deeper understanding of the human meaning of what one studied, but failed to grasp adequately, when one was young — namely that you do not need wisdom to love, but love needs wisdom to keep it alive when night begins to fall.

Much of what gets passed on silently or unknowingly during the education process germinates discretely, slowly, and often unpredictably, especially when it comes to the realm of spirit (what Yeats calls Art and Song). If the primary purpose of education is to prepare young people to inherit the world, its secondary purpose is to prepare them to become interlocutors later in life, that is, to give them the foundations on which they may find something meaningful to say to one another in the void left behind by estranged lovers, extinguished hopes, and dead companions. Aging and impending death allow a new kind of *logos* to flower, but only in those who spent endless hours of "long silence" under the student's lamp.

The wisdom of Yeats's aged lovers — what distinguishes them from those who have nothing to say to one another at their stage of life — is the vital afterlife of their youth, an afterlife that transfigures and thereby holds on to the love with which they loved each other in ignorance. Bodily decrepitude with wisdom retains its hold on this vitality. Bodily decrepitude without wisdom is merely bodily decrepitude taking its course in bewildered silence.

Continuing Education

If education has a goal, it is to increase the age of young people exponentially — to make them hundreds, if not thousands, of years older than they were when they entered the classroom or sat down with their student's lamp to enlarge their minds. For it is through books, or other forms of writing, that a culture transmits the inner core of its historical age.

Cultural rejuvenation takes place only if and when a culture acts its age, but a culture cannot act its age unless those who belong to its present learn how old they really are. In revealing our true age to us, education turns us into potential renewers of history. This is above all the case when those who are biologically young acquire an ancient cultural age through their schooling, their reading, or various other means. There is no surer way to invigorate youth than to en-age it, as it were.

Such is the paradox of human age in the cultural sphere: we get younger by becoming older. One of the blessings of the human condition, which is otherwise tragic and fraught with afflictions of every sort, is that, once it gets underway, the learning process never comes to an end, or at least never need come to an end. Neoteny thrives on the persistence of this youthful aptitude throughout our adulthood.

There is no more compelling image of human neoteny than

an adult reading a book from which he or she has something to learn. Occasionally I teach in my university's continuing studies program, which offers an array of courses in the humanities open to the public for modest enrollment fees. They tend to attract seasoned individuals, many of whom are retired, and the bliss of learning is so palpable among these continuing students that one wonders whether it takes a certain maturity, which arrives later and later in life these days, to learn what the humanities have to teach us. A great deal of humanistic education that used to take place successfully among a certain age group can now take place only at a later stage of life, if at all.

The dilemma is that a certain kind of learning presupposes a degree of maturity in the learner that is acquired largely through education, yet as the timing of the onset of such maturity gets more and more delayed, education becomes increasingly disconnected from those on whom the culture depends for its rejuvenation. To learn what it means to be an adult one must already have become one.

I will not speculate on the consequences of this paradox but will emphasize instead its brighter side, namely that human happiness in the future — or so I believe — will be more and more tied to institutions of adult education, which will take institutional forms that we can scarcely imagine at present. With a little luck, adulthood, especially in its later stages, will become the new arena for humanistic education, that is to say, for self-knowledge.

But what purpose will be served by educating these older "resurgent learners," as I would call them? It will serve no purpose at all, except the enhancement of life. In the human sphere learning is life, and life is learning. That is why there was a tremendous life-affirming spirit in Socrates's last pedagogical act. According to Emil Cioran's version of what transpired in the prison cell, where Socrates was surrounded by his most devoted disciples, Socrates was learning to play a new melody on the flute while his executioners were preparing the hemlock. "'What good will it do you,' he was asked, 'to know this tune before you die?'" That is exactly the wrong question to ask Socrates, whose final gesture showed his disciples that their teacher was first and foremost a learner, that learning is its own end, that there is no end to its project, because to be fully human means to prolong the process of learning until death itself brings its course to an end.

EPILOGUE

When I wrote, in the opening sentence of my preface, that the age of juvenescence began in America in the postwar period and from there moved eastward, against the traditional westerly drift of empire, I was referring to the global phenomenon known as Americanization, which is neither the cause nor the effect of our juvenescence but is, for reasons unknown, the dominant cultural form it takes at present. We tend to believe that we understand what it is, how it came about, and what it represents, yet Americanization remains a prodigious enigma, from both a cultural and a philosophical point of view. No philosophy of history could have foreseen its planetary triumph, and nothing in the cultural history of the West, not to mention non-Western societies, suggests that Americanization would become a world destiny, as it were. America may soon lose its geopolitical dominance, yet Americanization will continue for a long time to come to define our historical mode of being. This is at one level ironic, for Americanism has a way of defanging and even devouring history, even as it remakes it in its own image. I have no intention of delving into the sociological aspects of Americanism but will limit my concluding remarks to a few words about its relation to juvenescence, and the difficulties that this relation presents when it comes to gauging just how old we are in this strange historical age of ours.

One way of accounting for the ease and extent to which Americanism has triumphed the world over is to argue that it taps into, or wells up from, the collective subconscious of all other cultures. It is what that subconscious looks like when freed from its traditional inhibitions. Perhaps the one thing that tradition-based cultures have in common is a latent resentment against tradition itself — its rituals, dictates, and prohibitions, its tedious and tenacious self-sameness, and its pressures of conformity. This would explain why hardly anyone strives (or need strive) to become American but why almost everyone insists on the license that America stands for in the popular imagination. That, in turn, would explain why America can be wholeheartedly detested as a nation or geopolitical power without in the least compromising the sovereignty of Americanism.

In a conversation with my friend and Stanford colleague Michel Serres, I once wondered aloud about the worldwide reach of America's postwar popular culture, and Serres — a French philosopher and historian of science — responded with an elegant formula. While America is comprehensible from the perspectives of all other cultures, it is the perspective from which all other cultures are incomprehensible. I suspect that the formula comes from projective geometry. If you cast a light on a cube and project its shadow against a wall, you reduce a three-dimensional object to a two-dimensional square. While the square is "comprehensible" from the perspective of the cube, the reverse is not true, for the square is missing the cube's third dimension.

Is this what is going on when it comes to Americanism? Is America the phantasmatic wall on which all other cultures appear to themselves in two-dimensional form? If so, what is the source of its fascination? Why and how does the square win out over the cube? Is it because humankind cannot bear very much reality, as T. S. Eliot put it, or are there other factors at work?

While the two-dimensional square is only an analogy, who can deny that America first conquered the world not with its armies or undercover agents but through the promiscuous circulation of its motion pictures? That conquest continues today primarily through the sorcery of the screen, be it the movie screen, the television screen, the video game screen, the computer screen, or the cell-phone screen. America in this sense is more than a particular culture, nation, or world power; it is the great theater of geometric projection in which the whole world now appears to itself in a reduced form. Once a culture enters this space of projection there is no way to get back from the square to the cube. Eventually that culture becomes *incomprehensible to itself*. Or better, it becomes comprehensible to itself only from an "Americanized" perspective, the fantasy of America standing in for the lost dimension. That is precisely why, in a world that increasingly understands itself through the medium of the screen, America's postwar popular culture eventually appears as the only one that makes any sense.

I am tempted to change the analogy here and suggest that youth holds the secret to the universalism of American culture. No society on earth comes close to matching America's youthful imagination, its liberation of youthful energies, colors, forms, products, and narratives, all of which appeal directly to what is most neotenic or childlike in our nature. That America is comprehensible from the perspectives of all other cultures, while it is the perspective from which no other culture is comprehensible, would be explained by the fact that youth, while comprehensible to adults, does not comprehend adulthood.

Every such attempt at an explanation generates new enigmas, however. Americanism may be refashioning human society in its youthful image, yet it simply will not do to say that Lolita, from her juvenile perspective, cannot comprehend Humbert Humbert, while he, from his, can comprehend her. From the perspective of those who are older than her — of those who belong to an older cultural genome than she does — Lolita remains incomprehensible in her new brand of youth. Whether or not Humbert Humbert's fascination with her symbolizes old Europe's fascination with young America, Lolita is not just an adolescent girl on her way to womanhood. She is an adolescent girl who, even when she attains full womanhood, will continue to embody a historically unparalleled strain of youthfulness. No matter how old she gets she will always remain "younger" in mentality, looks, and lifestyle than the ancestors in her phylogenetic heritage. Her "age," which is also *our* age, has no precedent in world history, and where something has no precedent it is difficult if not impossible to comprehend.

That is why I believe that our juvenescent age is not merely a consequence of Americanization, but that Americanism, for reasons sociological analyses will never fully grasp, finds ways to tap into the deepest layers of the neotenic substrate of the collective human psyche. It has done so not in the mode of Vico's animistic religions but in distinctly modern modes deeply inflected by the later stages of what Vico called the human age. If the substance is the same, the idiom is different. By "substance" I mean the innate youthfulness of the species we have become over the course of our development.

That is also why I believe that our juvenescent age is not just another stage of cultural development in the unfolding of modern civilization but represents a momentous, yet chaotic event in the evolution of humanity itself. The future that this event holds in store for us is one that remains incomprehensible from the perspective of the cultural history that precedes it. That future may well be upon us already, for as each day passes our present confounds historical understanding. If wisdom serves to create a living memory by synthesizing past and present with a view to the future, wisdom in our age has been thrown for a loss.

In 1826 the Italian poet and thinker Giacomo Leopardi remarked the following about modern civilization:

> Modern civilization must not be considered simply as a continuation of ancient civilization, as its progression ... [W]hatever the filiation historically speaking between modern and ancient civilization, and the influence that the latter has on the former, especially at its birth and in its early development, logically speaking, these two civilizations, which are

essentially different, are and must be considered as two separate civilizations, or rather two different and distinct species of civilization, each actually complete in itself. (*Zibaldone*, 4171, entry from 1819)

The same could be said about the difference between modern civilization, which has already become "complete," and the successor civilization that is taking shape as we speak. The latter is still embryonic, indeterminate, and incomplete, yet whatever their historical filiation, the two must be considered distinct species of civilization. This of course assumes that the future will actually take the form of a new civilization, yet there is no compelling reason to believe that it will. It may turn out that humanity will evolve into a new kind of life form — one that dispenses altogether with civilization as we know it. I for one would not bet on this happening, yet no one at present can say what the future — assuming we have one — will look like. What we can say with relative certainty is that, whatever form it takes, the future will appear largely incomprehensible from the perspective of the past.

I set out to answer a simple question in this book: how old are we at this moment of our cultural history, when the age of juvenescence has not yet become the future to which it stands as a prelude? All we know for sure is that we are at once strangely young and immensely old, thanks to the extreme heterochrony of our present age, where the *puer* exists alongside the *senex*. As one gets younger, the other gets older. We have never before been so young, nor so old. To speak by means of a parable, I would say that today we contain within ourselves the ages of two literary characters who came into being during the decade when the process of Americanization began in earnest, namely the 1950s. In 1955 Nabokov published *Lolita* in France and Samuel Beckett published the English version of his novel *Molloy*. Together these two figures provide something of an answer to our basic question.

I remarked above that Lolita represents a different cultural type than her ancestors. She is not just an adolescent girl on her way to womanhood but a new specimen of humanity whose progeny will embody a historically unparalleled strain of youthfulness, even in their old age. In that sense we all share Lolita's age. As for Molloy, the following passage gives us a parabolic indication of how old he is, culturally speaking:

> Now my sick leg, I forget which, it is immaterial here, was in a condition neither to dig, because it was rigid, nor alone to support me, because it would have collapsed. I had so to speak only one leg at my disposal, I was virtually one-legged, and I would have been happier, livelier, amputated at the groin. And if they had removed a few testicles into the bargain I wouldn't have objected. For from such testicles as mine, dangling at mid-thigh at the end of a meager chord, there was nothing more to be squeezed, not a drop. So that *non che la speme il desiderio*, and I longed to see them gone, from the old stand where they bore false witness, for and against, in the lifelong charge against me. For if they accused me of having made a balls of it, of me, of them, they thanked me for it too, from the depths of their rotten bag, the right lower than the left, or inversely, I forget, decaying circus clowns. (*Molloy*, 46–47)

Molloy embodies the last leg of the long journey of his decaying civilization, whose immense age his testicles bear witness to from their "old stand." We who find ourselves at the end of that civilization and the beginning of a new one are at least as old as Molloy, yet we are also as young as Lolita's juvenile offspring. It would be misleading to say that our age is somewhere between the two, for the fact of the matter is that Lolita has gotten younger and Molloy has gotten older in the past half century. We who belong to the age of transitional juvenescence get older *and* younger along with them. Perhaps when Molloy reaches his true endpoint—I mean when he finally liquidates the paradox of those terminal words, "I can't go on, I will go on"—the senile countercurrent to our contemporary juvenescence will finally cease to agitate the currents that draw our age in several different directions at once.

I promised in my preface that I would not be offering prophecies. No one today can credibly claim to know how the future will turn out. I have been told that while all frogs begin their lives as tadpoles, not all tadpoles become frogs. It seems that in certain artificially controlled environments — and who will deny that our environments are increasingly artificial — some will remain tadpoles their entire lives. At this point in our cultural history we are becoming like the tadpoles of a new kind of humanity. It remains to be seen if one day we will become frogs.

NOTES

Since this book ranges widely in its topics and cultural references, the secondary works cited here represent only a small portion of the relevant bibliography. For the most part I cite articles and books that were directly pertinent, useful, or inspiring to me during the course of my research, as well as others I feel might be useful for the reader to consult. Unless otherwise indicated, all translations in the chapters and notes are mine.

Chapter One: Anthropos

THE INTRIGUING PHENOMENON OF AGE

The term *flatus vocis* was first introduced into philosophy and theology by the nominalist Roscelin de Compiègne (ca. 1050–ca. 1125), who held that the "universals" are mere sounds, without any substantial reality beyond the breath of the voice that names them. To be clear: I am not claiming that time is a universal or abstract object, rather that time's "reality" is bound to the age of phenomena. I would also like to clarify the following: when I speak of the age of the universe or the age of civilizations, I am not merely applying a biological metaphor to non-organic phenomena. Aging is not the prerogative of organisms. It is the flesh of time itself. Therefore — and this is crucial for the cultural history I pursue in this book — I do not share the hesitations of those who think the term "historical age" is a misleading figure of speech. If one believes, as I do, that even the biology of aging is affected by history, then history and age are linked by more than mere analogy. We age differently today than our ancestors did in the past, for we belong to a different age than they did; that is to say, we *are of a different age* than they were at our age, thanks to historical or cultural factors that distinguish our worlds from theirs.

Henri Bergson's theory of duration had the potential to become a compelling philosophy of age, yet the five pages that Bergson devotes to the aging process at the beginning of *Creative Evolution* (10–15) do little to fulfill that potential. In these pages Bergson understands age as the persistence of the past in the present—a crucial aspect of age, to be sure—yet he limits himself to reflecting on the "organic memory" that informs the aging process. His primary concern is to differentiate the vitality of living organisms from artificial systems (which he also calls "unorganized matter"). Unlike the latter, organisms carry "time" within their bodies. In his words, "The evolution of the living being, like that of the embryo, implies a continual recording of duration, a persistence of the past in the present, and so an appearance, at least, of organic memory" (13). From the perspective I adopt in this book, I find it altogether disappointing that Bergson contents himself with so little, that he is happy merely to insist that "real duration" amounts to "a hyphen, a connection link," or what he also calls "continuity of change." In sum, one cannot call Bergson's theory of duration a veritable philosophy of age. At the most—yet even this is doubtful—it contains the seeds of such a philosophy.

For Bergson's thinking about duration and organic form, see the first chapter of *Creative Evolution*, "The Evolution of Life—Mechanism and Teleology" (1–63). See also his *Duration and Simultaneity* (especially chapter 3, "Concerning the Nature of Time"), also included in *Henri Bergson: Key Writings*, edited by Keith Ansell-Pearson and John Mullarkey (205–22).

For a recent book on Bergson's philosophy of time, see Keith Ansell-Pearson, *Philosophy and the Adventure of the Virtual: Bergson and the Time of Life* (esp. 9–43). See also Suzanne Guerlac's excellent volume *Thinking in Time: An Introduction to Henri Bergson*. Frédéric Worms, arguably the foremost French-language Bergson scholar, has authored many studies on the French philosopher and his work. I found especially helpful his book *Bergson ou les deux sens de la vie*.

Heidegger speaks in many places about historical ages, for example in his classic essay "The Age of the World Picture," yet he had next to nothing to say about age as such. His most explicit comments on the topic—pronounced mostly on the occasion of his and some of his friends' sixtieth birthdays—were mostly undeveloped. Thus in 1949, when Heidegger turned sixty, he wrote in a letter, "Now it gets serious. Or is 60 only a number, the sign for something with which we calculate? Unconnected with the number, however, is the transition into the age [*das Alter*]." In another letter from the same year he wrote, "The age that begins with sixty years is the autumn of life. Autumn is the filled, settled [*ausgeglichene*], and therefore balancing season [*ausgleichende Zeit*]." Heidegger's commentator Andrew Mitchell, to whom I owe these references, is far more interesting than Heidegger himself when, in the introduction to his forthcoming book, *The Fourfold: Reading the Late Heidegger*, he writes, "From the midst of life, a receptivity is born. At 'the age' one senses what is not overtly present." Mitchell continues:

"One's very body senses the Heraclitean togetherness of things. The age is consequently an awakening to ... the belonging-together of what is, of what is always arriving. The age is an awareness of this and as such it is a way of beginning again."

For Heidegger's thoughts on "place" and "space," see Edward S. Casey, *The Fate of Place: A Philosophical History*. See also the two excellent books by Jeff Malpas: *Heidegger and the Thinking of Place* (esp. 1–69) and *Heidegger's Topology: Being, Place, World* (esp. 39–64). For other recent books relevant to this issue, see Alejandro A. Vallega, *Heidegger and the Issue of Space: Thinking on Exilic Grounds*, and Andrew Mitchell, *Heidegger among the Sculptors: Body, Space, and the Art of Dwelling*. I dwell on the topic in some depth in my book *The Dominion of the Dead* (17–36).

The two thinkers who have given due consideration to the phenomenon of age in their respective philosophies of history are Giambattista Vico and Hegel, both of whom I discuss at length in chapter 2.

For a recent, theoretically ambitious work on the poetry of Gerard Manley Hopkins, see Dennis Sobolev, *The Split World of Gerard Manley Hopkins: An Essay in Semiotic Phenomenology*. In his commentary on Hopkins's poem "Spring and Fall" (130–39), Sobolev compares it to the earlier poem "Spring and Death." Describing "Spring and Fall" as a text "strangely bereft of hope," he identifies its main theme as "the human existential (rather than metaphysical) condition, which is expressed in the girl's involuntary *memento mori*." (Sobolev's distinction between the metaphysical and existential is loosely analogous to my differentiation of time from age.)

Several philosophical readings of Leopardi in Italian scholarship have focused on the themes of "deception" and "illusion" in his work, as well as on his pessimism more broadly. I would draw attention here to Italian philosopher Emanuele Severino's *Il nulla e la poesia: Alla fine dell'età della tecnica: Leopardi*; Antonio Prete, *Il pensiero poetante* and *Finitudine e infinito: Su Leopardi*; and Nicholas Rennie, *Speculating on the Moment: The Poetics of Time and Recurrence in Goethe, Leopardi, and Nietzsche*. See also my own commentaries in *Forests: The Shadow of Civilization* (186–93), as well as my article "The Magic of Leopardi."

ANTHROPOS

The bibliography related to human cognition and its evolutionary history is practically endless. The book from which I have most benefited on the topic is *Origins of Intelligence: The Evolution of Cognitive Development in Monkeys, Apes, and Humans*, by Sue Taylor Parker and Michael L. McKinney. This impressive study (which I discuss in more detail in the next section) contains a vast bibliography of books and articles on the origins of human intelligence to which I refer the interested reader.

On wonder, see the article by my colleague Andrea Nightingale, to whom this book is dedicated, "On Wandering and Wondering: 'Theôria' in Greek Philosophy and Culture," as well as her book *Spectacles of Truth in Classical Greece*. See also Mary-Jane Rubenstein, *Strange Wonder: The Closure of Metaphysics and the Opening of Awe*.

On the role that neophilia plays in the psychic history of the human species, see Winifred Gallagher, *New: Understanding Our Need for Novelty and Change*. See also Michael North, *Novelty*, an intellectual history of the ways in which the concept of the "new" has been employed, to varying ends, in art, philosophy, religion, and science.

The excerpts I quote from Sophocles's Ode on Man come from Ralph Manheim's English translation of Martin Heidegger's *An Introduction to Metaphysics* (123-24). While perhaps not the most literal, it is, in my view, the most vivid and dramatic English rendition. For an exhaustive discussion of *Antigone* and its reception over the centuries, see George Steiner's magisterial book *Antigones*.

For a book-length study of the Sphinx myth, see Almut-Barbara Renger, *Oedipus and the Sphinx: The Threshold Myth from Sophocles through Freud to Cocteau*. See also the afterword to Alex Woloch's *The One vs. the Many* (319-36), as well as Freddie Rokem, "One Voice and Many Legs: Oedipus and the Riddle of the Sphinx." Lowell Edmunds, *Oedipus*, in the Routledge series "Gods and Heroes of the Ancient World," features an extensive bibliography of helpful related materials.

NEOTENY

I would like to make it clear that, while I accord a special importance to the role neoteny may have played in human evolution, my overall argument for what I call "cultural neoteny" does not depend on, or presuppose, the veracity of the claims that various evolutionary biologists have made in favor of human neoteny. I have examined those claims in detail, as well as those that argue against them. In my discussion of the evolutionary material I have relied mostly on the work of Stephen Jay Gould, above all his book *Ontogeny and Phylogeny*, as well as some of the essays in his collection *Ever Since Darwin: Reflections in Natural History* (see "The Child as Man's Real Father," 63-69; "Human Babies as Embryos," 70-78; "Size and Shape," 171-78; and "Sizing Up Human Intelligence," 179-85).

I am aware that Gould's strong advocacy for human neoteny is by no means uncontested or unproblematic. Perhaps the most frontal challenge to Gould comes from Parker and McKinney, in *Origins of Intelligence*, referenced in the previous section. The authors of this book describe their approach as "comparative developmental evolutionary studies," an approach that seeks to combine insights from the subdisciplines of developmental psychology, biological anthropology and comparative psychology, and evolutionary biology. Such a comprehensive framework allows them to track the cognitive development of humans alongside that of monkeys and apes, leading them to conclude that "the stages of development of human cognition roughly recapitulate the stages of their evolution" (xii). *Origins of Intelligence* synthesizes a massive amount of research and, while presenting novel ideas, is indebted to a substantial body of earlier work on human and primate intelligence. For the purposes of my own cultural history, the book is of particular interest because of the objections it raises to the "juvenilization model" so influentially promoted by Gould and others (on the juvenilization thesis and debates on underdevelopment versus overdevelopment, see chapter 12, "The Evolution and Development of the Brain," esp. 336–45). Against Gould, they argue in favor of evolutionary progress, defending the idea that humans are "the result of a general trend toward increasing complexity, both morphological and behavioral, that has characterized the history of life" (346).

If Parker and McKinney are right, then what they call "adultification" is at least, if not more, important for human evolution than juvenilization. I have no authority to evaluate the scientific soundness of their claims, yet I find it reassuring that my own theory of cultural neoteny also advances a theory of adultification of sorts. More precisely, I argue that juvenilization practically necessitates adultification. As I put it in the closing paragraph of chapter 1: "If it is true that the child is father of the man, it is because the child obliges the man to become a father, that is, to develop a degree of social, political, and moral maturity that is unheard of in the animal kingdom."

For Gould's treatment of Haeckel, see *Ontogeny and Phylogeny*, 76–85 and 167–206, where Gould discusses "the unsuccessful attempts of empirical cataloguers to refute Haeckel's theory of recapitulation." Gould's contention is that "the biogenetic law fell only when it became *unfashionable in approach* (due to the rise of experimental embryology) and finally *untenable in theory* (when the establishment of Mendelian genetics converted previous exceptions into new expectations)." Thus, Gould claims, "the biogenetic law was not disproved by a direct scrutiny of its supposed operation; it fell because research in related fields refuted its necessary mechanism" (168).

See also Robert J. Richards, *The Tragic Sense of Life: Ernst Haeckel and the Struggle over Evolutionary Thought*, especially chapter 5, "Evolutionary Morphology in the Darwinian Mode" (113–70). Richards criticizes past readers of Haeckel including, notably, Gould (as well as Peter Bowler) for distorting the relation between Darwin and Haeckel for ideological reasons, maximizing the differences between the two and unduly minimizing their similarities. Richards also criticizes Gould and others for both diminishing the importance of Haeckel's insights and exaggerating the pernicious ideological influence of his work.

Gould addresses recapitulation in part 1 of *Ontogeny and Phylogeny*, and neoteny in particular in part 2, esp. chapter 9 ("Progenesis and Neoteny") and chapter 10 ("Retardation and Neoteny in Human Evolution"). For his thoughts on Bolk, see 356–63.

Richards also discusses recapitulation extensively in *The Meaning of Evolution: The Morphological Construction and Ideological Reconstruction of Darwin's Theory*, esp. chapters 4–6. Here too, he takes Gould and others to task for reading their own political sensibilities back into Darwin's work and suppressing any similarities between Darwin and Haeckel, for example, by downplaying the importance of recapitulation in Darwin's work. Against Gould and other so-called antiprogressivists, Richards argues in favor of a (qualified) progressivist reading of Darwin's evolutionary theory. For a full treatment of the moral and social consequences of his interpretation, and for a critique of Gould's and others' revisionist readings, see also Richards, *Darwin and the Emergence of Evolutionary Theories of Mind and Behavior*.

On fetalization and neoteny, see, in addition to Gould, Ashley Montagu, *Growing Young*; Clive Bromhall, *The Eternal Child: How Evolution Has Made Children of Us All*; and Melvin Konner, *The Evolution of Childhood: Relationships, Emotion, Mind*. For a discussion of juvenilization in nature, see chapter 5 of Andreas Suchantke, *Eco-Geography*. For a sociological take on the phenomenon of juvenilization, see Marcel Danesi, *Forever Young: The Teen-aging of Modern Culture*; for a more philosophical take, see Bernard Stiegler, *Taking Care of Youth and the Generations*.

On childhood development, see Juan Carlos Gómez, *Apes, Monkeys, Children, and the Growth of Mind*; Ze'ev Hochberg, *Evo-Devo of Child Growth: A Treatise on Child Growth and Human Evolution*; and Barry Bogin, *Patterns of Human Growth* and *The Growth of Humanity*. On the role of play in childhood development, see the excellent collection *Play and Development*, edited by Artin Göncü and Suzanne Gaskins (esp. the editors' introduction, 3–18 and the contribution by Peter K. Smith, "Evolutionary Foundations and Functions of Play: An Overview," 21–50). See also *Developing Theories of Mind*, edited by Harris J. Astington, Paul L. Harris, and David R. Olson (esp. part 1, "Development Origins of Children's Knowledge of the Mind").

It is well known by now that our aptitude for learning has a cultural as well as a neurological basis. As primates age, their capacities to form new neuronal connections and modify existing ones — both of which are involved in learning — are significantly reduced; see Marcus Jacobson, "Development of Specific Neuronal Connections" (1969), quoted in Gould, *Ontogeny and Phylogeny*, 547). Human beings, by contrast, retain these capacities to a much greater extent as they age. One could say that even in our old age the child in us (in some of us, that is) continues to wonder, study, and learn. In Gould's words, "Human development is so strongly retarded that even mature adults retain sufficient flexibility for our adaptive status as a learning animal" (*Ontogeny and Phylogeny*, 401).

There are many biographies of Einstein, notably those by Ronald Clark, Albrecht Fölsing, Walter Isaacson, and Jürgen Neffe. Neffe quotes Einstein as saying, "When I ask myself how it happened that I in particular discovered the relativity theory, it seems to lie in the following circumstance. The normal adult never bothers his head about spacetime problems. Everything there is to be thought about it, in his opinion, has already been done in early childhood. I, on the contrary, developed so slowly that I only began to wonder about space and time when I was already grown up. In consequence I probed deeper into the problem than an ordinary child would have done." Neffe, *Einstein: A Biography*, 27. See also the chapter "Albert Einstein: The Perennial Child," in Howard Gardner, *Creative Minds* (87–136).

On plasticity, see Mary-Jane West-Eberhard, *Developmental Plasticity and Evolution*; Peter R. Huttenlocher, *Neural Plasticity: The Effects of Environment on the Development of the Cerebral Cortex*; and the excellent collection of essays in *La sinuosité du vivant*, edited by Patrizia d'Alessio (especially D'Alessio's essay on the phenomenon of elasticity, "Transmission des emotions de Fuller à Vygotsky," 15–30).

For a critical look at "transhumanist" dreams of immortality, see Francis Fukuyama, *Our Posthuman Future: Consequences of the Biotechnology Revolution*. For other recent books on the topic of prolonged life expectancies and the prospect of biological immortality, see Stephen Hall, *Merchants of Immortality: Chasing the Dream of Human Life Extension*; Elaine Dewar, *The Second Tree: Of Clones, Chimeras, and Quests for Immortality*; and Guy Brown, *The Living End: The New Sciences of Death, Ageing, and Immortality*.

THE ALBINO GORILLA

Several recent studies offer Darwinian-evolutionary accounts of the origins of storytelling and of the place of storytelling in human life. For anyone interested in the current debates, I recommend two issues of the journal *Critical Inquiry*. In the Winter 2011 issue (37, no. 2), Jonathan Kramnick's article "Against Literary Darwinism" (315–47) presents a comprehensive, forceful critique of recent literature on the subject by humanists and scientists alike. The Winter 2012 issue (38, no. 2) features responses to Kramnick by Paul Bloom, Brian Boyd, Joseph Carroll, Vanessa L. Ryan, G. Gabrielle Starr, and Blakey Vermeule, along with a response from Kramnick to his critics.

Image, Eye, and Art in Calvino: Writing Visibility, edited by Birgitte Grundtvig, Martin McLaughlin, and Lene Waage Petersen, offers a relevant collection of essays on Calvino, interpreting his work through the optic of "seeing" and "visibility." On Calvino and Copito de Nieve in particular, see my essay "Toward a Philosophy of Nature," in *Uncommon Ground: Rethinking the Human Place in Nature*, edited by William Cronon (447–60). See also Carrie Rohman's "On Singularity and the Symbolic: The Threshold of the Human in Calvino's *Mr. Palomar*"; Stefano Franchi's superb essay "Palomar, the Triviality of Modernity, and the Doctrine of the Void"; Brian Fitzgerald, "Animals, Evolution, Language:

Aspects of Whitehead in Italo Calvino's Palomar"; Isaac Rosier, "The Body, Eros, and the Limits of Objectivity in Calvino's Palomar"; and Sharon Wood, "The Reflections of Mr. Palomar and Mr. Cogito: Italo Calvino and Zbigniew Herbert."

For a documentary on the real-life gorilla Copito de Nieve, see *Snowflake: The White Gorilla*, first aired on PBS in 2005 and viewable online at http://video.pb s.org/video/1439146653.

For Heidegger on animality versus humanity, see *The Fundamental Concepts of Metaphysics* (esp. 186–273). Heidegger dwells at length in this book (based on a lecture course he gave in 1929–30) on the zoological work of theoretical biologist Jacob von Uexküll (201–64). For a much shorter discussion of Uexküll, largely derivative of Heidegger's analysis, see Giorgio Agamben's *The Open: Man and Animal* (39–46).

Uexküll's *A Foray into the Worlds of Animals and Humans: With a Theory of Meaning* was recently republished in English by the University of Minnesota Press. For an overview of biosemiotics, the field he helped establish, see *Introduction to Biosemiotics: The New Biological Synthesis*, edited by Marcello Barbieri. For a useful introductory article, see Kalevi Kull, "Jakob von Uexküll: An Introduction."

For a heavily Heidegger-indebted approach to "captivation," see Agamben, *The Open*, esp. 49–62. See also Donald Turner, "Humanity as Shepherd of Being: Heidegger's Philosophy and the Animal Other."

Jacques Derrida also discusses *Benommenheit*, or captivation, in volume 2 of his posthumous *The Beast and the Sovereign*. David Farrell Krell analyzes this seminar in *Derrida and Our Animal Others*. Krell is also the author of an earlier book, *Daimon Life*, that deals with these same issues of animality and humanity.

On anthropocentrism, see Gary Steiner's books *Anthropocentrism and Its Discontents: The Moral Status of Animals in the History of Western Philosophy*, *Animals and the Moral Community: Mental Life, Moral Status, and Kinship*, and *Animals and the Limits of Postmodernism*. See also Martha Nussbaum, "Humans and Other Animals," as well as the essays collected in *Anthropocentrism: Humans, Animals, Environments*, edited by Rob Boddice.

On the connection between speech and infancy, see Giorgio Agamben, *Infancy and History*, especially the title essay (11–64) and the second essay, "In Playland: Reflections on History and Play" (65–88).

FROM A COMMON SPRING

Freud's dictum "anatomy is destiny" comes from his 1912 essay "On the Universal Tendency to Debasement in the Sphere of Love." In context, it refers more to the positionality of the human genitals than to their gender, hence I am interpreting the saying more in light of Freud's general theories about sexual difference than in light of this essay's preoccupation with debasement in the sphere of erotic love.

For a helpful general introduction to feminist critiques of Freud, see Danielle Ramsey, "Feminism and Psychoanalysis," in *The Routledge Companion to Feminism and Postfeminism*, edited by Sarah Gamble (133–40). See also the essays in *Between Feminism and Psychoanalysis*, edited by Teresa Brennan; Mary Jo Buhle, *Feminism and Its Discontents: A Century of Struggle with Psychoanalysis*; and Juliet Mitchell, *Psychoanalysis and Feminism*.

On Ezra Pound and Chinese poetry, see Ming Xie, *Ezra Pound and the Appropriation of Chinese Poetry*. See also the critical edition of *The Chinese Written Character as a Medium for Poetry* by Ernest Fenollosa (posthumously edited by Pound).

In a personal communication, my friend and former Stanford colleague Weixing Su, who teaches literature at the University of Peking, wrote the following about Li Po's poem "The River Merchant's Wife." I quote from her letter with her permission:

This poem, "Song of Chokan," takes its title from the village of Chokan, the native village of both husband and wife, where apparently they also make their matrimonial home. In Li Po's time, this place was just south of Nanjing (then called Jinlin), but now it forms part of the much-expanded city. As the wife "writes" to her husband, it is early autumn — "the eighth month" on the lunar calendar, hence September rather than August, as in Pound's rendition. Up the Yangtze, from the port of Nanjing to the evocative destination she identifies — "far Ku-to-yen, by the river of the swirling eddies" (or "Yanyudui in Qutang Gorge") — her husband's westward journey has taken him over a thousand miles from home. In the version of Li Po's poem I have at hand, a few lines run somewhat differently from the English translation: "At sixteen you went afar / to Yanyudui in Qutang Gorge. / It was not to be touched in the fifth month, / the monkeys cried sorrowfully high above." Qutang Gorge is the first, i.e., westernmost, of the renowned Three Gorges on the Yangtze ("the narrows of the river Kiang" later in the poem), in present-day Sichuan province, and the most sublime and perilous of the three. Until the mid-twentieth century, a giant boulder named Yanyudui marked the entrance of this gorge. Every year "in the fifth month," or June, severe summer inundation would submerge the boulder under the torrential stream, turning it into a treacherous shoal "not to be touched." Such proverbial perils to which her husband's voyage is vulnerable must have given a sharper edge to the girl's sense of mortality, and vicariously she hears mortal lamentation in the cries of monkeys that were known to populate the mountainsides of the Three Gorges region. Upon his return, she is indeed eager to go far out to meet him, for Cho-Fu-Sa, a historic site on the Yangtze also known for its perilous shoals, is situated some two hundred miles west of her hometown. This place name, now spelt Chang Feng Sha, literally means "long drafts of sandy wind." (The boulder Yanyudui and the shoals at Cho-Fu-Sa, as I learned, have all been blown up by now for safer passage. Thus one by one we remove the edges of our mortality.)

According to the notes I have at hand, "Song of Chokan" was most likely composed during the poet's first visit to Nanjing in the year 726, when he was twenty-five. Li Po would have known firsthand, at least in part, the river merchant's journey. The year before he composed the poem, the poet had set out on his first great voyage out of mountain-encircled Sichuan province, his home since the age of four. Floating briskly down the Yangtze through the Three Gorges, "amid the ceaseless cries of monkeys on the river banks," as he wrote in a poem every schoolchild here knows by heart, he initiated a journey that was to take him far east, to Nanjing and beyond.

I am grateful to Weixing Su for reading a draft of this book prior to its publication. I have benefited greatly from her comments.

Regarding the cultural history of the timing of psychological maturation as well as the multiplication of stages between childhood and adulthood in our era, the following comments may be of interest to some readers. In 1904 G. Stanley Hall published his seminal book *Adolescence*, which "discovered" a transitional stage between youth and adulthood. Hall understood adolescence as more than a physiological phase of hormonal change. He argued that it emerged as a result of specific institutional changes that took place at the turn of the twentieth century, most notably the child-labor laws that mandated a minimum age of sixteen to enter the workforce and the universal-education laws that kept teenagers in secondary school. These developments in first-world societies prolonged the period of childhood and delayed, through institutional reforms, the advent of adulthood.

A century later an article by Jeffrey Arnett identified yet another transitional stage between youth and adulthood. Arnett applied the term "emerging adulthood" to the increasingly large proportion of first-world citizens in their twenties who have neither jobs nor families of their own. These emerging adults spend most of their time exploring professional, amorous, and worldview options, without committing to any of them. In Arnett's words, they have "left the dependency of childhood and adolescence … [but] not yet entered the enduring responsibilities that are normative in adulthood." Arnett, "Emerging Adulthood: A Theory of Development from the Late Teens through the Twenties," 469. Emerging adulthood is itself an emergent phenomenon, arising only recently, once again thanks to various social, economic, and technological luxuries that permit the onset of adulthood to be pushed further and further back for a certain class of people across the globe. All of which confirms yet again that a historical age, through its institutional dynamism, often has a direct impact on the aging process itself.

THE CHILD PROGENITOR

For Wordsworth's letter, see his *Fenwick Notes*.

On poetry and childhood in the Romantic era, see, Anna Wierda Rowland, *Romanticism and Childhood: The Infantilization of British Literary Culture*; Roni Natov, *The Poetics of Childhood*; Judith Plotz, *Romanticism and the Vocation of Childhood*; and G. Kim Blank, *Wordsworth and Feeling: The Poetry of an Adult Child*. On "Ode: Intimations of Immortality ...," see Geoffrey Durant, *Wordsworth and the Great System: A Study of Wordsworth's Poetic Universe*, 99–112. For a classic, still vibrant commentary on the ode, see Lionel Trilling, *The Liberal Imagination: Essays on Literature and Society*, 125–54.

For my reading of Wordsworth in general, I have benefited from *The Cambridge Companion to Wordsworth*, edited by Stephen Gill. Also, Douglas B. Wilson, *The Romantic Dream: Wordsworth and the Poet of the Unconscious*, and Geoffrey H. Hartman, *The Unremarkable Wordsworth*. For a recent study, see Paul H. Fry, *Wordsworth and the Poetry of What We Are*.

My reading of the nuances of Bonnefoy's poem "Une Voix" benefited from the insightful comments that my friend Samia Kassab offered on an early draft of these few pages of analysis. Kassab is the author of, among other works, *La métaphore dans la poésie de Baudelaire*. For some major works of Bonnefoy scholarship in English, see by Mary-Anne Caws, *Yves Bonnefoy*; John Naughton, *The Poetics of Bonnefoy*; and Robert Greene, *Searching for Presence*; and Michael G. Kelly, *Strands of Utopia*, chapters 5, 10, and 15. See also my late colleague Joseph Frank's foreword to *The Act and the Place of Poetry: Selected Essays* by Yves Bonnefoy, as well as his essay "Yves Bonnefoy: Notes of an Admirer," in Frank, *Responses to Modernity: Essays in the Politics of Culture*.

I believe Bonnefoy is the greatest French poet since Apollinaire. Much of his poetic corpus is available in English. Prominent translations include *Second Simplicity: New Poetry and Prose, 1991–2011*; *The Present Hour*; *The Arrière-Pays*; an edition (named after the collections it contains) comprising *Beginning and End of Snow* and *Where the Arrow Falls*; *The Curved Planks*; *In the Lure of Language*; *The Horizon*; *Yesterday's Wilderness Kingdom*; the collection *New and Selected Poems*; *The Lure and the Truth of Painting*; *In the Shadow's Light*; *On the Motion and Immobility of Douve*; *Early Poems 1947–1959*; *The Act and Place of Poetry*;

Things Dying Things Newborn; *Poems 1959–1975* (a translation of *Pierre écrite* and *Dans le leurre du soleil*); and *Words in Stone*.

Chapter Two: Wisdom and Genius

SAPIENTIA

Nowadays few people use the label *Homo sapiens sapiens*, given that the other major subspecies of *Homo sapiens* — namely *Homo sapiens idaltu* — has long been extinct. Some believe that the Denisovans as well as *Homo rhodesiensis*, various fossils of which were discovered recently, should also be considered subspecies of *Homo sapiens*. The status of the Neanderthals remains ambiguous. Many consider them a subspecies as well (hence the label *Homo sapiens neanderthalensis*). In my book *The Dominion of the Dead*, I claim that humanity is not a species but a way of being mortal, hence that the Neanderthals, who seem to have possessed an awareness of death (evidenced by burial rituals), should be regarded as human in the essential cultural sense of the term, even if they do not belong to our biological species (see p. 34). If it could be shown that they maintained long-term relations with the dead, that would be enough, from my point of view, to consider them "sapient" in both of the senses I discuss in this chapter (namely, both ingenious and wise).

My use of the term "wisdom" in this book shares a family resemblance with the conventional conceptions and connotations, yet it also deviates significantly from them. For an excellent history of the world's wisdom traditions, see Robert Sternberg, *Wisdom: Its Nature, Origins, and Development*.

Abbott Payson Usher's *A History of Mechanical Inventions*, originally published in 1929, remains a classic historical account of technological innovation over the centuries. See also Lewis Mumford's "Renewal of Life" series, starting with *Technics and Civilization*, first published in 1934. Also excellent is the two-volume *Technology in Western Civilization*, edited by Melvin Kranzberg and Carroll W. Pursell. Among more recent publications, see Arnold Pacey's books *Technology in World Civilization: A Thousand-Year History* and *The Maze of Ingenuity*, and *An Encyclopedia of the History of Technology*, edited by Ian McNeil. McNeil subsequently edited, with Lance Day, the *Biographical Dictionary of the History of Technology*, which expands upon some of the most notable figures of the earlier encyclopedia. More popular works include Donald Cardwell's *Wheels, Clocks, and Rockets*. For more recent introductory volumes, see James E. McClellan III and Harold Dorn, *Science and Technology in World History: An Introduction*, and Daniel Headrick, *Technology: A World History*. See also T. K. Derry and Trevor I. Williams, *A Short History of Technology*. I am especially taken with Friedrich Kittler's more theoretically oriented work on technology, media, and information systems, *Literature, Media, and Information Systems* and

Gramophone, Film, Typewriter (Optical Media and Discourse Networks 1800/1900 are also excellent volumes). For a sociological examination of the development of network culture, see my colleague Fred Turner's book From Counterculture to Cyberculture; for accounts of more recent digital innovation, Johnny Ryan, A History of the Internet and the Digital Future, and Katie Hafner and Matthew Lyon, Where Wizards Stay Up Late: The Origins of the Internet; and for an ambitious theory of media transformation, Marshall T. Poe, A History of Communications: Media and Society from the Evolution of Speech to the Internet.

A NOTE ON AGE AND WISDOM

I take the H. L. Mencken quote from Wayne Booth, The Art of Growing Older: Writers on Living and Aging (186). This well-conceived book contains excerpts by writers across the ages on the topic of growing older, interspersed with reflections and commentaries by Booth. The quotes from Montaigne in this section also come from Booth's volume (232–33). There have been many studies on varying conceptions of, and attitudes toward, "old age" in Western culture. I would draw attention here to Georges Minois, History of Old Age: From Antiquity to the Renaissance (originally published as Histoire de la vieillesse). On Montaigne and aging, see Hugo Friedrich, Montaigne, 258–300.

The perceived vulgarization, if not decline, of civilization is a prevalent, almost universal, sentiment in world cultures (see the notes under the heading "Generation Gaps" below). Classic works on the theme of the decline of civilization, which go beyond the impressionism of sentiment, include Oswald Spengler, The Decline of the West; Edward Gibbon, The History of the Decline and Fall of the Roman Empire; and Arnold Toynbee, A Study of History (see volumes 4–6 on the "breakdowns" and "disintegrations" of civilizations). See also E. A. Thompson, Romans and Barbarians: The Decline of the Western Empire, and J. G. A. Pocock's Barbarism and Religion, vol. 3, The First Decline and Fall. For an ecological account of select cases of dramatic societal decline and collapse, see Jared Diamond, Collapse: How Societies Choose to Fail or Succeed.

THE RIVER AND THE VOLCANO

Quotations from the Timaeus are from Benjamin Jowett's translation of the Dialogues; see vol. 3, 443–47. For an older treatment of Plato's myth of Atlantis, see Phyllis Young Forsyth, Atlantis: The Making of Myth. For a more recent treatment, see the user-friendly volume by the esteemed French historian and classicist Pierre Vidal-Naquet, The Atlantis Story: A Short History of Plato's Myth.

Much of the field of cultural geography in the Anglophone world has been shaped by the work of Carl Sauer. Those interested in his founding role should read the essays dedicated to his life and work in the volume Carl Sauer on Cul-

ture and Landscape: Readings and Commentaries, edited by William M. Denevan and Kent Mathewson. On historical geography in general, see *Geography and History: Bridging the Divide*, edited by Alan R. H. Baker, as well as Baker's earlier volume, coedited with Mark Billinge, *Period and Place, Research Methods in Historical Geography*. Other titles include *Human Geography: Society, Space, and Social Science*, edited by Derek Gregory, Ron Martin, and Graham Smith; *Historical Geography: Progress and Prospect*, edited by Michael Pacione; and Robert A. Dodgshon, *Society in Time and Space: A Geographical Perspective on Change*. See also the critical discussion in Leonard Guelke, *Historical Understanding in Geography: An Idealist Approach*, esp. chapter 1; *The Cultural Geography Reader*, edited by Timothy S. Oakes and Patricia L. Price; and *People, Land and Time: A Historical Introduction to the Relations between Landscape, Culture, and Environment*, edited by Peter Atkins, Ian Gordon Simmons, and Brian K. Roberts. I am grateful to my Stanford colleague Martin W. Lewis, a historical geographer and author of, among other works, the 1997 book *The Myth of Continents: A Critique of Metageography* (with Karen E. Wigen), for expanding my understanding of the discipline of geography; I discuss the topic with him on my radio show and podcast *Entitled Opinions* (November 9, 2011).

For a useful comparative study of the relations and differences between Egyptian, Greek, and Roman civilizations, see Charles Freeman, *Egypt, Greece, and Rome: Civilizations of the Ancient Mediterranean*. I also profited from Nicolas Grimal, *A History of Ancient Egypt*, and Ian Shaw, *The Oxford History of Ancient Egypt*.

There are notable precedents (Ibn Khaldun, for example), yet Giambattista Vico is arguably the most important and compelling modern proponent of a cyclical theory of history. (For more on Vico see the notes under the heading "Heterochrony" below.) For a more recent, sociologically oriented version of cyclical history, see the work of Arthur Meier Schlesinger, above all *The Cycles of American History*, a book influenced by his father Arthur M. Schlesinger Sr., author of *Paths to the Present*. An influential precursor to their work can be found in the ideas of nineteenth-century political economist Wilhelm Georg Friedrich Roscher, author of the five-volume *System der Volkwirthschaft* and *Principles of Political Economy*.

For the importance of the classical tradition to the American founders and to American education generally in the eighteenth and nineteenth centuries, see *The Culture of Classicism: Ancient Greece and Rome in American Intellectual Life 1780–1910*, by my Stanford colleague Caroline Winterer. I discuss this topic with her in my radio show and podcast *Entitled Opinions* (January 18, 2011).

For useful introductions to the history of the scientific method, see Barry Gower, *Scientific Method: A Historical and Philosophical Introduction*, as well as the essays in *Histories of Scientific Observation*, edited by Lorraine Daston and Elizabeth Lunbeck. See also Peter J. Bowler and Iwan Rhys Morus, *Making Modern Science: A Historical Survey*, and Jan Golinski, *Making Natural Knowledge*. Paul Karl Feyerabend's *Against Method* remains a classic in its genre, as does Thomas Kuhn's *The Structure of Scientific Revolutions*, two books to which I am especially indebted in these pages.

Walter Benjamin's important essay "Theses on the Philosophy of History" can be found in *Illuminations*, 253–64 (see esp. 257–58 for the thesis on the angel). For Benjamin's "angel of history," see Stéphane Mosès, *The Angel of History: Rosenzweig, Benjamin, Scholem*, and O. K. Werckmeister, "Walter Benjamin's Angel of History, or the Transfiguration of the Revolutionary into the Historian." See also Giorgio Agamben, "Walter Benjamin and the Demonic: Happiness and Historical Redemption," in *Potentialities* (138–59).

The quotes from Saint-Exupéry come from his essay "The Tool," in *Wind, Sand, and Stars* (41–47). This collection was originally published in French as *Terre des hommes*. Jean-Paul Sartre briefly discusses this essay from a related but different perspective than my own in the first volume of *Critique of Dialectical Reason* (452–53).

The concept of "deep time" was developed by the Scottish geologist James Hutton (see his four-volume *Theory of the Earth*). Stephen Jay Gould provides an excellent discussion of its discovery in *Time's Arrow, Time's Cycle* (1–20, 61–98). See also Stephen Baxter, *Ages in Chaos: James Hutton and the Discovery of Deep Time*; Henry Gee, *In Search of Deep Time: Beyond the Fossil Record to a New History of Life*; Dennis R. Dean, *James Hutton and the History of Geology*; and M. J. S. Rudwick's impressive *Bursting the Limits of Time: The Reconstruction of Geohistory in the Age of Revolution*. Wai Chee Dimock has recently applied the concept of deep time to the study of American literature (see *Through Other Continents: American Literature across Deep Time*), as has Sabrina Ferri with respect to French and Italian literature of the eighteenth and nineteenth centuries. In her recently completed book manuscript, *The Past in Ruins: History and Nature in Eighteenth- and Early-Nineteenth-Century Italy*, Ferri treats, among other things, the impact of the discovery of the age of the earth on the poetic and historiographical imagination in the period that connects Giambattista Vico to Giacomo Leopardi. See also her articles on geology and the poetics of ruins: "Lazzaro Spallanzani's Hybrid Ruins: A Scientist at Serapis and Troy" and "Time in Ruins: Melancholy and Modernity in the Pre-Romantic Natural Picturesque."

For more on the evolutionary concept and role of heterochrony, see Michael L. McKinney and Ken McNamara, *Heterochrony: The Evolution of Ontogeny*; *Heterochrony in Evolution: A Multidisciplinary Approach*, edited by Michael L. McKinney; and *Evolutionary Change and Heterochrony*, edited by Ken McNamara. For a more recent work, see Miriam Zelditch, *Beyond Heterochrony: The Evolution of Development*.

For excellent, comprehensive accounts of Hegel's thought, see Charles Taylor, *Hegel*, and Terry Pinkard, *Hegel: A Biography*. See also *The Cambridge Companion to Hegel*, edited by Frederick Beiser. For an approach focused on the role of memory in Hegel's system, see Rebecca Comay, *Memory in Hegel and Heidegger*. In part 2 of *Hegel, Haiti, and Universal History*, Susan Buck-Morss offers a compelling discussion of Hegel's philosophy of history, with many pertinent analyses of universal history (79–152).

Vico has a number of excellent Anglophone commentators, including R. G. Collingwood, Isaiah Berlin, Samuel Beckett, Donald Verene, Hayden White, Giorgio Tagliacozzo, Giuseppe Mazzotta, Mark Lilla, Peter Burke, and Sandra Luft (see bibliography for titles). I have commented on Vico at some length in two of my previous books, *Forests* (3–60, 133–42, 164–70) and *The Dominion of the Dead* (esp. 17–54, 72–105).

On the theme of disenchantment, see the classic study by Charles Edward Montague, *Disenchantment*, as well as Max Weber, *The Sociology of Religion*. See also the excellent book by Marcel Gauchet, *The Disenchantment of the World*. On the theme of "reenchantment," see *The Re-Enchantment of the World: Secular Magic in a Rational Age*, edited by Joshua Landy and Michael Saler, which includes an exhaustive bibliography on disenchantment. On disenchantment and secularization, see Charles Taylor's magisterial study *A Secular Age*.

For a review of the religious foundations of Roman piety, see W. Warde Fowler's extraordinary Gifford Lectures, collected and published as *The Religious Experience of the Roman People*. See also Valerie M. Warrior's useful introduction *Roman Religion* (esp. 25–70). On patriarchy and piety, see Peter Garnsey and Richard Saller, *The Roman Empire: Economy, Society and Culture*. For an analysis of Aeneas's piety in particular, see Eve Adler, *Vergil's Empire: Political Thought in the Aeneid* (167–92, 219–300).

Those interested in reading the source of the Greek theogony I draw on in this section may consult Glenn Most's critical edition of Hesiod's *Theogony* in the Loeb Classical Library series (in the same volume are Hesiod's *Works and Days* and *Testimonia*). *Greek Mythology and Poetics*, by Gregory Nagy, remains a classic study. See also Yves Bonnefoy, *Greek and Roman Mythologies*, and the *Cambridge Companion to Greek Mythology*, edited by Roger D. Woodard.

For generational conflict in Greece and Rome, see the excellent collection *The Conflict of Generations in Ancient Greece and Rome*, edited by Stephen Bertman. For an interesting study of Oedipal conflict between the generations of Greek gods, see Richard S. Caldwell, *The Origin of the Gods: A Psychoanalytic Study of Greek Theogonic Myth*. See also Elizabeth S. Belfiore, *Murder among Friends: A Violation of Philia in Greek Tragedy*.

GENERATION GAPS

On the topic of social embeddedness and generativity, see Gunhild O. Hagestad and Peter Uhlenberg, "The Social Separation of Old and Young: A Root of Ageism." For a much broader treatment of the family dynamics of age and generations, see Ingrid A. Connidis, *Family Ties and Aging*.

The *locus classicus* of sociological generation gaps is the so-called Strauss-Howe generational theory. William Strauss and Neil Howe's 1991 book *Generations* deals specifically with American history across the centuries; several other coauthored works have been published since then. Karl Mannheim's work is an important precursor; see his essay "The Problem of Generations." For a recent sociological commentary on these and other related issues, see also Karen Foster, *Generation, Discourse, and Social Change*, and Jennifer Cole and Deborah Durham, *Generations and Globalization: Youth, Age and Family in the New World Economy*. On the generation gap of the 1960s and its political aftermath, see Rebecca E. Klatch, *A Generation Divided: The New Left, the New Right, and the 1960s*.

I suggest in this chapter that deep generation gaps prevail in societies informed by "insurrectional" rather than "pious" forms of cultural heterochrony, yet the sentiment of estrangement among the elderly vis-à-vis the younger generations is a recurrent motif in many world cultures. *In Praise of Shadows*, written in 1933 by the Japanese writer Jun'ichirō Tanizaki, contains a passage that is worth quoting here, as it resonates with some of the main themes of my chapter 2:

It struck me [recently] that old people everywhere have the same laments. The older we get the more we seem to think that everything was better in the past. ... Never has there been an age that people have been satisfied with. But in recent years the pace of progress has been so precipitous that conditions in our own country [Japan] go somewhat beyond the ordinary. The changes that have taken place since the Restoration of 1867 must be at least as great as those of the preceding three and a half centuries.

It will seem odd, I suppose, that I should go on in this vein, as if I too were grumbling in my dotage. Yet of this I am convinced, that the conveniences of modern culture cater exclusively to youth, and that the times grow increasingly inconsiderate of old people. (39)

Tanizaki overstates the case, to be sure, since a number of the conveniences of modern culture cater to the old as well as the young, yet there is no question that the introduction of new conveniences alter the life worlds of a given society or culture. World alteration, almost by definition, unsettles older people more than younger people, whether the new conveniences cater specifically to the young or not. See, in chapter 4, the sections headed "*Amor Mundi* and a Poem about Going" and "The New Ones" for my discussion of this dynamic.

TRAGIC WISDOM

For an approach to Greek tragic theater that emphasizes the elements I consider most crucial, see Rush Rehm's remarkable books *Greek Tragic Theater* and *The Play of Space: Spatial Transformation in Greek Tragedy*. Another book that I found especially insightful is Daniel Mendelsohn's *Gender and the City in Euripides's Political Plays*. H. D. F. Kitto's *Greek Tragedy* remains an invaluable introduction to the tragic genre among the Greeks. On the emergence of that genre, see Glen Most's "Generating Genres: The Idea of the Tragic." Other useful works, among a great many, include David Wiles, *Mask and Performance in Greek Tragedy: From Ancient Festival to Modern Experimentation*; R. B. Rutherford, *Greek Tragic Style: Form, Language, and Interpretation*; and James Barrett, *Staged Narrative: Poetics and the Messenger in Greek Tragedy*. For an inspired, free-ranging reflection on tragedy across the ages and across genres, see Terry Eagleton, *Sweet Violence: The Idea of the Tragic*. See also J. M. Bernstein's entry on "Tragedy," chapter 3 in *The Oxford Handbook of Philosophy and Literature*, edited by Richard Eldridge, who himself discusses tragedy in "What Can Tragedy Matter for Us?," chapter 8 in his *The Persistence of Romanticism*.

On *King Lear*, I have been especially inspired by Stanley Cavell's "The Avoidance of Love: A Reading of *King Lear*," as well as William Elton's magisterial *King Lear and the Gods*. For an analysis of Shakespeare's corpus through the lens of age and ages, see David Bevington's books *Shakespeare: The Seven Ages of Human Experience* and *Shakespeare's Ideas: More Things in Heaven and Earth*.

Chapter Three: Neotenic Revolutions

PREAMBLE

A neotenic revolution, as I conceive it, has a dynamic that is altogether sui generis. The case studies I deal with in this chapter put into relief exactly what that dynamic consists of. I have surveyed various other theories of revolution, if only to gauge how they contrast with my own. In this regard I have profited from an essay by my colleague Dan Edelstein, "Do We Want a Revolution without a Revolution? Reflections on Political Authority," which discusses the problems entailed by theorizing revolution and contains a useful bibliography of some of the most notable theories; of note are Reinhart Koselleck's essay "Historical Criteria of the Modern Concept of Revolution," and Alain Rey's *Révolution: Histoire d'un mot*. For an account of the emergence of what we now think of as "revolution," see Keith Baker's *Inventing the French Revolution* (esp. 203–23). See also the essays collected in *The Age of Cultural Revolutions: Britain and France, 1750–1820*, edited by Colin Jones and Dror Wahrman. Finally, I found helpful two books edited by John Foran, *Theorizing Revolutions* and *The Future of Revolutions*, as well as one edited by Foran, David Lane, and Andreja Zivkovic, *Revolution in the Making of the Modern World*.

SOCRATIC GENIUS

On Socrates, see Gregory Vlastos, *Socrates, Ironist and Moral Philosopher*. See also the *Cambridge Companion to Socrates*, edited by Donald Morrison, and *A Companion to Socrates*, edited by Sara Ahbel-Rappe and Rachana Kamtekar. These volumes contain thorough bibliographies of the countless excellent books and essays devoted to the figure of Socrates. For studies of Socratic philosophy and its ongoing relevance in our day, I would draw special attention to two essay collections by Alexander Nehamas: *The Art of Living: Socratic Reflections from Plato to Foucault* and *Virtues of Authenticity: Essays on Plato and Socrates*. A classic study of Socrates's putative corruption of the Athenian youth is C. D. C. Reeve, *Socrates in the Apology*. On Socrates and his politics, see Richard Kraut, *Socrates and the State*.

In *De Senectute* (*On Old Age*), Cicero uses the term *adulescentia* in his discussion of the four main stages of life. *Adulescentia* comes after youth (*pueritia*, seventeen or younger) and before middle age (*aetas media*, forty or older). Thus, the Roman concept of *adulescentia* is by no means identical with the modern concept of adolescence, which we consider a psychological, hormonal, and institutional stage of transition from puberty to adulthood. The classic study of adolescence in the latter, modern sense is Stanley Hall's foundational book *Adolescence*, which has lost little of its relevance since its publication some nine decades ago. On this difference between Roman and modern concepts of adolescence, see Marc Kleijwegt, *Ancient Youth: The Ambiguity of Youth and the Absence of Adolescence in Greco-Roman Society*, and Christian Laes, *Children in the Roman Empire: Outsiders Within*. On the rise of the modern view of adolescence, see also (among many other studies) Sarah E. Chinn, *Inventing Modern Adolescence: The Children of Immigrants in Turn of the Century America*; Joseph F. Kett, *Rites* of Passage: Adolescence in America, 1790 to the Present; Marcel Danesi, Cool: The Signs and Meanings of Adolescence; and Louise J. Kaplan's personal recollection Adolescence: The Farewell to Childhood.

Quotations from the *Republic* are from Benjamin Jowett's translation of the *Dialogues*; see vol. 3, 5–6. For other perspectives on the figure of Cephalus, see Terence Irwin, *Plato's Ethics* (170–71); Nickolas Pappas, *The Routledge Guide Book to Plato and the Republic* (30–32); and Stanley Rosen, "Cephalus and Polemarchus." For an interpretation that shares affinities with mine, see C. D. C. Reeve, "Cephalus, Odysseus, and the Importance of Experience."

PLATONIC WISDOM

For a fine collection of essays that question the standard account of the transition from *mythos* to *logos* in Greek culture, see *From Myth to Reason? Studies in the Development of Greek Thought*, edited by Richard Buxton. I find particularly helpful the contribution by Glenn Most, "From Logos to Mythos" (25–50). Buxton is also author of two fine studies on Greek mythology, *Imaginary Greece* and *Myths and Tragedies in Their Ancient Greek Contexts*. One of the finest treatments of Plato's engagement with myth and various literary genres is Andrea Nightingale, *Genres in Dialogue*. See also the essays collected in *Plato and Myth: Studies in the Use and Status of Platonic Myths*, edited by Catherine Collobert, Pierre Destrée, and Francisco J. Gonzalez. In the same series, see *Plato and the Poets*, edited by Pierre Destrée and Fritz-Gregor Herrmann. Other valuable studies include *Plato's Myths*, edited by Catalin Partenie; *Plato the Myth Maker* by Luc Brisson; and the Oxford World Classics volume on Plato's *Selected Myths*. See also Jonathan Lear, "Allegory and Myth in Plato's *Republic*."

On the figure of Socrates in Plato's dialogues, see Gregory Vlastos's chapter "Socrates *Contra* Socrates in Plato," in *Socrates: Ironist and Moral Philosopher* (45–80), as well as Vlastos, *Socratic Studies*, 87–108. See also Sandra Peterson, *Socrates and Philosophy in the Dialogues of Plato*.

THE CHILD AND THE KINGDOM

For those interested in what I call Christianity's "theology of the child," I recommend, among other studies, *The Child in Christian Thought*, edited by Marcia JoAnn Bunge; *The Child in the Bible*, edited by Marcia J. Bunge, Terence E. Fretheim, and Beverly Roberts Gaventa; and *Let the Little Children Come to Me: Childhood and Children in Early Christianity*, edited by Cornelia B. Horn and John W. Martens.

On Nietzsche and Christianity, see Jörg Salaquarda, "Nietzsche and the Judaeo-Christian Tradition"; on Nietzsche and transvaluation, see Kathleen

Marie Higgins, "Rebaptizing Our Evil: On the Revaluation of All Values." See also the section on revaluation in Brian Leiter, *The Routledge Guidebook to Nietzsche on Morality* (26–35). An especially good recent study is Bernard Reginster, *The Affirmation of Life: Nietzsche on Overcoming Nihilism*.

On the "fools for Christ" tradition that drew inspiration from Saint Paul's words in 1 Corinthians, see the magisterial *Holy Fools in Byzantium and Beyond*, by Sergey Ivanov.

Several contemporary philosophers have not only engaged Paul in depth but also appropriated him in one way or another. See, for example, Alain Badiou, *Saint Paul: The Foundation of Universalism*; Giorgio Agamben, *The Time That Remains: A Commentary on the Letter to the Romans*; and Slavoj Zizek, "The Politics of Truth or Alain Badiou as a Reader of St. Paul." See also *Saint Paul among the Philosophers*, edited by John D. Caputo and Linda Martin Alcoff, for more essays on Saint Paul in contemporary European philosophy.

On Saint Paul in general, and his theology of conversion in particular, see Richard Peace, *Conversion in the New Testament: Paul and the Twelve*; also, *The Cambridge Companion to St. Paul*, edited by James D. G. Dunn, esp. part 3, with sections by Alan F. Segal, Graham N. Stanton, L. W. Hurtado, Luke Timothy Johnson, and Brian Rosner. See also James D. G. Dunn, *The Theology of Paul the Apostle*, for a fine study on various aspects of Paul's thinking.

For a classic study on the theology of baptism, see George Raymond Beasley-Murray, *Baptism in the New Testament*. See also the collection *Dimensions of Baptism: Biblical and Theological Studies*, edited by Stanley E. Porter and Anthony R. Cross, as well as the massive volume *Ablution, Initiation, and Baptism: Late Antiquity, Early Judaism, and Early Christianity*, edited by David Hellholm, Tor Vegge, Oyvind Norderval, and Christer Hellholm. For a more recent monograph about baptism, see Everett Ferguson, *Baptism in the Early Church: History, Theology, and Liturgy in the First Five Centuries*.

For my philosophical thinking about Christianity, I have also found interesting the work of Karl Rahner, whose most important work is *Foundations of Christian Faith*. See Thomas Sheehan's excellent book *Karl Rahner: The Philosophical Foundations*. See also *The Cambridge Companion to Karl Rahner*, edited by Declan Marmion and Mary E. Hines; Karen Kilby, *Karl Rahner: Theological Philosophies*; and Patrick Burke, *Reinterpreting Rahner: A Critical Study of His Major Themes*.

CHRISTIAN WISDOM

Concerning pagan attacks on Christianity and the early church fathers' defense against them, I have relied heavily on the detailed accounts provided by Jaroslav Pelikan in his magisterial five-volume work *The Christian Tradition* (volume 1,

The Emergence of the Catholic Tradition, is my main source in this section). See also John Granger Cook, *The Interpretation of the Old Testament in Greco-Roman Paganism*, and *Paganism and Christianity, 100–425 C.E.: A Sourcebook*, edited by Ramsay MacMullen and Eugene Lane. For the centuries beyond those that I discuss here, see *Christianity and Paganism, 350–750: The Conversion of Western Europe*, edited by J. N. Hillgarth, and Ramsay MacMullen, *Christianity and Paganism in the Fourth to Eighth Centuries*. Another book that I found especially useful is Avery Cardinal Dulles, *A History of Apologetics*.

On Christian and pagan debates about the relative antiquity of their respective traditions, see Arthur Droge's excellent *Homer or Moses? Early Christian Interpretations of the History of Culture*. On the history of the concept of *logos spermatikos*, see the outstanding article by R. Holte, "Logos Spermatikos: Christianity and Ancient Philosophy According to Saint Justin's Apologies." For more on Justin Martyr's use of this Stoic concept, see Susan Wendel, "Interpreting the Descent of the Spirit," as well as her book *Scriptural Interpretation and Community Self-Definition in Luke-Acts and the Writings of Justin Martyr*. Another quite useful volume on early Christianity is Peter Lampe, *From Paul to Valentinus: Christians at Rome in the First Two Centuries*.

On Christian typology, see John J. O'Keefe, "Typology"; O'Keefe and R. R. Reno, *Sanctified Vision: An Introduction to Early Christian Interpretations of the Bible*; Leonhardt Goppelt, *Typos: The Typology Interpretation of the Old Testament in the New*; and Sydney Greidanus, *Preaching Christ from the Old Testament: A Contemporary Hermeneutical Method*.

THE CHILD OF ENLIGHTENMENT

For Hegel's views of the Enlightenment, see "Spirit," part B, section II, "The Enlightenment," in *Phenomenology of Spirit* (328–54). See also the essays in *Hegel on the Modern World*, edited by Ardis B. Collins, and the older study by Lewis P. Hinchman, *Hegel's Critique of the Enlightenment*. See also — among a number of other excellent studies — Frederick Beiser, *Hegel*; Allen Wood, *Hegel's Ethical Thought*; and Frederick Neuhouser, *Foundations of Hegel's Social Theory: Actualizing Freedom*.

On Galileo's role as one of the founders of modern scientific method, the list of titles is vast. For an excellent introductory volume, see *The Cambridge Companion to Galileo*, edited by Peter Machamer. For the ins and outs of his trial, see William R. Shea and Mariano Artigas, *Galileo in Rome: The Rise and Fall of a Troublesome Genius*. See also Maurice Finocchiaro's work, including his books *The Galileo Affair: A Documentary History*, *Retrying Galileo, 1633–1992*, and the *Routledge Guidebook to Galileo's Dialogue*.

In *Forests: The Shadow of Civilization*, I discuss from another point of view Descartes's lament that we cannot be born as adults, with the full use of our reason, but must pass through a period of childhood; see the section "The Ways of Method" (108–13).

Kant's views about Enlightenment have received considerable scholarly attention. I would note here Katerina Deligiorgi, *Kant and the Culture of Enlightenment*, and Michel Foucault's important reflections in his essay "What Is Enlightenment?"

On reason, modernity, and maturity, see David Owen, *Maturity and Modernity: Nietzsche, Weber, Foucault, and the Ambivalence of Reason* (on maturity and Kant in particular, 7–15). On Kant's views of human nature, see Allen Wood, "Kant and the Problem of Human Nature"; Robert B. Louden, *Kant's Human Being* and *Kant's Impure Ethics*; and Patrick R. Frierson, *Freedom and Anthropology in Kant's Moral Philosophy*. See also Michel Foucault's doctoral dissertation of 1961, published in English as *Introduction to Kant's Anthropology*. Directly pertinent to my analysis is an excellent essay by Herbert Dreyfus and Paul Rabinow, "What Is Maturity?" in Foucault, *Critical Reader*, 109–21.

DECLARING INDEPENDENCE

One of the studies from which I learned the most concerning the Declaration of Independence is *Declaring Independence*, by my late Stanford colleague Jay Fliegelman. See also Pauline Maier, *American Scripture: Making the Declaration of Independence*, and Gary Wills, *Inventing America: Jefferson's Declaration of Independence*. My reading of the small "neotenic revolution" of the opening sentence is strictly my own. I have written about in it in another context in "The Book from Which Our Literature Springs." When he changed the word "sacred" to "self-evident," Benjamin Franklin believed he was regrounding the truths in question on reason instead of faith, yet in my interpretation of the term, "self-evidence" contains — whether wittingly or not — a creative retrieval and reprojection of the Christian heritage of faith, traditionally defined (as I point out in this section) as the "evidence of things unseen."

On the Lockean legacy of the Declaration's concept of "government by consent of the governed," see Gillian Brown, *The Consent of the Governed*.

THE AMERICAN CONSTITUTION

My historical review of the events, ideas, and sources of the American Constitution is heavily indebted to the work of Gordon S. Wood, above all his magisterial book *The Creation of the American Republic: 1776–1787*. Most of the direct quotes in this section come from this book.

Roger Williams, founder of the colony of Rhode Island, was a fascinating figure of the first wave of American Puritanism. Perry Miller writes eloquently about him in *Roger Williams: His Contribution to the American Tradition*. On

Williams as a forerunner of the doctrine of separation of church and state, see Timothy L. Hall, *Separating Church and State: Roger Williams and Religious Liberty*; John M. Barry, *Roger Williams and the Creation of the American Soul: Church, State, and the Birth of Liberty*; and Edwin S. Gaustad, *Liberty of Conscience: Roger Williams in America*.

On the Federalists' suspicion of popular democracy, see Wood, *Creation of the American Republic*, 483–531.

GETTYSBURG

For Emerson's views on slavery, see *Emerson's Antislavery Writings*, edited by Len Gougeon and Joel Myerson. On the fratricidal and sacrificial origins of Rome's founding, see René Girard's remarkable meditation in his "Collective Violence and Sacrifice in Shakespeare's Julius Caesar." For a very different perspective, see Cynthia J. Bannon, *The Brothers of Romulus: Fraternal "Pietas" in Roman Law, Literature, and Society*. Both in *Discourses on Livy* and *The Prince*, Machiavelli insists on the sanguinary, sacrificial nature of Rome's founding, attributing Rome's greatness to that inaugural act of fratricide by Romulus. See book 1 of the *Discourses* (esp. 100–104). On Rome's beginnings, see also Alexandre Grandazzi, *The Foundation of Rome: Myth and History*; H. H. Scullard, *A History of the Roman World, 753 to 146 BC*; and Augusto Fraschetti, *The Foundation of Rome*.

I have analyzed the Gettysburg Address from other perspectives both in my book *The Dominion of the Dead* (27–30) and in "America: The Struggle to Be Reborn." There are countless commentaries on Lincoln's Address. I would draw special attention here to the one by Garry Wills, *Lincoln at Gettysburg: The Words That Remade America*.

Chapter Four: Amor Mundi

CLARIFICATIONS

Hannah Arendt's first introduced her concept of "natality" in *The Human Condition*. She meant by the term the ever-present possibility that human beings, either on their own or in concert with one another, can undertake actions that will bring something new into the world. To be human means to be capable of world-altering initiatives. Or as Arendt herself puts it in one of the more moving pages of *The Human Condition*:

> The miracle that saves the world, the realm of human affairs, from its normal, "natural" ruin is ultimately the fact of natality, in which the faculty of action is ontologically rooted. It is, in other words, the birth of new men

and the new beginning, the action they are capable of by virtue of being born. Only the full experience of this capacity can bestow upon human affairs faith and hope, those two essential characteristics of human existence which Greek antiquity ignored altogether, discounting the keeping of faith as a very uncommon and not too important virtue and counting hope among the evils of illusion in Pandora's box. It is this faith in and hope for the world that found perhaps its most glorious and most succinct expression in the few words with which the Gospels announced their "glad tidings": "A child has been born unto us." (247)

In the broadest terms, my efforts in this book have been focused on clarifying and evaluating the inner cultural dynamics of natality in order to determine whether, and to what extent, our contemporary juvenescence has the character of a "miracle that saves the world" from its natural ruin, or whether it represents instead a historically unusual form of such ruin. As my epilogue makes clear, a definitive answer to this question is not available to us at this point.

On Arendt's thinking about natality, see Patricia Bowen-Moore, *Hannah Arendt's Philosophy of Natality*, and Peg Birmingham, *Hannah Arendt and Human Rights: The Predicament of Common Responsibility* (esp. 4–34, "The Event of Natality: The Ontological Foundation of Human Rights"). Among recent articles, see Jonathan Schell, "A Politics of Natality"; Margarete Durst, "Birth and Natality in Hannah Arendt"; Miguel Vatter, "Natality and Biopolitics in Hannah Arendt"; Mavis Louise Biss, "Arendt and the Theological Significance of Natality"; and Jeffrey Champlin, "Born Again: Arendt's 'Natality' as Figure and Concept." Arendt has an army of excellent commentators (see *The Cambridge Companion Guide to Hannah Arendt*, edited by Dana Villa, for an extensive bibliography). The gold-standard biography is *Hannah Arendt: For Love of the World*, by Elizabeth Young-Bruehl. For its depth of thought and keen insights into Arendt's thinking, I recommend Roger Berkowitz's introduction to *Thinking in Dark Times*, edited by Berkowitz, Thomas Keenan, and Jeffrey Katz (1–16), as well as several of the excellent essays included in this collection.

In his notebook, Paul Valéry wrote, "La connaissance s'étend comme un arbre, par un procédé identique à lui-même: en se répétant. Novat reiterando" (*Cahiers*, 3:273). In my own English translation: "Knowledge extends like a tree, by a process identical to itself: that is, by repeating itself. Novat reiterando [Renewal through repetition]." An excellent collection of essays on this remarkable French poet is *Reading Paul Valéry: Universe in Mind*, edited by Paul Gifford and Brian Stimpson. Another fine study is Christine M. Crow, *Paul Valéry and the Poetry of Voice*.

Michael North offers an interesting account of the origins and transmission of Ezra Pound's famous slogan "Make it new" in his compelling book *Novelty: A History of the New* (162–71).

On Dante's appropriation of the pagan tradition, see Kevin Brownlee, "Dante and the Classical Poets," and Michelangelo Picone, "Dante and the Classics." See also Winthrop Wetherbee, *The Ancient Flame: Dante and the Poets*, and *The Poetry of Allusion: Virgil and Ovid in Dante's Commedia*, edited by Rachel Jacoff and Jeffrey Schnapp.

On Petrarch, see *Petrarch: A Critical Guide to the Complete Works*, edited by Victoria Kirkham and Armando Maggi. See also Giuseppe Mazzotta's superb *The Worlds of Petrarch*. On Petrarch's humanism, see Gur Zak, *Petrarch's Humanism and the Care of the Self*.

For Nietzsche and philology, see James I. Porter, *Nietzsche and the Philology of the Future*. For Nietzsche and ancient philosophy, see Jessica Berry, *Nietzsche and the Ancient Skeptical Tradition*. See also the essays in *Nietzsche and Antiquity: Reaction and Response to the Classical Tradition*, edited by Paul Bishop. Tracy Strong discusses Nietzsche and the Greeks in chapter 6 of his *Friedrich Nietzsche and the Politics of Transfiguration*, as does Dennis J. Schmidt in chapter 5 of his *On Germans and Other Greeks: Tragedy and Ethical Life*. See also *Nietzsche as Scholar of Antiquity*, edited by Anthony K. Jensen and Helmut Heit.

CHANGING THE WORLD

On genius, see Darrin MacMahon, *Divine Fury*, a recent book that offers an interesting and engaging history of the notion of individual genius.

On Hannah Arendt and "amor mundi," see Marieke Borren's remarkable dissertation "Amor Mundi: Hannah Arendt's Political Phenomenology of the World" (http://dare.uva.nl/document/469656). See also Svetlana Boym's moving pages on Hannah Arendt in *Another Freedom* (24–30, 224–32, 255–65). See also Sigrid Weigel, "Sounding Through—Poetic Difference—Self-Translation: Hannah Arendt's Thoughts and Writings between Different Languages, Cultures, and Fields."

On Walter Benjamin and the "destructive character," see Irving Wohlfarth, "No-Man's-Land: On Walter Benjamin's 'Destructive Character,'" which is also included in a valuable collection of essays, *Walter Benjamin's Philosophy: Destruction and Experience*, edited by Andrew Benjamin and Peter Osborne.

AMOR MUNDI AND A POEM ABOUT GOING

On Larkin's poem "Going, Going," see the fine commentary by Rob Rollison, "Going, Going, by Philip Larkin," on the website *The Poetry Room*. For scholarship on Larkin in general, here is a small sample: Janice Rossen, *Philip Larkin: His Life's Work*; Tijana Stojkovic, *"Unnoticed in the Casual Light of Day": Philip Larkin and the Plain Style*; *Philip Larkin: The Man and His Work*, edited by Dale Salwak; Salem Hassan, *Philip Larkin and His Contemporaries*; Stephen Cooper,

Philip Larkin: Subversive Writer; and Richard Palmer, *Such Deliberate Disguises: The Art of Philip Larkin*.

THE NEW ONES

On the role of children in ancient Greece, see, in addition to the works cited in the "Platonic Wisdom" section of chapter 3, *Coming of Age in Ancient Greece: Images of Childhood from the Classical Past*, edited by Jenifer Neils and John Howard Oakley; Mark Golden, *Children and Childhood in Classical Athens*; and *The Conflict of Generations in Ancient Greece and Rome*, edited by Stephen Bertman.

On Greek *paideia*, or education, see Werner Jaeger's multivolume *Paideia: The Ideals of Greek Culture*.

On Bergson, perception, and memory, see G. William Barnard, *Living Consciousness: The Metaphysical Vision of Henri Bergson*, and Leonard Lawlor, *The Challenge of Bergsonism*, among other recent studies.

YOUNG LOVE

On D. H. Lawrence, see Robert E. Montgomery, *The Visionary D. H. Lawrence: Beyond Philosophy and Art*; Jack Stewart, *The Vital Art of D. H. Lawrence: Vision and Expression*; and the three-volume *Cambridge Biography of D. H. Lawrence*, by John Worthen, Mark Kinkead-Weekes, and David Ellis. I am especially indebted to the fine studies of Lawrence's work by Keith M. Sagar, books such as *The Art of D. H. Lawrence* and *D. H. Lawrence: Life into Art*. My reflections on Lawrence in this section are indebted to Sagar's inspired work, which quotes abundantly from Lawrence's corpus.

For a particularly thoughtful reflection on Emerson and his essay "Experience," see Stanley Cavell's essay, "Finding as Founding: Taking Steps in Emerson's 'Experience.'" See also the discussion of the essay in my review of Emerson's journals entitled "Emerson: The Good Hours."

AFTER LONG SILENCE

On Yeats's poem "After Long Silence," see the masterful essay by Marjorie Perloff, "How to Read a Poem: W. B. Yeats's 'After Long Silence.'"

Machiavelli's letter to Vettori, dated December 10, 1513, is quoted from *Machiavelli and His Friends*, edited and translated by J. B. Atkinson and David Sices (262–65). On the letter, see John Najemy, *Between Friends: Discourses of Power and Desire in the Machiavelli-Vettori Letters of 1513–1515*. See also the *Cambridge Companion to Machiavelli*, edited by John Najemy, and the essays in *Machiavelli and Republicanism*, edited by Gisela Bock, Quentin Skinner, and

Maurizio Viroli. On Machiavelli, I have also been particularly inspired by my personal exchanges with the Italian scholar Gabriele Pedullà.

The most compelling image of what I call the "reverential posture" of the reader is found, in my view, in Wallace Stevens's poem "The House Was Quiet and the World Was Calm":

The house was quiet and the world was calm.
The reader became the book; and summer night

Was like the conscious being of the book.
The house was quiet and the world was calm.

The words were spoken as if there was no book,
Except that the reader leaned above the page,

Wanted to lean, wanted much most to be
The scholar to whom his book is true, to whom

The summer night is like a perfection of thought.
The house was quiet because it had to be.

The quiet was part of the meaning, part of the mind:
The access of perfection to the page.

And the world was calm. The truth in a calm world,
In which there is no other meaning, itself

Is calm, itself is summer and night, itself
Is the reader leaning late and reading there.

Those who today still engage in deep reading are like Stevens's "reader leaning late," for historically speaking the hour is late indeed, even if the world is far from quiet.

We might note that the recent recommendations of Common Core State Standards for schools in America do not further the cause of wisdom. The standards, which have been adopted by forty-six states, recommend that 50 percent of fourth-grade reading and 70 percent of twelfth-grade reading be "informational" rather than "literary," explaining that "most of the required reading in college and workforce training programs is informational in structure and content; postsecondary education programs typically provide students with both a higher volume of such reading than is generally required in K–12 schools and comparatively little scaffolding." As the *San Francisco Chronicle* put it in an editorial comment: "English teachers across the country are moving Shakespeare and Keats off of the Syllabus and asking students to read federal reports and Malcolm Gladwell instead. Out with *Macbeth* and in with Fed-Views by the Federal Reserve Bank of San Francisco" ("Literary Retreat," December 2, 2012). Learning the basic skills of informational reading will no doubt help students get through college with more proficiency. What they will have to descant upon later in their lives is another matter.

CONTINUING EDUCATION

The anecdote about Socrates on his deathbed is cited by Italo Calvino in his essay "Why Read the Classics," in *The Uses of Literature* (134). He is referring to an apocryphal version of Socrates's final moments by the Romanian wrier Emil Cioran. The translation comes from *The Uses of Literature*.

WORKS CITED

Adler, Eve. *Vergil's Empire: Political Thought in the Aeneid*. Lanham, MD: Rowman and Littlefield, 2003.

Agamben, Giorgio. *Infancy and History: Essays on the Destruction of Experience*. Translated by Liz Heron. New York: Verso, 1993.

———. *The Open: Man and Animal*. Translated by Kevin Attell. Palo Alto, CA: Stanford University Press, 2004.

———. *Potentialities*. Translated by Daniel Heller-Roazen. Palo Alto, CA: Stanford University Press, 1999.

———. *The Time That Remains: A Commentary on the Letter to the Romans*. Translated by Patricia Dailey. Palo Alto, CA: Stanford University Press, 2005.

Ahbel-Rappe, Sara, and Rachana Kamtekar, eds. *A Companion to Socrates*. Malden, MA: Wiley-Blackwell, 2006.

Ansell-Pearson, Keith. *Philosophy and the Adventure of the Virtual: Bergson and the Time of Life*. London: Routledge, 2002.

Arendt, Hannah. *The Human Condition*. Chicago: University of Chicago Press, 1958.

———. "On Humanity in Dark Times: Thoughts about Lessing." In *Men in Dark Times*. Translated by Clara Winston and Richard Winston, 3–31. New York: Harcourt Brace Jovanovich, 1968.

Arnett, Jeffrey. "Emerging Adulthood: A Theory of Development from the Late Teens through the Twenties." *American Psychologist* 55, no. 5 (2000): 469–80.

Astington, Harris J., Paul L. Harris, and David R. Olson, eds. *Developing Theories of Mind*. Cambridge: Cambridge University Press, 1988.

Atkins, Peter, Ian Gordon Simmons, and Brian K. Roberts, eds. *People, Land, and Time: The Relations between Landscape, Culture, and Environment*. London: Arnold, 1998.

Atkinson, James, and David Sices, eds. *Machiavelli and His Friends: Their Personal Correspondence*. Dekalb: Northern Illinois University Press, 1996.

Badiou, Alain. *Saint Paul: The Foundation of Universalism*. Translated by Ray Brassier. Palo Alto, CA: Stanford University Press, 2003.

Baker, Alan R. H., ed. *Geography and History: Bridging the Divide*. Cambridge: Cambridge University Press, 2003.

Baker, Alan R. H., and Mark Billinge, eds. *Period and Place: Research Methods in Historical Geography*. Cambridge: Cambridge University Press, 1982.

Baker, Keith Michael. *Inventing the French Revolution*. Cambridge: Cambridge University Press, 1990.

Bannon, Cynthia J. *The Brothers of Romulus: Fraternal "Pietas" in Roman Law, Literature, and Society*. Princeton, NJ: Princeton University Press, 1997.

Barbieri, Marcello, ed. *Introduction to Biosemiotics: The New Biological Synthesis*. Dordrecht, Netherlands: Springer, 2007.

Barnard, G. William. *Living Consciousness: The Metaphysical Vision of Henri Bergson*. Albany: State University of New York Press, 2011.

Barrett, James. *Staged Narrative: Poetics and the Messenger in Greek Tragedy*. Berkeley: University of California Press, 2002.

Barry, John M. *Roger Williams and the Creation of the American Soul: Church, State, and the Birth of Liberty*. New York: Viking, 2012.

Baxter, Stephen. *Ages in Chaos: James Hutton and the Discovery of Deep Time*. New York: Forge, 2004.

Beasley-Murray, George Raymond. *Baptism in the New Testament*. Grand Rapids, MI: Eerdmans, 1962.

Beckett, Samuel. "Dante ... Bruno ... Vico ... Joyce" (1929). In *Modernism: An Anthology*, edited by Lawrence Rainey, 1061–72. Malden, MA: Wiley-Blackwell, 2005.

———. *Three Novels: Molloy, Malone Dies, The Unnamable*. New York: Grove Press, 2009.

Beiser, Frederick, ed. *The Cambridge Companion to Hegel*. Cambridge: Cambridge University Press, 1993.

———. *Hegel*. New York: Routledge, 2005.

Belfiore, Elizabeth S. *Murder among Friends: A Violation of Philia in Greek Tragedy*. Oxford: Oxford University Press, 2000.

Benjamin, Andrew, and Peter Osborne, eds. *Walter Benjamin's Philosophy: Destruction and Experience*. London: Routledge, 1994.

Benjamin, Walter. "The Destructive Character." In *Reflections: Essays, Aphorisms, Autobiographical Writings*, edited by Peter Demetz, 301–3. New York: Schocken, 1986.

———. "Theses on the Philosophy of History." In *Illuminations: Essays and Reflections*, edited by Hannah Arendt, translated by Harry Zohn, 253–64. New York: Houghton Mifflin Harcourt, 1968.

Bergson, Henri. *Creative Evolution* (1907). Edited by Keith Ansell-Pearson, Michael Kolkman, and Michael Vaughan. Translated by Arthur Mitchell. Basingstoke, UK: Palgrave MacMillan, 2007.

———. *Duration and Simultaneity* (1922). Translated by Leon Jacobson. Indianapolis, IN: Bobbs-Merrill, 1965.

———. *Henri Bergson: Key Writings*. Edited by Keith Ansell-Pearson and John Mullarkey. New York: Continuum, 2002.

———. *Matter and Memory* (1896). Translated by N. M. Paul and W. S. Palmer. New York: Zone Books, 1991.

Berkowitz, Roger, Thomas Keenan, and Jeffrey Katz, eds. *Thinking in Dark Times: Hannah Arendt on Ethics and Politics*. New York: Fordham University Press, 2009.

Berlin, Isaiah. *Three Critics of the Enlightenment: Vico, Hamann, Herder*. Edited by Henry Hardy. Princeton, NJ: Princeton University Press, 2000.

Bernstein, J. M. "Tragedy." In *The Oxford Handbook of Philosophy and Literature*, edited by Richard T. Eldridge, 71–94. Oxford: Oxford University Press, 2009.

Berry, Jessica. *Nietzsche and the Ancient Skeptical Tradition*. Oxford: Oxford University Press, 2011.

Bertman, Stephen, ed. *The Conflict of Generation in Ancient Greece and Rome*. Amsterdam: Grüner, 1976.

Bevington, David. *Shakespeare's Ideas: More Things in Heaven and Earth*. Malden, MA: Wiley-Blackwell, 2008.

———. *Shakespeare: The Seven Ages of Human Experience*. 2nd ed. Malden, MA: Wiley-Blackwell, 2005.

Birmingham, Peg. *Hannah Arendt and Human Rights: The Predicament of Common Responsibility*. Bloomington: Indiana University Press, 2006.

Bishop, Paul, ed. *Nietzsche and Antiquity: Reaction and Response to the Classical Tradition*. Rochester, NY: Camden House, 2004.

Biss, Mavis Louise. "Arendt and the Theological Significance of Natality." *Philosophy Compass* 7, no. 11 (2012): 762–71.

Blank, G. Kim. *Wordsworth and Feeling: The Poetry of an Adult Child*. Cranbury, NJ: Associated University Presses, 1995.

Bock, Gisela, Quentin Skinner, and Maurizio Viroli, eds. *Machiavelli and Republicanism*. Cambridge: Cambridge University Press, 1990.

Boddice, Rob, ed. *Anthropocentrism: Humans, Animals, Environments*. Leiden, Netherlands: Brill, 2011.

Bogin, Barry. *The Growth of Humanity*. New York: Wiley-Liss, 2001.

———. *Patterns of Human Growth*. 2nd ed. Cambridge: Cambridge University Press, 1999.

Bonnefoy, Yves. *The Act and the Place of Poetry: Selected Essays*. Edited and translated by John Naughton. Chicago: University of Chicago Press, 1989.

————, ed. *Greek and Egyptian Mythologies*. Translated under the direction of Wendy Doniger. Chicago: University of Chicago Press, 1992.

————. *New and Selected Poems*. Edited by John Naughton and Anthony Rudolf. Translated by Galway Kinnell, Anthony Rudolph, Richard Pevear, Emily Grosholz, John Naughton, and Richard Stamelman. Chicago: University of Chicago Press, 1995.

————. *Pierre écrite*. Paris: Mercure de France, 1965.

————. *The Present Hour*. Translated by Beverly Bie Brahic. Calcutta: Seagull Books, 2013.

————. *Second Simplicity: New Poetry and Prose, 1991–2011*. Translated by Hoyt Rogers. New Haven, CT: Yale University Press, 2012.

————. *Words in Stone*. Translated by Susanna Lang. Amherst, MA: University of Massachusetts Press, 1976.

Booth, Wayne, ed. *The Art of Growing Older: Writers on Living and Aging*. Chicago: University of Chicago Press, 1996.

Borren, Marieke. "Amor Mundi: Hannah Arendt's Political Phenomenology of the World." PhD dissertation, University of Amsterdam, 1997.

Bowen-Moore, Patricia. *Hannah Arendt's Philosophy of Natality*. Basingstoke, UK: Macmillan, 1989.

Bowler, Peter J., and Iwan Rhys Morus. *Making Modern Science: A Historical Survey*. Chicago: University of Chicago Press, 2005.

Boym, Svetlana. *Another Freedom: The Alternative History of an Idea*. Chicago: University of Chicago Press, 2010.

Brennan, Teresa, ed. *Between Feminism and Psychoanalysis*. London: Routledge, 1989.

Brisson, Luc. *Plato the Myth Maker*. Edited and translated by Gerald Naddaf. Chicago: University of Chicago Press, 1998.

Bromhall, Clive. *The Eternal Child: How Evolution Has Made Children of Us All*. London: Ebury Press, 2003.

Brown, Gillian. *The Consent of the Governed: The Lockean Legacy in Early American Culture*. Cambridge, MA: Harvard University Press, 2001.

Brown, Guy. *The Living New: The New Sciences of Death, Ageing, and Immortality*. Basingstoke, UK: Macmillan, 2008.

Brownlee, Kevin. "Dante and the Classical Poets." In *The Cambridge Companion to Dante*, 2nd ed., edited by Rachel Jacoff, 141–60. Cambridge: Cambridge University Press, 2007.

Buck-Morss, Susan. *Hegel, Haiti, and Universal History*. Pittsburgh, PA: Pittsburgh University Press, 2009.

Buhle, Mary Jo, *Feminism and Its Discontents: A Century of Struggle with Psychoanalysis*. Cambridge, MA: Harvard University Press, 2009.

Bunge, Marcia JoAnn, ed. *The Child in Christian Thought*. Grand Rapids, MI: Eerdmans, 2001.

Bunge, Marcia JoAnn, Terence E. Fretheim, and Beverly Roberts Gaventa, eds. *The Child in the Bible*. Grand Rapids, MI: Eerdmans, 2008.

Burke, Patrick. *Reinterpreting Rahner: A Critical Study of His Major Themes*. New York: Fordham University Press, 2002.

Burke, Peter. *Vico*. Oxford: Oxford University Press, 1985.

Buxton, Richard, ed. *From Myth to Reason? Studies in the Development of Greek Thought*. Oxford: Oxford University Press, 2001.

———. *Imaginary Greece: The Contexts of Mythology*. Cambridge: Cambridge University Press, 1994.

———. *Myths and Tragedies in Their Ancient Greek Contexts*. Oxford: Oxford University Press, 2013.

Caldwell, Richard S. *The Origins of the Gods: A Psychoanalytic Study of Greek Theogonic Myth*. Oxford: Oxford University Press, 1989.

Calvino, Italo. *Mr. Palomar*. Translated by William Weaver. New York: Harcourt Brace Jovanovich, 1985.

———. *The Uses of Literature*. Translated by Patrick Creagh. New York: Harcourt Brace Jovanovich, 1986.

Caputo, John D., and Linda Martin Alcoff, eds. *St. Paul among the Philosophers*. Bloomington: Indiana University Press, 2009.

Cardwell, Donald. *Wheels, Clocks, and Rockets*. New York: W. W. Norton, 2001. Originally published as *The Norton History of Technology* (1994).

Casey, Edward S. *The Fate of Place: A Philosophical History*. Berkeley: University of California Press, 1997.

Cavell, Stanley. "The Avoidance of Love: A Reading of *King Lear*." In *Must We Mean What We Say?*, rev. ed., 267–356. Cambridge: Cambridge University Press, 2002.

———. *Disowning Knowledge in Seven Plays of Shakespeare*. Rev. ed. Cambridge: Cambridge University Press, 2003.

———. "Finding as Founding: Taking Steps in Emerson's 'Experience.'" In *Emerson's Transcendental Etudes*, edited by David Justin Hodge, 110–40. Palo Alto, CA: Stanford University Press, 2003.

Caws, Mary-Anne. *Yves Bonnefoy*. Boston: Twayne, 1984.

Champlin, Jeffrey. "Born Again: Arendt's 'Natality' as Figure and Concept." *The Germanic Review: Literature, Culture, and Theory* 88, no. 2 (2013): 150–64.

Chinn, Sarah E. *Inventing Modern Adolescence: The Children of Immigrants in Turn of the Century America*. New Brunswick, NJ: Rutgers University Press, 2009.

Cicero. *De Senectute, De Amicitia, De Divinatione*. Translated by William Falconer. Loeb Classical Library (Book 154). Cambridge, MA: Harvard University Press, 1923.

Cole, Jennifer, and Deborah Lynn Durham. *Generations and Globalization:*

Youth, Age, and Family in the New World Economy. Bloomington: Indiana University Press, 2007.

Collingwood, R. G. *The Idea of History* (1946). Edited by Jan van der Dussen. Oxford: Oxford University Press, 1994.

Collins, Ardis, ed. *Hegel on the Modern World*. Albany: State University of New York Press, 1995.

Collobert, Catherine, Pierre Destrée, and Francisco J. Gonzalez, eds. *Plato's Myths: Studies in the Use and Study of Platonic Myth*. Leiden, Netherlands: Brill, 2012.

Cook, John Granger. *The Interpretation of the Old Testament in Greco-Roman Paganism*. Peabody, MA: Hendrickson, 2002.

Comay, Rebecca. *Memory in Hegel and Heidegger*. Palo Alto, CA: Stanford University Press, 2011.

Connidis, Ingrid Arnet. *Family Ties and Aging*. 2nd ed. Thousand Oaks, CA: Pine Forge Press (Sage), 2010.

Conrad, Joseph. *Lord Jim: A Tale* (1900). New York: Penguin Classics, 2000.

Cooper, Stephen. *Philip Larkin: Subversive Writer*. Brighton, UK: Sussex Academic Press, 2004.

Crow, Christine M. *Paul Valéry and the Poetry of Voice*. Cambridge: Cambridge University Press, 1982.

d'Alessio, Patrizia, ed. *La sinuosité du vivant*. Paris: Hermann Éditeurs, 2011.

Danesi, Marcel. *Cool: The Signs and Meanings of Adolescence*. Toronto: University of Toronto Press, 1994.

———. *Forever Young: The Teen-aging of Modern Culture*. Toronto: University of Toronto Press, 2003.

Dante. *The Divine Comedy*. 3 vols.: *Inferno, Purgatorio, Paradiso* (ca. 1308–1321). Translated by Robert M. Durling and Ronald L. Martinez. Oxford: Oxford University Press, 1996, 2003, 2010.

Daston, Lorraine, and Elizabeth Lunbeck, eds. *Histories of Scientific Observation*. Chicago: University of Chicago Press, 2011.

Dean, Dennis R. *James Hutton and the History of Geology*. Ithaca, NY: Cornell University Press, 1992.

Deligiorgi, Katerina. *Kant and the Culture of Enlightenment*. Albany: State University of New York Press, 2005.

Denevan, William, and Kent Mathewson, eds. *Carl Sauer on Culture and Landscape: Readings and Commentaries*. Baton Rouge: Louisiana State University Press, 2009.

Derrida, Jacques. *The Beast and the Sovereign*, vol. 2. Edited by Michel Lisse, Marie-Louise Mallet, and Ginette Michaud. Translated by Geoffrey Bennington. Chicago: University of Chicago Press, 2011.

Derry, T. K., and Trevor I. Williams. *A Short History of Technology from the Earliest Times to AD 1900*. Oxford: Oxford University Press, 1961.

Descartes, René. *Discourse on Method and Meditations on First Philosophy* (1637). Translated by D. A. Cress. Indianapolis: Hackett, 1995.

Destrée, Pierre, and Fritz Gregor-Herrmann, eds. *Plato and the Poets.* Leiden, Netherlands: Brill, 2011.

Dewar, Elaine. *The Second Tree: Of Clones, Chimeras, and Quests for Immortality.* New York: Carroll and Graf, 2004.

Diamond, Jared. *Collapse: How Societies Choose to Fail or Succeed.* New York: Penguin, 2005.

Dimock, Wai Chee. *Through Other Continents: American Literature across Deep Time.* Princeton, NJ: Princeton University Press, 2006.

Dodgshon, Robert A. *Society in Time and Space: A Geographical Perspective on Change.* Cambridge: Cambridge University Press, 1998.

Droge, Arthur. *Homer or Moses? Early Christian Interpretations of the History of Culture.* Tübingen: Mohr, 1989.

Dulles, Avery Cardinal. *A History of Apologetics.* Eugene, OR: Wipf and Stock, 1999.

Dunn, James D. G., ed. *The Cambridge Companion to Saint Paul.* Cambridge: Cambridge University Press, 2003.

———. *The Theology of Paul the Apostle.* Grand Rapids, MI: Eerdmans, 1998.

Durant, Geoffrey. *Wordsworth and the Great System: A Study of Wordsworth's Poetic Universe.* Cambridge: Cambridge University Press, 1970.

Durst, Margarete. "Birth and Natality in Hannah Arendt." *Analecta Husserliana* 79 (2004): 777–97.

Eagleton, Terry. *Sweet Violence: The Idea of the Tragic.* Malden, MA: Blackwell, 2003.

Edelstein, Dan. "Do We Want a Revolution without a Revolution? Reflections on Political Authority." *French Historical Studies* 35, no. 2 (2012): 269–89.

Edmunds, Lowell. *Oedipus.* Abingdon, UK: Routledge, 2006.

Eldridge, Richard. "What Can Tragedy Matter for Us?" In *The Persistence of Romanticism*, 145–64. Cambridge: Cambridge University Press, 2001.

Eliot, T. S. *The Four Quartets* (1943). New York: Mariner Books, 1968.

Elton, William. *King Lear and the Gods.* Lexington: University Press of Kentucky, 1966.

Emerson, Ralph Waldo. *Emerson's Antislavery Writings.* Edited by Len Gougeon and Joel Myerson. New Haven, CT: Yale University Press, 1995.

———. "Experience" (1844). In *The Essential Writings of Ralph Waldo Emerson*, edited by Brooke Atkinson. New York: Modern Library, 2009.

———. *The Spiritual Emerson: Essential Writings.* Edited by David M. Robinson. Boston: Beacon Press, 2003.

Fenollosa, Ernest, and Ezra Pound. *The Chinese Written Character as a Medium for Poetry: A Critical Edition.* Edited by Haun Saussy, Jonathan Stalling, and Lucas Klein. New York: Fordham University Press, 2008.

Ferguson, Everett. *Baptism in the Early Church: History, Theology, and Liturgy in the First Five Centuries*. Grand Rapids, MI: Eerdmans, 2009.

Ferri, Sabrina. "Lazzaro Spallanzani's Hybrid Ruins: A Scientist at Serapis and Troy." *Studies in Eighteenth-Century Culture* 43 (2014): 169–96.

———. *The Past in Ruins: History and Nature in Eighteenth- and Early Nineteenth-Century Italy*. Forthcoming.

———. "Time in Ruins: Melancholy and Modernity in the Pre-Romantic Natural Picturesque." *Italian Studies* (forthcoming, 2014).

Feyerabend, Paul Karl. *Against Method*. 3rd ed. New York: Verso, 1993.

Finocchiaro, Maurice. *The Galileo Affair: A Documentary History*. Berkeley: University of California Press, 1989.

———. *Retrying Galileo, 1633–1992*. Berkeley: University of California Press, 2005.

———. *The Routledge Companion to Galileo's Dialogue*. Abingdon, UK: Routledge, 2013.

Fitzgerald, Brian. "Animals, Evolution, Language: Aspects of Whitehead in Italo Calvino's Palomar." *Spunti e ricerche: Rivista d'Italianistica* 10 (1994): 43–61.

Fliegelman, Jay. *Declaring Independence: Jefferson, Natural Language, and the Culture of Performance*. Palo Alto, CA: Stanford University Press, 1993.

Foran, John, ed. *The Future of Revolutions: Rethinking Radical Change in the Age of Globalization*. New York: Zed Books, 2003.

———, ed. *Theorizing Revolutions*. London: Routledge, 1997.

Foran, John, David Lane, and Andreja Zivkovic, eds. *Revolution in the Making of the Modern World: Social Identities, Globalization, and Modernity*. Abingdon, UK: Routledge, 2008.

Forsyth, Phyllis Young. *Atlantis: The Making of Myth*. Montreal: McGill-Queen's University Press, 1980.

Foster, Karen. *Generation, Discourse, and Social Change*. Abingdon, UK: Routledge, 2013.

Foucault, Michel. *Introduction to Kant's Anthropology*. Edited by Roberto Nigro. Translated by Roberto Nigro and Kate Briggs. Los Angeles: Semiotext(e), 2008.

———. "What Is Enlightenment?" In *The Foucault Reader*, edited by Paul Rabinow, 32–50. New York: Pantheon, 1984.

Fowler, W. Warde. *The Religious Experience of the Roman People*. London: Macmillan, 1911.

Franchi, Stefano. "Palomar, the Triviality of Modernity, and the Doctrine of the Void." *New Literary History* 28, no. 4 (1997): 757–78.

Frank, Joseph. *Responses to Modernity: Essays in the Politics of Culture*. New York: Fordham University Press, 2012.

Fraschetti, Augusto. *The Foundation of Rome*. Edinburgh: Edinburgh University Press, 2005.

Freeman, Charles. *Egypt, Greece, and Rome: Civilizations of the Ancient Mediterranean*. 2nd ed. Oxford: Oxford University Press, 1996.

Freud, Sigmund. "On the Universal Tendency to Debasement in the Sphere of Love" (1912). In *The Freud Reader*, edited by Peter Gay, 394–400. New York: W. W. Norton, 1989.

Friedrich, Hugo. *Montaigne* (1949). Edited by Philippe Desan. Translated by Dawn Eng. Berkeley: University of California Press, 1991.

Frierson, Patrick R. *Freedom and Anthropology in Kant's Moral Philosophy*. Cambridge: Cambridge University Press, 2003.

Fry, Paul H. *Wordsworth and the Poetry of What We Are*. New Haven, CT: Yale University Press, 2008.

Fukuyama, Francis. *Our Posthuman Future: Consequences of the Biotechnology Revolution*. New York: Picador, 2002.

Gallagher, Winifred. *New: Understanding Our Need for Novelty and Change*. New York: Penguin, 2011.

Gardner, Howard. "Albert Einstein: The Perennial Child." In *Creative Minds: An Anatomy of Creativity Seen through the Lives of Freud, Einstein, Picasso, Stravinsky, Eliot, Graham, and Gandhi*, 87–136. New York: Basic Books, 1993.

Garnsey, Peter, and Richard Saller. *The Roman Empire: Economy, Society, and Culture*. Berkeley: University of California Press, 1987.

Gauchet, Marcel. *The Disenchantment of the World: A Political History of Religion*. Translated by Oscar Burge. Princeton, NJ: Princeton University Press, 1997.

Gaustad, Edwin S. *Liberty of Conscience: Roger Williams in America*. Valley Forge, PA: Judson Press, 1999.

Gee, Henry. *In Search of Deep Time: Beyond the Fossil Record to a New History of Life*. New York: Free Press, 1999.

Gibbon, Edward. *The History of the Decline and Fall of the Roman Empire* (1776–1788). Edited and abridged by David Womersley. New York: Penguin, 2001.

Gifford, Paul, and Brian Stimpson, eds. *Reading Paul Valéry: Universe in Mind*. Cambridge: Cambridge University Press, 1998.

Gill, Stephen, ed. *The Cambridge Companion to Wordsworth*. Cambridge: Cambridge University Press, 2003.

Girard, René. "Collective Violence and Sacrifice in Shakespeare's Julius Caesar." *Salmagundi* 88–89 (Fall 1990–Winter 1991): 399–419.

Golden, Mark. *Children and Childhood in Classical Athens*. Baltimore, MD: Johns Hopkins University Press, 1990.

Golding, William. *The Lord of the Flies*. New York: Penguin, 2011.

Golinski, Jan. *Making Natural Knowledge: Constructivism and the History of Science*. Chicago: University of Chicago Press, 1998.

Gómez, Juan Carlos. *Apes, Monkey, Children, and the Growth of Mind*. Cambridge, MA: Harvard University Press, 2004.

Göncü, Artin, and Suzanne Gaskin, eds. *Play and Development: Evolutionary, Sociocultural, and Functional Perspectives*. Hillsdale, NJ: Lawrence Erlbaum, 2007.

Goppelt, Leonhardt. *Typos: The Typological Interpretation of the Old Testament in the New* (1939). Grand Rapids, MI: Eerdmans, 1982.

Gould, Stephen Jay. *Ever Since Darwin: Reflections in Natural History*. New York: W. W. Norton, 1992.

————. *Ontogeny and Phylogeny*. Cambridge, MA: Harvard University Press, 1977.

————. *Time's Arrow, Time's Cycle: Myth and Metaphor in the Discovery of Geological Time*. Cambridge, MA: Harvard University Press, 1987.

Gower, Barry. *Scientific Method: A Historical and Philosophical Introduction*. Abingdon, UK: Routledge, 1997.

Grandazzi, Alexandre. *The Foundation of Rome: Myth and History*. Translated by Jane Marie Todd. Ithaca, NY: Cornell University Press, 1997.

Greene, Robert W. *Searching for Presence: Yves Bonnefoy's Writings on Art*. Amsterdam: Rodopi, 2004.

Gregory, Derek, Ron Martin, and Graham Smith, eds. *Human Geography: Society, Space, and Social Science*. Minneapolis: University of Minnesota Press, 1994.

Greidanus, Sydney. *Preaching Christ from the Old Testament: A Contemporary Hermeneutical Method*. Grand Rapids, MI: Eerdmans, 1999.

Grimal, Nicolas. *A History of Ancient Egypt*. Oxford: Wiley-Blackwell, 1992.

Grundtvig, Birgitte, Martin McLaughlin, and Lene Waage Petersen, eds. *Image, Eye, and Art in Calvino*. London: Legenda, 2007.

Guelke, Leonard. *Historical Understanding in Geography: An Idealist Approach*. Cambridge: Cambridge University Press, 1982.

Guerlac, Suzanne. *Thinking in Time: An Introduction to Henri Bergson*. Ithaca, NY: Cornell University Press, 2006.

Hafner, Katie, and Matthew Lyon. *Where Wizards Stay Up Late: The Origins of the Internet*. New York: Simon and Schuster, 1998.

Hagestad, Gunhild O., and Peter Uhlenberg. "The Social Separation of Old and Young: A Root of Ageism." *Journal of Social Issues* 61, no. 2 (2005): 343–60.

Hall, Granville Stanley. *Adolescence: Its Psychology and Its Relation to Physiology, Anthropology, Sex, Crime, Religion, and Education*. 2 vols. New York: D. Appleton, 1904.

Hall, Stephen. *Merchants of Immortality: Chasing the Dream of Human Life.* New York: Houghton Mifflin, 2003.

Hall, Timothy L. *Separating Church and State: Roger Williams and Religious Liberty.* Bloomington: Indiana University Press, 1998.

Harrison, Robert Pogue. "America: The Struggle to Be Reborn." *New York Review of Books,* October 25, 2012, 64–68.

———. "The Book from Which Our Literature Springs." *New York Review of Books,* February 9, 2012, 40–45.

———. *The Dominion of the Dead.* Chicago: University of Chicago Press, 2003.

———. "Emerson: The Good Hours." *New York Review of Books,* October 28, 2010, 25–28.

———. *Forests: The Shadow of Civilization.* Chicago: University of Chicago Press, 1992.

———. "The Magic of Leopardi." *New York Review of Books,* February 10, 2011, 34–38.

———. "Toward a Philosophy of Nature." In *Uncommon Ground: Rethinking the Human Place in Nature,* edited by William Cronon, 447–60. New York: W. W. Norton, 1996.

Hartman, Geoffrey H. *The Unremarkable Wordsworth.* Minneapolis: University of Minnesota Press, 1987.

Hassan, Salem Kadhem. *Philip Larkin and His Contemporaries: An Air of Authenticity.* Basingstoke, UK: Macmillan, 1988.

Headrick, Daniel. *Technology: A World History.* Oxford: Oxford University Press, 2009.

Hegel, G. W. F. *Introduction to the Philosophy of History* (1840). Translated by Leo Rauch. Indianapolis, IN: Hackett, 1988.

———. *Phenomenology of Spirit* (1807). Translated by A. V. Miller with an analysis by J. N. Findlay. Oxford: Oxford University Press, 1977.

Heidegger, Martin. "The Age of the World Picture" (1938). In *The Question Concerning Technology and Other Essays.* Translated by William Lovitt, 115–54. New York: Harper and Row, 1977.

———. *Being and Time* (1927). Translated by Joan Staumbaugh. Albany: State University Press of New York, 1996.

———. *The Fundamental Concepts of Metaphysics: World, Finitude, Solitude.* Translated by William McNeil and Nicholas Walker. Indianapolis: Indiana University Press, 1995.

———. *An Introduction to Metaphysics* (1935). Translated by Ralph Manheim. New Haven, CT: Yale University Press, 1959.

Hellholm, David, Tor Vegge, Oyvind Norderval, and Christer Hellholm, eds. *Ablution, Initiation, and Baptism: Late Antiquity, Early Judaism, and Early Christianity.* 3 vols. Berlin: Walter de Gruyter, 2011.

Higgins, Kathleen Marie. "Rebaptizing Our Evil: On the Revaluation of All Values." In *A Companion to Nietzsche*, edited by Keith Ansell-Pearson, 404–18. Oxford: Wiley-Blackwell, 2011.

Hillgarth, J. N., ed. *Christianity and Paganism, 350–750: The Conversion of Western Europe*. Rev. ed. Philadelphia: University of Pennsylvania Press, 1986.

Hinchman, Lewis P. *Hegel's Critique of the Enlightenment*. Gainesville: University Presses of Florida, 1984.

Hochberg, Ze'ev. *Evo-Devo of Child Growth: A Treatise on Child Growth and Human Evolution*. New York: Wiley-Blackwell, 2012.

Holte, R. "Logos Spermatikos: Christianity and Ancient Philosophy According to Saint Justin's Apologies." *Studia Theologica* 12, no. 1 (1958): 109–68.

Hopkins, Gerard Manley. *Gerald Manley Hopkins: The Major Works*. Edited by Catherine Phillips. Oxford: Oxford University Press, 2002.

Horn, Cornelia B., and John W. Martens, eds. *Let the Little Children Come to Me: Childhood and Children in Early Christianity*. Washington, DC: Catholic University of America Press, 2009.

Huttenlocher, Peter R. *Neural Plasticity: The Effects of Environment on the Development of the Cerebral Cortex*. Cambridge, MA: Harvard University Press, 2002.

Huxley, Aldous. *After Many a Summer Dies the Swan* (1939). Chicago: Ivan R. Dee, 1993.

Irwin, Terence. *Plato's Ethics*. Oxford: Oxford University Press, 1995.

Ivanov, Sergey. *Holy Fools in Byzantium and Beyond*. Translated by Simon Franklin. Oxford: Oxford University Press, 2006.

Jacoff, Rachel, and Jeffrey Schnapp, eds. *The Poetry of Allusion: Virgil and Ovid in Dante's Commedia*. Palo Alto, CA: Stanford University Press, 1991.

Jaeger, Werner. *Paideia: The Ideals of Greek Culture*. Translated by Gilbert Highet. Oxford: Oxford University Press, 1986.

Jensen, Anthony K., and Helmut Heit, eds. *Nietzsche as Scholar of Antiquity*. London: Bloomsbury, 2014.

Jones, Colin, and Dror Wahrman, eds. *The Age of Cultural Revolutions: Britain and France, 1750–1820*. Berkeley: University of California Press, 2002.

Kant, Immanuel. *Perpetual Peace and Other Essays*. Translated by Ted Humphries. Indianapolis, IN: Hackett, 1983.

Kaplan, Louise J. *Adolescence: The Farewell to Childhood*. New York: Simon and Schuster, 1995.

Kelly, Michael G. *Strands of Utopia: Spaces of Poetic Work in Twentieth-Century France*. London: Legenda, 2008.

Kett, Joseph F. *Rites of Passage: Adolescence in America, 1790 to the Present*. New York: Basic Books, 1977.

Kilby, Karen. *Karl Rahner: Theological Philosophy*. London: Routledge, 2004.

Kirkham, Victoria, and Armando Maggi, eds. *Petrarch: A Critical Guide to the Complete Works.* Chicago: University of Chicago Press, 2009.

Kirkpatrick, Robin, ed. *English and Italian Literature from Dante to Shakespeare.* London: Longman, 1995.

Kittler, Friedrich. *Discourse Networks 1800/1900.* Translated by Michael Metteer and Chris Cullens. Palo Alto, CA: Stanford University Press, 1990.

———. *Gramophone, Film, Typewriter.* Translated by Geoffrey Winthrop-Young and Michael Wutz. Palo Alto, CA: Stanford University Press, 1999.

———. *Literature, Media, and Information Systems.* Edited by John Johnston. Abingdon, UK: Routledge, 2012.

———. *Optical Media.* Translated by Anthony Enns. Cambridge, UK: Polity Press, 2009.

Kitto, H. D. F. *Greek Tragedy.* Abingdon, UK: Routledge Classics, 2011.

Klatch, Rebecca E. *A Generation Divided: The New Left, the New Right, and the 1960s.* Berkeley: University of California Press, 1999.

Kleijwegt, Marc. *Ancient Youth: The Ambiguity of Youth and the Absence of Adolescence in Greco-Roman Society.* Amsterdam: J. C. Gieben, 1991.

Konner, Melvin. *The Evolution of Childhood: Relationships, Emotion, Mind.* Cambridge, MA: Harvard University Press, 2010.

Koselleck, Reinhart. "Historical Criteria of the Modern Concept of Revolution." In *Futures Past: On the Semantics of Historical Time.* Translated by Keith Tribe, 43–57. Rev. ed. New York: Columbia University Press, 2013.

Kramnick, Jonathan. "Against Literary Darwinism." *Critical Inquiry* 37, no. 2 (Winter 2011): 315–47.

Kranzberg, Melvin, and Carroll W. Pursell, eds. *Technology in Western Civilization.* 2 vols. Oxford: Oxford University Press, 1967.

Kraut, Richard. *Socrates and the State.* Princeton, NJ: Princeton University Press, 1987.

Krell, David Farrell. *Daimon Life: Heidegger and Life-Philosophy.* Bloomington: Indiana University Press, 1992.

———. *Derrida and Our Animal Others.* Bloomington: Indiana University Press, 2013.

Kuhn, Thomas. *The Structure of Scientific Revolutions: 50th Anniversary Edition.* Chicago: University of Chicago Press, 2012.

Kull, Kalevi. "Jakob von Uexküll: An Introduction." *Semiotica* 134 (2001): 1–59.

Laes, Christian. *Children in the Roman Empire: Outsiders Within.* Cambridge: Cambridge University Press, 2011.

Lampe, Peter. *From Paul to Valentinus: Christians at Rome in the First Two Centuries.* Translated by Michael Steinhauser. London: Continuum, 2003.

Landy, Joshua, and Michael Saler, eds. *The Re-Enchantment of the World: Secular Magic in the Rational Age.* Palo Alto, CA: Stanford University Press, 2009.

Larkin, Philip. *Collected Poems*. Edited by Anthony Thwaite. New York: Farrar, Straus, and Giroux, 2004.

Lawlor, Leonard. *The Challenge of Bergsonism*. London: Continuum, 2004.

Lawrence, D. H. *Phoenix: The Posthumous Papers of D. H. Lawrence*. 2 vols. Edited by Edward McDonald (vol. 1), Warren Roberts and Harry T. Moore (vol. 2). London: Heinemann, 1936, 1958.

———. *Selected Poems*. Edited by Keith M. Sagar. New York: Penguin, 1986.

Lear, Jonathan. "Allegory and Myth in Plato's Republic." In *The Blackwell Guide to Plato's Republic*, edited by Gerasimos Santas, 25–43. Malden, MA: Blackwell, 2006.

Leiter, Brian. *The Routledge Guidebook to Nietzsche on Morality*. London: Routledge, 2002.

Leopardi, Giacomo. *Canti*. Translated by Jonathan Galassi. New York: Farrar, Straus, and Giroux, 2010.

———. *Zibaldone*. Edited by Michael Caesar and Franco d'Intino. Translated by Kathleen Baldwin, Richard Dixon, David Gibbons, Ann Goldstein, Gerard Slowey, Martin Thom, and Pamela Williams. New York: Farrar, Straus, and Giroux, 2013.

Lewis, Martin K., and Karen E. Wigen. *The Myth of Continents: A Critique of Metageography*. Berkeley: University of California Press, 1997.

Lilla, Mark. *G. B. Vico: The Making of an Antimodern*. Cambridge, MA: Harvard University Press, 1994.

Louden, Robert B. *Kant's Human Being: Essays on His Theory of Human Nature*. Oxford: Oxford University Press, 2011.

———. *Kant's Impure Ethics: From Rational Beings to Human Beings*. Oxford: Oxford University Press, 2002.

Luft, Sandra Rudnick. *Vico's Uncanny Humanism: Reading the New Science between Modern and Postmodern*. Ithaca, NY: Cornell University Press, 2003.

Luther, Martin. *Commentary on Galatians*. Translated by Jay P. Green Sr. Lafayette, IN: Sovereign Grace Publishers, 2001.

———. *Martin Luther's Basic Theological Writings*. 3rd ed. Edited by Timothy F. Lull and William R. Russell. Minneapolis, MN: Fortress Press, 2012.

Machamer, Peter, ed. *The Cambridge Companion to Galileo*. Cambridge: Cambridge University Press, 1998.

Machiavelli, Niccolò. *Discourses on Livy* (1531). Translated by Leslie J. Walker and revised by Brian J. Richardson. New York: Penguin Classics, 2003.

———. *The Prince* (1532). Translated by Tim Parks. New York: Penguin, 2009.

MacMahon, Darrin. *Divine Fury: A History of Genius*. New York: Basic Books, 2013.

MacMullen, Ramsay. *Christianity and Paganism in the Fourth to Eighth Centuries.* New Haven, CT: Yale University Press, 1997.

MacMullen, Ramsay, and Eugene Lane, eds. *Paganism and Christianity, 100–425 CE: A Sourcebook.* Minneapolis, MN: Fortress Press, 1992.

Maier, Pauline. *American Scripture: Making the Declaration of Independence.* New York: Knopf, 1997.

Malpas, Jeff. *Heidegger and the Thinking of Place: Explorations in the Topology of Being.* Cambridge, MA: MIT Press, 2012.

———. *Heidegger's Topology: Being, Place, World.* Cambridge, MA: MIT Press, 2006.

Mannheim, Karl. "The Problem of Generations." In *Essays on the Sociology of Knowledge* (1936). In *Collected Works of Karl Mannheim,* 5:276–320. Abingdon, UK: Routledge, 2000.

Marmion, Declan, and Mary E. Hines, eds. *The Cambridge Companion to Karl Rahner.* Cambridge: Cambridge University Press, 2005.

Mazzotta, Giuseppe. *The New Map of the World: The Poetic Philosophy of Giambattista Vico.* Princeton, NJ: Princeton University Press, 1999.

———. *The Worlds of Petrarch.* Durham, NC: Duke University Press, 1999.

McClellan, James E., III, and Harold Dorn. *Science and Technology in World History: An Introduction.* 2nd ed. Baltimore, MD: Johns Hopkins University Press, 2006.

McKinney, Michael L., ed. *Heterochrony in Evolution: A Multidisciplinary Approach.* New York: Plenum Press, 1988.

McKinney, Michael L., and Ken McNamara. *Heterochrony: The Evolution of Ontogeny.* New York: Plenum Press, 1991.

McNamara, Ken, ed. *Evolutionary Change and Heterochrony.* Chichester, UK: Wiley, 1995.

McNeil, Ian, ed. *An Encyclopedia of the History of Technology.* London: Routledge, 1990.

McNeil, Ian, and Lance Day, eds. *Biographical Dictionary of the History of Technology.* London: Routledge, 1996.

Mendelsohn, Daniel. *Gender and the City in Euripides's Political Plays.* Oxford: Oxford University Press, 2002.

Miller, Perry. *Roger Williams: His Contribution to the American Tradition.* Indianapolis, IN: Bobbs-Merrill, 1953.

Minois, Georges. *History of Old Age: From Antiquity to Renaissance.* Translated by Sarah Hanburg Tenison. Chicago: University of Chicago Press, 1987.

Mitchell, Andrew. *The Fourfold: Reading the Late Heidegger.* Evanston, IL: Northwestern University Press, 2014.

———. *Heidegger among the Sculptors: Body, Space, and the Art of Dwelling.* Palo Alto, CA: Stanford University Press, 2010.

Mitchell, Juliet. *Psychoanalysis and Feminism.* New York: Basic Books, 2000.

Montagu, Ashley. *Growing Young.* 2nd ed. Westport, CT: Greenwood, 1989.

Montague, Charles. *Disenchantment.* New York: Brentano's, 1922.

Montaigne, Michel de. *The Complete Essays* (1580). Translated by M. A. Screech. New York: Penguin Classics, 2003.

Montgomery, Robert E. *The Visionary D. H. Lawrence: Between Philosophy and Art.* Cambridge: Cambridge University Press, 1994.

Morrison, Donald R, ed. *The Cambridge Companion to Socrates.* Cambridge: Cambridge University Press, 2011.

Mosès, Stéphane. *The Angel of History: Rosenzweig, Benjamin, Scholem.* Translated by Barbara Harshav. Palo Alto, CA: Stanford University Press, 2009.

Most, Glenn. "From Logos to Mythos." In *From Myth to Reason? Studies in the Development of Greek Thought*, edited by Richard Buxton, 25–50. Oxford: Oxford University Press, 2001.

———. "Generating Genres: The Idea of the Tragic." In *Matrices of Genre*, edited by Mary Depew and Dirk Obbink, 15–35. Cambridge, MA: Harvard University Press, 2000.

———, ed. and trans. *Hesiod: Theogony, Works and Days, Testimonia.* Loeb Classical Library. Cambridge, MA: Harvard University Press, 2006.

Mumford, Lewis. *Technics and Civilization* (1934). Chicago: University of Chicago Press, 2010.

Nagy, Gregory. *Greek Mythology and Poetics.* Ithaca, NY: Cornell University Press, 1990.

Najemy, John. *Between Friends: Discourses of Power and Desire in the Machiavelli-Vettori Letters of 1513–1515.* Princeton, NJ: Princeton University Press, 1993.

———, ed. *The Cambridge Companion to Machiavelli.* Cambridge: Cambridge University Press, 2010.

Naughton, John. *The Poetics of Bonnefoy.* Chicago: University of Chicago Press, 1984.

Natov, Roni. *The Poetics of Childhood.* Abingdon, UK: Routledge, 2006.

Neffe, Jürgen. *Einstein: A Biography.* Translated by Shelley Frisch. New York: Farrar, Straus, and Giroux, 2007.

Nehamas, Alexander. *The Art of Living: Socratic Reflections from Plato to Foucault.* Berkeley: University of California Press, 1998.

———. *Virtues of Authenticity: Essays on Plato and Socrates.* Princeton, NJ: Princeton University Press, 1999.

Neils, Jenifer, and John Howard Oakley, eds. *Coming of Age in Ancient Greece: Images of Childhood from the Classical Past.* New Haven, CT: Yale University Press, 2003.

Neuhouser, Frederick. *Foundations of Hegel's Social Theory: Actualizing Freedom.* Cambridge, MA: Harvard University Press, 2000.

Nietzsche, Friedrich. *Basic Writings of Nietzsche*. Edited and translated by Walter Kaufmann. Rev. ed. New York: Random House, 2011.

———. *The Gay Science: With a Prelude in Rhymes and an Appendix of Songs*. Translated by Walter Kaufmann. New York: Vintage, 1974.

———. *The Portable Nietzsche*. Edited and translated by Walter Kaufmann. New York: Penguin, 1977.

Nightingale, Andrea. *Genres in Dialogue: Plato and the Construct of Philosophy*. Cambridge: Cambridge University Press, 1995.

———. "On Wandering and Wondering: "Theôria" in Greek Philosophy and Culture." *Arion* 9 (2001): 23–58.

———. *Spectacles of Truth in Classical Greece. Theoria in Its Cultural Context*. Cambridge: Cambridge University Press, 2004.

North, Michael. *Novelty: A History of the New*. Chicago: University of Chicago Press, 2013.

Nussbaum, Martha. "Humans and Other Animals: The Neo-Stoic View Revised." In *Upheavals of Thought: The Intelligence of Emotions,* 89–138. Cambridge: Cambridge University Press, 2001.

Oakes, Timothy S., and Patricia L. Price, eds. *The Cultural Geography Reader*. Abingdon, UK: Routledge, 2008.

O'Keefe, John. "Typology." In *A Dictionary of Jewish-Christian Relations*, edited by Edward Kessler and Neil Wenborn, 431. Cambridge: Cambridge University Press, 2005.

O'Keefe, John J., and R. R. Reno. *Sanctified Vision: An Introduction to Early Christian Interpretations of the Bible*. Baltimore, MD: Johns Hopkins University Press, 2005.

Owen, David. *Maturity and Modernity: Nietzsche, Weber, Foucault, and the Ambivalence of Reason*. Abingdon, UK: Routledge, 1994.

Pacey, Arnold. *The Maze of Ingenuity: Ideas and Idealism in the Development of Technology*. 2nd ed. Cambridge, MA: MIT Press, 1992.

———. *Technology in World Civilization: A Thousand-Year History*. Cambridge, MA: MIT Press, 1991.

Pacione, Michael, ed. *Historical Geography: Progress and Prospect*. London: Croom Helm, 1987.

Palmer, Richard. *Such Deliberate Disguises: The Art of Philip Larkin*. London: Continuum, 2008.

Pappas, Nickolas. *The Routledge Guidebook to Plato and the Republic*. Abingdon, UK: Routledge, 1995.

Parker, Sue Taylor, and Michael McKinney, eds. *Origins of Intelligence: The Evolution of Cognitive Development in Monkeys, Apes, and Humans*. Baltimore, MD: Johns Hopkins University Press, 1999.

Peace, Richard. *Conversion in the New Testament: Paul and the Twelve*. Grand Rapids, MI: Eerdmans, 1999.

Pelikan, Jaroslav. *The Christian Tradition*. Vol. 1, *The Emergence of the Catholic Tradition*. Chicago: University of Chicago Press, 1971.

Perloff, Marjorie. "How to Read a Poem: W. B. Yeats's 'After Long Silence.'" http://marjorieperloff.com/stein-duchamp-picasso/yeats-silence/

Peterson, Sandra. *Socrates and Philosophy in the Dialogues of Plato*. Cambridge: Cambridge University Press, 2011.

Picone, Michelangelo. "Dante and the Classics." In *Dante: Contemporary Perspectives*, edited by Amilcare Iannucci, 51–73. Toronto: University of Toronto Press, 1997.

Plato. *The Dialogues of Plato translated into English with Analyses and Introductions by Benjamin Jowett, MA in Five Volumes*. 3rd ed., rev. and corrected. Oxford: Oxford University Press, 1892.

———. *Selected Myths*. Edited by Catalin Partenie. Translated by Robin Waterfield, C. C. W. Taylor, and David Gallop. Oxford: Oxford University Press, 2004.

Plotz, Judith. *Romanticism and the Vocation of Childhood*. Basingstoke, UK: Palgrave Macmillan, 2001.

Pocock, J. G. A. *Barbarism and Religion*. Vol. 3, *The First Decline and Fall*. Cambridge: Cambridge University Press, 2003.

Poe, Edgar Allan. *The Complete Poetry of Edgar Allan Poe*. New York: Penguin, 2008.

Poe, Marshall T. *A History of Communications: Media and Society from the Evolution of Speech to the Internet*. Cambridge: Cambridge University Press, 2011.

Porter, James I. *Nietzsche and the Philology of the Future*. Palo Alto, CA: Stanford University Press, 2000.

Porter, Stanley E., and Anthony R. Cross, eds. *Dimensions of Baptism: Biblical and Theological Studies*. New York: Sheffield Academic Press, 2002.

Pound, Ezra. *The Cantos of Ezra Pound* (1934). New York: New Directions, 1996.

———. *Early Poems*. Edited by Thomas Crofts. Mineola, NY: Dover, 1996.

Prete, Antonio. *Finitudine e infinito: Su Leopardi*. Milan: Feltrinelli, 1998.

———. *Il pensiero poetante*. Rev. ed. Milan: Feltrinelli, 2006.

Rahner, Karl. *Foundations of Christian Faith: An Introduction to the Idea of Christianity*. New York: Crossroad, 1978.

Reeve, C. D. C. "Cephalus, Odysseus, and the Importance of Experience." In *Blindness and Reorientation: Problems in Plato's Republic*, 35–52. Oxford: Oxford University Press, 2013.

———. *Socrates in the Apology: An Essay on Plato's Apology of Socrates*. Indianapolis, IN: Hackett, 1989.

Reginster, Bernard. *The Affirmation of Life: Nietzsche on Overcoming Nihilism*. Cambridge, MA: Harvard University Press, 2006.

Rehm, Rush. *Greek Tragic Theater*. Abingdon, UK: Routledge, 1992.

———. *The Play of Space: Spatial Transformation in Greek Tragedy*. Princeton, NJ: Princeton University Press, 2002.

Renger, Almut-Barbara. *Oedipus and the Sphinx: The Threshold Myth from Socrates through Freud to Cocteau*. Chicago: University of Chicago Press, 2013.

Rennie, Nicholas. *Speculating on the Moment: The Poetics of Time and Recurrence in Goethe, Leopardi, and Nietzsche*. Göttingen, Germany: Wallstein-Verlag, 2005.

Rey, Alain. *Révolution: Histoire d'un mot*. Paris: Gallimard, 1989.

Richards, Robert J. *Darwin and the Emergence of Evolutionary Theories of Mind and Behavior*. Chicago: University of Chicago Press, 1987.

———. *The Meaning of Evolution: The Morphological Construction and Ideological Reconstruction of Darwin's Theory*. Chicago: University of Chicago Press, 1992.

———. *The Tragic Sense of Life: Ernst Haeckel and the Struggle over Evolutionary Thought*. Chicago: University of Chicago Press, 2008.

Rohman, Carrie. "On Singularity and the Symbolic: The Threshold of the Human in Calvino's *Mr. Palomar*," *Criticism* 51, no. 1 (Winter 2009): 63–78.

Rokem, Freddie. "One Voice and Many Legs: Oedipus and the Riddle of the Sphinx." In *Untying the Knot: On Riddles and Other Enigmatic Modes*, edited by Galit Hasan-Rokem and David Shulman, 255–70. Oxford: Oxford University Press, 1996.

Rollison, Rob. "Going, Going, by Philip Larkin." *The Poetry Room* website, May 29, 2012. http://thepoetryroom.com/2012/05/29/going-going-by-philip-larkin/

Rosen, Stanley. "Cephalus and Polemarchus." In *Plato's Republic: A Study*, 19–37. New Haven, CT: Yale University Press, 2005.

Rosier, Isaac. "The Body, Eros, and the Limits of Objectivity in Calvino's Palomar." *Italian Quarterly* 35 (1998): 23–33.

Rossen, Janice. *Philip Larkin: His Life's Work*. Iowa City: University of Iowa Press, 1989.

Rowland, Anna Wierda. *Romanticism and Childhood: The Infantilization of British Literary Culture*. Cambridge: Cambridge University Press, 2012.

Rubenstein, Mary-Jane. *Strange Wonder: The Closure of Metaphysics and the Opening of Awe*. New York: Columbia University Press, 2008.

Rudwick, M. J. S. *Bursting the Limits of Time: The Reconstruction of Geohistory in the Age of Revolution*. Chicago: University of Chicago Press, 2005.

Rutherford, R. B. *Greek Tragic Style: Form, Language, and Interpretation*. Cambridge: Cambridge University Press, 2012.

Ryan, Johnny. *A History of the Internet and the Digital Future*. London: Reaktion, 2010.

Sagar, Keith M. *The Art of D. H. Lawrence*. Cambridge: Cambridge University Press, 1966.

———. *D. H. Lawrence: Life into Art*. New York: Viking, 1985.

Saint-Exupéry, Antoine de. "The Tool." In *Wind, Sand, and Stars* (1939). Translated by Lewis Galantière, 41–47. New York: Penguin, 1966.

Salaquarda, Jörg. "Nietzsche and the Judaeo-Christian Tradition." In *The Cambridge Companion to Nietzsche*, edited by Bernd Magnus and Kathleen Marie Higgins, 90–118. Cambridge: Cambridge University Press, 1996.

Salwak, Dale, ed. *Philip Larkin: The Man and His Work*. London: Macmillan, 1989.

Schell, Jonathan. "A Politics of Natality." *Social Research* 69, no. 2 (2002): 461–71.

Schlesinger, Arthur Meier. *The Cycles of American History*. New York: Houghton Mifflin, 1999.

Schlesinger, Arthur M., Sr. *Paths to the Present*. New York: Macmillan, 1949.

Schmidt, Dennis J. *On Germans and Other Greeks: Tragedy and Ethical Life*. Bloomington: Indiana University Press, 2001.

Scullard, H. H. *A History of the Roman World, 753 to 146 BC* (1935). Abingdon, UK: Routledge Classics, 2013.

Severino, Emanuele. *Il nulla e la poesia: Alla fine dell'età della tecnica: Leopardi*. Milan: Rizzoli, 1990.

Shakespeare, William. *The Complete Pelican Shakespeare*. 2nd rev. ed. Edited by Stephen Orgel and A. R. Braunmuller. New York: Penguin Classics, 2002.

———. *The Complete Works of Shakespeare*. 7th ed. Edited by David Bevington. New York: Longman, 2013.

Shaw, Ian. *The Oxford History of Ancient Egypt*. Oxford: Oxford University Press, 2000.

Shea, William R., and Mariano Artigas. *Galileo in Rome: The Rise and Fall of a Troublesome Genius*. Oxford: Oxford University Press, 2003.

Sheehan, Thomas. *Karl Rahner: The Philosophical Foundations*. Athens: Ohio University Press, 1987.

Smith, Peter K. "Evolutionary Foundations and Functions of Play: An Overview." In *Play and Development: Evolutionary, Sociocultural, and Functional Perspectives*, edited by Artin Göncü and Suzanne Gaskin, 21–50. Hillsdale, NJ: Lawrence Eribaum, 2007.

Sobolev, Dennis. *The Split World of Gerard Manley Hopkins: An Essay in Semiotic Phenomenology*. Washington, DC: Catholic University of America Press, 2011.

Sophocles. *The Three Theban Plays: Antigone, Oedipus the King, Oedipus at Colonus*. Translated by Robert Fagles. New York: Penguin Classics, 1984.

Spengler, Oswald. *The Decline of the West* (1918–1923). Abridged ed. Oxford: Oxford University Press, 1991.

Steiner, Gary. *Animals and the Limits of Postmodernism*. New York: Columbia University Press, 2013.

———. *Animals and the Moral Community: Mental Life, Moral Status, and Kinship*. New York: Columbia University Press, 2008.

———. *Anthropocentrism and Its Discontents: The Moral Status of Animals in the History of Western Philosophy*. Pittsburgh, PA: University of Pittsburgh Press, 2005.

Steiner, George. *Antigones*. Oxford: Clarendon Press, 1984.

Sternberg, Robert, ed. *Wisdom: Its Nature, Origins, and Development*. Cambridge: Cambridge University Press, 1990.

Stevens, Wallace. *The Collected Poems of Wallace Stevens*. New York: Knopf, 1990.

Stewart, Jack. *The Vital Art of D. H. Lawrence: Vision and Expression*. Carbondale: Southern Illinois University Press, 1999.

Stiegler, Bernard. *Taking Care of Youth and the Generations*. Translated by Stephen Barker. Palo Alto, CA: Stanford University Press, 2010.

Stojkovic, Tijana. *"Unnoticed in the Casual Light of Day": Philip Larkin and the Plain Style*. Abingdon, UK: Routledge, 2006.

Strauss, William, and Neil Howe. *Generations: The History of America's Future, 1584 to 2069*. New York: Harper Collins, 1991.

Strong, Tracy B. *Nietzsche and the Politics of Transfiguration*. Berkeley: University of California Press, 1975.

Suchantke, Andreas. *Eco-Geography: What We See When We Look at Landscapes*. Translated by Norman Skillen. Great Barrington, MA: Lindisfarne Books, 2001.

Tagliacozzo, Giorgio, ed. *Vico: Past and Present*. Atlantic Highlands, NJ: Humanities Press, 1981.

Tagliacozzo, Giorgio, and Donald Verene, eds. *Giambattista Vico's Science of Humanity*. Baltimore, MD: Johns Hopkins University Press, 1976.

Tanizaki, Jun'ichirō. *In Praise of Shadows*. Translated by Thomas J. Harper and Edward G. Seidensticker. New York: Vintage, 2001.

Taylor, Charles. *Hegel*. Cambridge: Cambridge University Press, 1979.

———. *A Secular Age*. Cambridge, MA: Harvard University Press, 2007.

Thompson, E. A. *Romans and Barbarians: The Decline of the Western Empire*. Madison: University of Wisconsin Press, 1982.

Toynbee, Arnold. *A Study of History*. 12 vols. Oxford: Oxford University Press, 1934–1961. See also the abridgments by D. C. Somervell (Oxford, 1946–47, 1960).

Trilling, Lionel. *The Liberal Imagination: Essays on Literature and Society* (1950). New York: New York Review of Books, 2008.

Turner, Donald. "Humanity as Shepherd of Being: Heidegger's Philosophy and the Animal Other." In *Heidegger and the Earth: Essays in Environmen-*

tal Philosophy, edited by Ladelle McWorther and Gail Senstad, 144–68. Toronto: University of Toronto Press, 2009.

Turner, Fred. *From Counterculture to Cyberculture*. Chicago: University of Chicago Press, 2006.

Uexküll, Jakob von. *A Foray into the Worlds of Animals and Humans: With a Theory of Meaning* (1934). Translated by Joseph D. O'Neil. Minneapolis: University of Minnesota Press, 2010.

Usher, Abbott Payson. *A History of Mechanical Inventions*. Rev. ed. Cambridge, MA: Harvard University Press, 1954.

Vallega, Alejandro A. *Heidegger and the Issue of Space: Thinking on Exilic Grounds*. University Park: Pennsylvania State University Press, 2003.

Vatter, Miguel. "Natality and Biopolitics in Hannah Arendt." *Revista de Ciencia Politica* 26, no. 2 (2006): 137–59.

Verene, Donald P. *Knowledge of Things Human and Divine: Vico's New Science and Finnegans Wake*. New Haven, CT: Yale University Press, 2003.

———. *Vico's Science of Imagination*. Ithaca, NY: Cornell University Press, 1981.

Vico, Giambattista. *The New Science* (1744). Revised and unabridged edition. Translated by Thomas G. Bergin and Max H. Frisch. Ithaca, NY: Cornell University Press, 1984.

Vidal-Naquet, Pierre. *The Atlantis Story: A Short History of Plato's Myth*. Translated by Janet Lloyd. Exeter, UK: University of Exeter Press, 2007.

Villa, Dana, ed. *The Cambridge Companion to Hannah Arendt*. Cambridge: Cambridge University Press, 2000.

Vlastos, Gregory. *Socrates, Ironist and Moral Philosopher*. Cambridge: Cambridge University Press, 1991.

———. *Socratic Studies*. Edited by Myles Burnyeat. Cambridge: Cambridge University Press, 1994.

Warrior, Valerie. *Roman Religion*. Cambridge: Cambridge University Press, 2006.

Weber, Max. *The Sociology of Religion* (1920). Translated by Ephraim Fischoff. Boston: Beacon Press, 1963.

Weigel, Sigrid. "Sounding Through—Poetic Difference—Self-Translation: Hannah Arendt's Thoughts and Writings between Different Languages, Cultures, and Fields." In *German Intellectuals in New York: A Compendium on Exile after 1933*, edited by Eckart Goebel and Sigrid Weigel, 55–79. Berlin: Walter de Gruyter, 2012.

Wendel, Susan. "Interpreting the Descent of the Spirit." In *Justin Martyr and His Worlds*, edited by Sara Parvis and Paul Foster, 95–103. Minneapolis, MN: Fortress Press, 2007.

———. *Scriptural Interpretation and Community Self-Definition in Luke-Acts and the Writings of Justin Martyr*. Leiden, Netherlands: Brill, 2011.

Werckmeister, O. K. "Walter Benjamin's Angel of History, or the Transfiguration of the Revolutionary into the Historian." *Critical Inquiry* 22 (1996):
239–67. Reprinted in Peter Osborne, ed., *Walter Benjamin: Modernity*
(Abingdon, UK: Routledge, 2005).

West-Eberhard, Mary-Jane. *Developmental Plasticity and Evolution*. Oxford:
Oxford University Press, 2003.

Wetherbee, Winthrop. *The Ancient Flame: Dante and the Poets*. Notre Dame,
IN: University of Notre Dame Press, 2008.

White, Hayden. *The Fiction of Narrative: Essays on History, Literature, and
Theory 1957–2007*. Edited by Robert Doran. Baltimore, MD: Johns Hopkins
University Press, 2010.

———. *Metahistory: The Historical Imagination in Nineteenth-Century Europe*.
Baltimore, MD: Johns Hopkins University Press, 1973.

Wiles, David. *Mask and Performance in Greek Tragedy: From Ancient Festival to
Modern Experimentation*. Cambridge: Cambridge University Press, 2007.

Wills, Gary. *Inventing America: Jefferson's Declaration of Independence*. New
York: Houghton Mifflin, 1978.

———. *Lincoln at Gettysburg: The Words That Remade America*. New York:
Simon and Schuster, 1992.

Wilson, Douglas B. *The Romantic Dream: Wordsworth and the Poet of the
Unconscious*. Lincoln: University of Nebraska Press, 1993.

Winterer, Caroline. *The Culture of Classicism: Ancient Greece and Rome in
American Intellectual Life, 1780–1910*. Baltimore, MD: Johns Hopkins University Press, 2002.

Wohlfarth, Irving. "No-Man's-Land: On Walter Benjamin's 'Destructive Character.'" *Diacritics* 8 (1978): 47–65.

Woloch, Alex. *The One vs. the Many*. Princeton, NJ: Princeton University Press,
2009.

Wood, Allen. *Hegel's Ethical Thought*. Cambridge: Cambridge University Press,
1990.

———. "Kant and the Problem of Human Nature." In *Essays on Kant's
Anthropology*, edited by Brian Jacobs and Patrick Kain, 38–59. Cambridge:
Cambridge University Press, 2003.

Wood, Gordon S. *The Creation of the American Republic: 1776–1787*. Chapel
Hill: University Press of North Carolina, 1969.

Wood, Sharon. "The Reflections of Mr. Palomar and Mr. Cogito: Italo Calvino
and Zbigniew Herbert." *MLN* 109, no. 1 (1994): 128–41.

Woodard, Roger D., ed. *The Cambridge Companion to Greek Mythology*. Cambridge: Cambridge University Press, 2007.

Wordsworth, William. *Fenwick Notes*. Electronic edition edited by Jared Curtis.
Humanities-Ebooks.co.uk. Originally published in 1993 by Bristol Classical
Press.

———. *The Major Works, including The Prelude*. Edited by Stephen Gill. Oxford: Oxford University Press, 2008.

Worms, Frédéric. *Bergson ou les deux sens de la vie*. 2nd ed. Paris: PUF, 2013.

Worthen, John, Mark Kinkead-Weekes, and David Ellis. *The Cambridge Biography of D. H. Lawrence*. 3 vols. Cambridge: Cambridge University Press, 1992, 1996, 1998.

Xie, Ming. *Ezra Pound and the Appropriation of Chinese Poetry*. New York: Garland, 1999.

Yeats, W. B. *The Collected Works of W. B. Yeats*. Vol. 1, *The Poems*. 2nd ed. Edited by Richard J. Finneran. New York: Scribner, 1997.

Young-Bruehl, Elizabeth. *Hannah Arendt: For Love of the World*. 2nd ed. New Haven, CT: Yale University Press, 2004.

Zak, Gur. *Petrarch's Humanism and the Care of the Self*. Cambridge: Cambridge University Press, 2010.

Zelditch, Miriam. *Beyond Heterochrony: The Evolution of Development*. New York: Wiley-Liss, 2001.

Žižek, Slavoj. "The Politics of Truth or Alain Badiou as a Reader of Saint Paul." In *The Ticklish Subject: The Absent Center of Political Ontology*, 127–70. New York: Verso, 1999.

INDEX